The Philadelphia Story

*To all the coaches, managers, and general managers
who lost their jobs in the struggle to turn the City of Losers
into the City of Winners.*

THE PHILADELPHIA STORY

A City of Lo̶s̶e̶r̶s Winners

FRANK DOLSON

Icarus Press
South Bend, Indiana
1981

THE PHILADELPHIA STORY
Copyright © 1981 by Frank Dolson

Manufactured in the United States of America.

Icarus Press, Inc.
Post Office Box 1225
South Bend, Indiana 46624

81 82 83 84 10 9 8 7 6 5 4 3 2 1

Library of Congress Cataloging in Publication Data

Dolson, Frank.
    The Philadelphia story.

    Includes index.
    1. Sports—Pennsylvania—Philadelphia—History.
I. Title.
GV584.P46D64   796'.09748'll   81-7201
ISBN 0-89651-600-8   AACR2

Contents

Introduction

PHILADELPHIA HAS BEEN CALLED BY SOME—MOSTLY PHILADEL-phians, I suppose—the best sports city in the United States. OK, maybe it is; maybe it isn't. Instead of arguing the point, let's just say Philadelphia is the unique sports city in the United States.

For years Philadelphia's teams were uniquely bad. Now they're uniquely good. But good or bad, up or down, there's always been a special quality about Philadelphia, its teams, and its fans—a sort of My-God-what's-going-to-happen-next quality that sets them aside from the others. Even during the bad years, when the losses piled up and the sports writing critics attacked full blast and the boos grew deafening, there were always some truly memorable happenings that prevented monotony from setting in—some special thrills, some especially bitter disappointments, and, above all, some laughs. Always some laughs.

Where else but in Philadelphia could . . .

—the ice crack under the weight of a Zamboni machine on opening night, forcing the postponement of a professional hockey game?

—a man selected as NBA Coach of the Year wind up getting fired?

—part of the roof blow off a new indoor arena, leaving the city's National Hockey League team homeless for the stretch drive in its first season?

—the pro basketball team lose 73 of 82 games?

—a baseball manager whose team has just been mathematically eliminated late in the season, falling seven games behind with six to go, refuse to give up?

—the needling get so rough at a major sports banquet

7

that the featured speaker, Howard Cosell, threatens to walk out?

—a baseball team that's leading by six-and-a-half games with twelve games to go lose the pennant by a game?

—a hockey team get knocked out of a berth in the Stanley Cup playoffs on a goal scored with four seconds to go in the final game of the regular season?

—the pro football team go eleven consecutive years (from 1967 through 1977) without a winning season and the baseball team go through a thirty-one-year stretch (from 1918 through 1948) in which they managed one winning season?

—a baseball team compete in two World Series and three National League championship series prior to 1980 and win only a single game at home?

—fans get so worked up about a losing football team that they hire a plane to circle the stadium trailing a sign that asks for the coach's scalp?

Philadelphia has become very much a pro sports town in the last decade or so, but even on the college level the city has managed to stand out in the crowd, to soar to giddy highs and plunge to sickening lows. The crazy thing is, some of the teams that provided the giddy highs also were responsible for the sickening lows.

There was the St. Joseph's College basketball team, coached by Jack Ramsay, that reached the NCAA's final four . . . and had it all wiped out by a point-shaving scandal. And Philadelphia's next final-four basket ball team, a Jack Kraft-coached, Howard Porter-led Villanova squad that made it all the way to the championship game against UCLA . . . and also wound up in disgrace when it was revealed that its star player had signed a pro contract early in the season. Talk about ups and downs, highs and lows, how about the University of Pennsylvania, which secretly hired a new football coach for 1960 in August of 1959 and wound up a laughingstock when the old coach, Steve Sebo, led the school to a 7-1-1 season and its only Ivy League championship in '59?

We've had a lot to cheer about in Philadelphia, and a lot to jeer about, which may explain why Philadelphians are so accomplished at doing both. We've come to realize, I think, that as bad as the bad years were, they served a useful purpose—making the good years, when they finally arrived, seem even better. We learned to live with adversity in Philadelphia, to wait for next year, and the year after that, and the year after *that*, to smile as well as swear at our frequently flawed sports heroes because—dammit—they *were* pretty funny at times.

It's fascinating covering sports in the Philadelphia area, but it isn't easy, as the late Harry Hoffman, long-time writer for an Atlantic City newspaper, discovered one opening day at old Connie Mack Stadium. The game had just ended and, with a deadline staring him in the face, Hoffman ran down to the clubhouse, got some quotes, dashed out a quick story, and headed for the nearest telephone booth to dictate the hot news to the office. The booth he chose happened to be on the main floor of the ball park, in the home plate area, and Harry placed his call, got through with no difficulty, and began talking.

Everything was progressing smoothly until somebody pushed open the door to Hoffman's booth, stuck a sharp object in the writer's back, and informed him that he was being held up. Poor Harry. There he was, on deadline, trying to rush word of the Phillies' latest opening-day defeat to the eagerly waiting sports fans in Atlantic City, and some no-good so-and-so—a Mets' fan probably—had picked this inopportune time to rob him.

But Philadelphia-area sportswriters are a tough breed, and come hell or high water, come victory or defeat, come a confrontation with a raving manager or a screaming owner or a post-game robber, the story must get in. So, Harry would explain to his friends later, he simply kept talking, all the while handing over his wallet and assorted other valuables to the robber who had joined him in the phone booth.

Hoffman's conversation with the guy taking his story over the phone must have been a classic. "And then," he was likely saying, "the Phillies loaded the bases in the bottom of the fourth when . . . excuse me a second. I'm being held up. Yeah, here's the wallet. Now try to be quiet, will you? I'm right on deadline . . . no, not you, Joe. Now where was I? Oh yeah . . ."

Let the record show that Harry's story got in, even as the robber got away. We can only hope that Harry's considerable losses were covered in his expense account.

Now don't get the idea that Harry Hoffman's experience was commonplace in the life of a Philadelphia sportswriter. Let's just say that nobody was particularly surprised when Harry revealed what had happened.

One thing you've got to say about the sports scene in Philadelphia —it's lively. Maybe we went years without winning very many games. Maybe our teams set new standards of mediocrity. But life was never dull.

In the twenty-five years I've covered sports in Philadelphia a few incidents stand out in bold relief, which is what some of those Phillie teams could have used in the bad years.

I'll never forget the time—it was in the second half of the 1966 season—when the Eagles, coached by Joe Kuharich, were whipped, 27-7, by the Cleveland Browns at Cleveland Stadium. Kuharich was never very popular with the press, but at that stage he and I had a decent relationship. By the time I walked into the visiting coach's office—after spending some time with the winners—only three men were there: Kuharich, Eagles' owner Jerry Wolman, and Jesse Abramson, a highly respected New York sportswriter.

Jesse, bless him, was a hard-hitting, fast-talking, no-holds-barred type of guy. He did his homework, and he asked tough questions. On this day, he had no trouble thinking up plenty of toughies to ask, but the interview had hit a snag when I got there. Jesse was growling. Joe was snarling. Jerry was wincing. Finally, just a minute or so after my arrival, Abramson turned and marched out, much to the apparent relief of Kuharich and Wolman.

They seemed so agitated by Jesse's questioning, and they greeted me so warmly, that I didn't have it in my heart to pick up where Abramson had left off. So I murmured hello, asked a couple of innocuous questions, received routine answers, and was just preparing to depart when Joe Kuharich turned to Jerry Wolman in this rather large, bare room under cavernous Cleveland Stadium and said, "Now why don't all sportswriters ask those kinds of questions? Why can't they all be as smart as Frank Dolson?"

Somewhat flustered by this totally unexpected—and richly undeserved—testimonial from the coach of the Philadelphia Eagles, I thanked him and made a beeline for the door, leaving Joe and Jerry alone to continue their discussion on how brilliant I was. One problem. The door I chose led not to the corridor in the bowels of the stadium, but to a closet. Slamming it shut behind me, I found myself completely in the dark, a state that Joe Kuharich and others would accuse me of being in on several occasions in the years that followed. There I was, standing in a pitch-black closet, momentarily too embarrassed to reopen the door, nod a second farewell to Joe and Jerry, and search for the right door. To this day I can imagine what Joe Kuharich said to Jerry Wolman as they stared at that closet door, waiting for me to come out.

I suspect it went something like this: "See, Jerry, that's the smart one. Can you imagine what those other dummies who write sports in Philadelphia are like?"

Another very special episode involved a basketball coach whose name was Roy Rubin and whose team, the 1972-73 Philadelphia 76ers, were the worst in National Basketball Association history. Yes, even worse than the expansion Dallas Mavericks have been. Rubin, a successful small-college coach, was a friendly man who wanted very much to be liked and to be accepted in the crazy world of pro basketball. Trouble was, he was saddled with an absolutely gosh-awful team that wasted no time in showing its true colors: black and blue (with red faces). The 76ers opened the Rubin Era—some callous critics called it the Rubin Error— by losing its first fifteen games.

The law of averages finally caught up with Rubin and his heroes on a Saturday night in San Antonio, Texas, the site of a 76ers–Houston Rockets game that will not be found in any NBA highlights film. Somehow, the 76ers won the game, a historic event that produced minimal excitement among Philly fans and writers alike. The truth was, the 76ers were so bad then that the local papers didn't bother to send writers on most of their road trips, employing "stringers" instead.

Quite obviously, Rubin was dying to talk to somebody following this epic game, dying to let the world—or at least the Delaware Valley— know all that went into this stirring upset. Since no Philly writers were present, Roy did the next best thing: He decided to call one of them long-distance. As luck would have it, he picked me.

It was rather late by the time Roy called. Since I had an early-morning plane to catch the next day, I was sound asleep when the phone rang. Now understand, I didn't really know Roy Rubin very well. He hadn't been in town very long, and, quite frankly, nobody expected him to stay very long the way things were going. So I was absolutely flabbergasted at receiving this postmidnight call from San Antonio.

The conversation went something like this:

"Hello . . . hello. Is this you, Frank?"

"Uh, yes. Who's this?"

"This is Roy."

"Roy who?"

"Roy Rubin. [Pause] Of the 76ers."

"Roy Rubin?"

"That's right, Frank. I'm in San Antonio. I just had to call you. I guess you know by now that we won."

"Gee, uh, no, I didn't know. Who'd you beat?"

"Houston, Frank. We beat the Houston Rockets."

"Well, congratulations, Roy. I mean, that's really something, beating the Houston Rockets and all that."

"The thing is, Frank, I figured you'd probably have some questions you'd want to ask me. So go ahead. Shoot. Ask me anything you want to know."

"Questions?"

"Yeah, questions about the game. Questions about anything. You must have something you want to know."

"Well, there is one thing."

"Yeah, yeah, what's that?"

"Do you have any idea what time it is?"

That unforgettable after-hours, long-distance conversation ended there rather abruptly, as I recall. But now that I think about it, it *was* nice of Roy to call. And the man definitely showed some class. I mean, he didn't even phone collect.

There were, of course, a few other memorable moments along the way. Like the time I was covering a minor-league hockey team called the Philadelphia Ramblers—long before the big-league Flyers arrived on the scene—and the club was in Charlotte, North Carolina, for the Eastern Hockey League championship playoffs. The Ramblers were staying in the Coliseum Motel, a short walk from the rink, and rooms were a bit scarce, so I wound up staying with the team's scoring star, a winger named Bill Kurtz.

Kurtz and I had something in common. We both liked to sleep late. The coach, a man named Edgar (Chirp) Brenchley, had other ideas. Chirp set a team meeting for 10–something in the morning on game day and had the switchboard operator call all the rooms with a 9 o'clock wake-up call. I happened to be nearer the phone than Kurtz, so when it rang I rolled over, picked it up, grunted something, hung up, and went back to sleep. Kurtz never even stirred. Next thing we knew the phone was ringing again. The meeting had already started . . . and no Bill Kurtz. Brenchley was livid.

"Where is he?" he bellowed into the phone.

"Right here," I told him, "sleeping."

"Sleeping. Didn't you get a wake-up call?"

"Uh, I think so, but I must have answered the phone and hung up."

"Oh you did, did you? Well, that's a dollar-a-minute fine for every minute he's late. And since it's your fault he's late, you're going to pay the fine." And with that, Chirp slammed down the phone.

I can't prove this, of course, but I believe on that day—some twenty-four years ago—I became the first sportswriter to be fined by a coach because one of his players overslept and missed a team meeting. Chirp was an all-right guy, though. He let me win it back playing gin rummy.

Well, I could go on like this for pages, but I think you get the idea. Philadelphia is not your routine sports town. Never has been. Never will be. There's something special about its teams; they are never, *never* run-of-the-mill, and covering them is never, *never* run-of-the-mill.

It was in Philadelphia that Bill Giles, the executive vice- president of the Phillies, came up with the bright idea of pepping up an opening-night by having a character called Kiteman soar down a ramp built in the upper deck in center field and land on the playing field carrying the "first ball." To nobody's great surprise, Kiteman crashed. He was merely keeping in step with Philadelphia sports tradition.

Bad luck followed the city's sports teams long before Bill Giles and Kiteman arrived. Take, for example, August 4, 1944, when Philadelphia decided to pay homage to Connie Mack, "the grand old man of baseball" who owned and managed the Philadelphia A's almost from the day the game was invented. The affair was dubbed Connie Mack's "Golden Jubilee" because it saluted his fifty years as a big-league manager, and everything was in readiness for a big celebration at the ball park. So what happened? On that very day they had a streetcar strike in Philadelphia.

That's the way things go there—or at least went for a long time. The first All-Star Game in Philly got rained out in the sixth inning. The nice, new arena built there—called the Spectrum—lost part of its roof in a windstorm the first year and had to be closed for repairs. But even a hole in the roof provided Philly teams with a unique opportunity. I mean, when the 76ers and the Flyers said "the sky's the limit" in those days, they weren't kidding. Whatever you do, though, don't get the idea that only the sportswriters had it tough in Philadelphia. The announcers had their trying times too.

It was in Philadelphia—where else?—that ABC's Howard Cosell, the voice of Monday Night Football, had to leave before a game was completed. The site was Franklin Field on the University of Pennsylvania campus, where the Eagles played in the pre¢Veterans Stadium years. The opponents were the New York Giants.

There's something about those Monday night games. The crowd was unusually boisterous. It was almost a Super Bowl atmosphere, and the freezing temperature didn't seem to put a damper on the excitement. If anything, it encouraged the consumption of even more liquor than usual and thus got the fans even more revved up. And there, in the middle of all that commotion, was Howard. If Philadelphia was ready for his first Monday Night Football visit, he wasn't quite ready for Philadelphia. Cosell didn't make it through the second half, and never heard the end of it. His, uh, friends in the press box hinted strongly that he was drunk— with liquor, not power—and his legion of loyal loathers out there in teeveeland were only too happy to accept that as the gospel.

What actually happened, Cosell explained later, was downright frightening. "Suddenly," he said, "I couldn't articulate.

I couldn't stand up. I threw up all over Dandy [Don Meredith]. I was scared to death."

Cosell left Franklin Field, returning to New York City by cab, and was home by 3:30 in the morning. "At seven," he said, "I was having my electrocardiogram. I thought I had a heart attack."

Actually, he had picked up a virus that attacked the middle ear. "It was the scariest time I ever had in my life," he said. "I really mean it."

That'll teach ABC to play Monday night games in Philadelphia.

Cosell wasn't the only sports "voice" to have problems in Philadelphia. Talk about a black cloud, take By Saam. For thirty-eight years he did the play-by-play of A's games and Phillies games. For thirty-eight years he waited for a Philadelphia team to get into a World Series—and when it finally happened, when that joyous day finally arrived and the Phillies won the 1950 National League pennant, what was Saam doing? A's games, that's what. Given the choice, he'd made the wrong one.

And then there was Stu Nahan, now a West Coast sportscaster who, once upon a time, was the first radio-TV voice of the Philadelphia Flyers and doubled in the afternoon as the host of a kiddie show. In the latter capacity Nahan climbed into a space suit and called himself Captain Philadelphia. Well, the good captain met his downfall one day when, instead of a space suit, he put on goalie's pads and took a turn in the nets during a Flyers' practice session. Nahan, in truth, had been a minor-league goaltender in his younger days, but that experience didn't help him on this day. The captain got hit in the mouth and came out with a lip swollen at least three times its normal size. Wouldn't you know it? Of all the "superheroes" who kept popping up on TV screens, it had to be one named Captain Philadelphia who was forced to face the world with a fat lip.

But that was in the old days, before Philadelphia—with the help of its sports team—changed its image. This, then, is a very personal, very opinionated, largely loving look at the joke that turned serious, at the City of Losers that became the City of Winners.

1

Second Prize, Two Weeks in Philadelphia

THE FLYERS WON BACK-TO-BACK STANLEY CUPS. THE CITY WENT ga-ga. Freddie Shero, the inscrutable one, the guy who wrote those thought-provoking sayings on the blackboard and taught that wonderful "system," had become as much a part of Philadelphia as cheese steaks. Everybody loved Freddie Shero. Everybody laughed at his eccentricities and read great significance into his most banal utterances. Great fella, they all said. How clever of the Flyers to pluck him out of the New York Rangers' farm system.

Beautiful, eh? At long last, the joke was on New York. The Rangers were lousy. The Flyers, thanks in large part to good old Freddie, were no. 1.

And so what did good old Philadelphia Freddie do? He picked up and went to New York to coach the Rangers.

It wasn't the first time that Philly and its sports fans had been jilted. The 76ers won the pro basketball championship in 1967—won it so convincingly that thirteen years later the NBA would honor Wilt Chamberlain and friends as the greatest team in the history of the league. Ah, but what happened in '68? First, the Boston Celtics overcame a 3–1 deficit to beat the Sixers in seven games; then Wilt went west, signing with the Los Angeles Lakers, and Alex Hannum, the coach of the best-ever team, fled to Denver.

It almost seemed as if a little—maybe a not-so-little—black cloud hovered over Philadelphia and its sports teams. The cloud made road trips too.

In 1969, the baseball All-Star Game was held in Washington, D.C., where a gigantic rainstorm hit a few hours before game time, washing out baseball's "100th birthday party," which was being held under a brightly colored canvas tent pitched on the grounds of an armory across the street from Robert F. Kennedy Stadium. When it became obvious that the game would not be played that night, the guests—by now, wet and miserable—looked for ways to get back to their homes or hotels. There was mass confusion for a while . . . but not for the Phillies family. Even though the baseball team was a disaster area in those days, the front office was on the ball. Bob Carpenter and John Quinn had a chauffeured limousine waiting. Into the limo climbed the Phillie execs, understandably pleased with themselves for having such marvelous foresight. There was only one problem with their seemingly foolproof plan. The limousine broke down on the way back to the hotel.

Occasionally that little black cloud that hovered over Veterans Stadium during Phillie home stands turned on the opposition as well. Early in the 1976 season, the Atlanta Braves turned an apparent defeat into a ninth-inning victory over the Phillies with a big, walk-filled rally that so inspired Atlanta Braves owner Ted Turner that he leaped out of his front row box, rushed across the field, and hugged all the players he could reach. Then Turner dashed to the clubhouse shouting, "We're going all the way. You bet your sweet ass we are." Poor fella didn't realize that Philadelphia was not the place to utter such remarks. His Braves promptly embarked on the longest losing streak of the major-league season.

There was one occasion, however, when the management of the Phillies took advantage of that little black cloud. This was back in the Connie Mack Stadium era; in fact, it was in 1964, the year the Phillies almost won the pennant.

The Los Angeles Dodgers were in town, winding up a series, and a Hall-of-Fame-bound lefthander named Sandy Koufax was scheduled to face the Phillies that night, a fact that didn't fill Phillie manager Gene Mauch's heart with overwhelming joy and optimism. But Mauch was a smart cookie, and he set his mind to the task of finding a way not to lose to Koufax. Enter that little black cloud.

To be honest about it, the cloud seen in the vicinity of the ball park early that afternoon wasn't very black. If you were describing it, white and fleecy might have been the words that came most

readily to mind. But it *was* a cloud. And it *was* little. And Gene
Mauch got a brainstorm. He called general manager John Quinn
and suggested that the game be postponed. Recalling the incident
years later, Mauch said, "A drop of rain fell about 1:30, and I told
John, 'Call it.' "

John called it. The game was rescheduled for later in the
season. Ah, but don't count that little black cloud short. In the
makeup game, Phillies first baseman Frank Thomas broke his
thumb, an injury that contributed greatly to the Phillies' failure to
hold onto first place.

There were times when nothing seemed to go right in
Philadelphia when it came to sports events. A classic foul-up occurred in July 1959,when the city hosted an event of genuine international significance—the first dual track meet between the United
States and the Soviet Union ever held in this country. Naturally,
careful plans were laid. No detail was overlooked. The city, *The
Philadelphia Inquirer* (which sponsored the meet), the Amateur
Athletic Union—everybody involved went to great lengths to
make sure that nothing went wrong.

And nothing did—until the morning the Russians arrived.

They landed in New York's Idlewild (now Kennedy) Airport
early on a Monday morning, went through customs, and boarded
two chartered buses for the trip to Philadelphia. There were
seventy-four in the traveling party, including athletes, officials,
and interpreters. To guarantee a safe, speedy journey, the Pennsylvania State police were alerted to meet the buses at the Valley
Forge exit of the Pennsylvania Turnpike and provide an escort into
downtown Philly. It seemed like a great idea—and it would have
worked beautifully, except for one small oversight. The buses
failed to turn off the New Jersey Turnpike onto the Pennsy Turnpike; instead of going to Philadelphia by way of Valley Forge, the
Russians went by way of Camden, New Jersey.

When the horrible truth dawned on the sportswriter assigned
to direct the lead bus—modesty forbids me to reveal my identity—it was too late to turn back. The Russians were tired of
traveling; they wanted to get to their destination. So, the police
escort at Valley Forge notwithstanding, it was Camden or bust.

Unfortunately, nobody ever bothered to stop long enough to
pick up a phone and notify the Pennsylvania State Police, who re-

mained totally in the dark. So did the Soviet head coach, Gavrial Korobkov, meet director Ken Doherty, and AAU officials Dan Ferris and Jim Simms, who made the trip from New York to Philadelphia by car. Naturally, they went by way of Valley Forge, as planned, and they sat there, at the interchange, along with the police escort, waiting for the Russians to show up. For forty-five minutes they waited, getting more and more nervous as time passed. And then the big moment arrived. Two buses appeared at the toll gate. The police escort revved up its motors and prepared to lead the way to Philadelphia. It took a few minutes, and a few wails of the siren, before the police and the Soviet coach and the officials realized the buses were carrying ordinary, everyday American commuters —albeit slightly startled ordinary, everyday American commuters. Luckily, nobody ever made a big thing out of the comedy of errors. The city was having enough fun poked at it in those days as it was.

Philadelphia not only lost track teams, as well as football, baseball, and basketball games in those days, but coin tosses too. The most momentous flip took place in March 1974, when the Philadelphia 76ers met the Portland Trail Blazers in the biggest competition of the season for either team: the coin toss to decide which last-place club would get the rights to Bill Walton. Don't laugh. The 76ers and the Trail Blazers had worked hard to get the opportunity to flip over the UCLA center, the former losing fifty-seven games to bring up the rear in the East, the latter losing fifty-five games to stave off all challengers in the West.

So the interested parties gathered in the Cinema Room of the Beverly Hills Hotel for what basketball lovers were billing as the Flip of the Decade, maybe even the Flip of the Century. Those with a feel for history noted that the coin used for the great event was a 1946 half-dollar. The man in charge—hereafter to be known as the flipper—was none other than the commissioner of the league, Walter Kennedy. At the appointed time Kennedy flipped. It was up to Irv Kosloff, then the owner of the 76ers, to make the call. He cried heads, and the fifty-cent piece came down tails, proving that even when it came to flips the 76ers of that era were flops.

Considering the stature of the athlete involved—hereafter to be known as the flippee—you'd have thought the NBA would have made it a best-of-seven flip, or at least a best-of-three. But no, this was a single elimination tournament. So Walton went to Portland, where he stayed healthy long enough to beat the 76ers out of one pro basketball championship.

If you think that 1974 coin toss was rotten luck, Philly was going so bad in the late '60s that even when it won it lost. That was the sad state of affairs in 1968 when the prize for the worst record in professional football was the draft rights to O. J. Simpson, the great Southern Cal running back who was destined to become an all-time National Football League star.

As the season wore on it became obvious that the race for O. J. had narrowed down to a two-team affair, involving the Philadelphia Eagles and the Buffalo Bills. For quite a while it appeared that the Eagles were simply too weak for even the Bills to "undercome" them. Helped along no doubt by the boos of their fans, the Eagles lost their first eleven games and had O. J. virtually gift-wrapped for delivery to Philadelphia. Then a crazy thing happened—the Eagles won two games in a row. First they beat the Lions in the Detroit mud. Then they came home and whipped the New Orleans Saints. The two-game winning streak was just enough to cost them O. J.

The Eagles-Saints game, billed in some quarters as the "Boycott Bowl" because some fans tried to push an organized boycott, was the win that really hurt. The man who did the most to make it possible was Tom Woodeshick, who received the game ball from his smiling teammates. "I'll take a victory anytime. Anytime, at all," said Woodeshick, who coincidentally was also a running back. "I don't care what the cost is . . . . I don't want him here. If he came here, I'd have to put on lineman's pads and block. I'd get two carries a game." Thus inspired, Woody carried the ball eighteen times against the Saints . . . and O. J. landed in Buffalo. Those are the breaks.

For years, it seemed, the joke was always on Philadelphia. All you had to do was listen to practically any stand-up comic deliver a routine. Some of them told traveling salesman jokes. Some of them told Polish jokes. Some of them told political jokes. Almost all of them told Philadelphia jokes.

"I was in Philadelphia last Sunday," they'd say, "but it was closed."

Or, "We're running a contest. First prize is a one-week vacation in Philadelphia. Second prize is two weeks."

Or . . . well, you get the idea.

It may have been amusing to New Yorkers, two hours up the New Jersey Turnpike to the north. It may have been a barrel of laughs for Washingtonians, a two-and-a-half to three-hour drive to the south. It may have kept the natives rolling in the aisles in Walla-Walla and Peoria and the rest of the country. But the people who lived in Philadelphia stopped laughing at those jokes a long time before the comedians stopped telling them.

Want to know how bad it got? Even comics who had gone on to their happy resting place were credited—or accused, depending on your point of view—of knocking Philadelphia. A case in point was W. C. Fields. Well-circulated legend had it that the fabled movie funnyman, a one-time Philadelphian, had his tombstone inscribed with these words: "All in all, I would rather be in Philadelphia." Several versions of the Fields' "epitaph" surfaced, including one popularized by Californians that went, "I'd rather be dead in California than alive in Philadelphia."

Since Fields' grandson, W. C., III, lived in California, it wasn't at all surprising that he favored the latter version. Young Fields was an oarsman, and in the mid-'60s he visited Philadelphia to compete in the pair without coxswain at the National Rowing Regatta on the Schuylkill, the river that only Philadelphians—and well-educated Philadelphians, at that—can spell. You'll have to admit it took rare courage for a man whose name was W. C. Fields, III, to show his face in Philly, but there he was, in the town his grandfather allegedly hated as much as he hated children.

A delightful fellow, W. C.'s grandson, and on that particular visit, at least, he was the kind of athlete native-born Philadelphians could appreciate. Together with his partner, he finished last. When the race was over he cheerfully talked about old granddad, and about that much-publicized epitaph. No such thing really existed, the young man confirmed but, he added quickly, old W. C. had expressed such opinions many times. "He'd always make jokes about Philadelphia."

Well, why not? In those days almost everybody made jokes about Philadelphia. Even Jackie Gleason, whose make-believe life as Brooklyn bus driver Ralph Cramden was less than thrilling, managed to get in an occasional jab at the city to the south. "What can I do in Philadelphia on Sunday?" Gleason was asked on one of his shows. "What can you do in Philadelphia *any* day," he replied. Philadelphia has changed tremendously since those jokes saw the light of day, just as Philadelphia's sports teams have changed tremendously. But the joke writers haven't packed up and left. They just looked for—and found—other Philadelphia targets, including the frequently booing fans who turn out in great numbers to watch their "heroes" in action on the sports front, and the sportswriters who help to make and/or break those heroes.

"Philadelphia fans," said Pat Williams, the 76ers' general manager, at the annual blood-letting known as the Philadelphia Sports Writers Banquet, "are the type who will scream from the sixtieth row of the bleachers about the ref who missed a marginal call in the interior line—and then they can't find their car in the parking lot."

There is nothing quite like the Philadelphia dinner, for which we should all be thankful. The writers rip the "honored" athletes. The athletes, in turn, rip the writers. The crowd—more than 1,000 strong—rises to the occasion by doing what it does best. It boos.

Ripping has become such an art form at the Philly dinner that even the guest speakers occasionally find themselves fair game. Or maybe even unfair game. Howard Cosell thought it was decidedly unfair in 1972 when, as he sat at the head table awaiting his turn to address the assembled throng, I introduced "Amateur Athlete of the Year" Marty Liquori by saying, "I'll make this very brief. I know a lot of you want to leave early so you can get out of here before Howard goes on."

Cosell did not join in the laughter.

"We're hopeful and confident that late this summer in Munich," I went on, "Marty Liquori will gain the greatest honor that an amateur athlete can attain: an interview on national television with Howard Cosell. Despite that, Marty has assured us that he will go all out in an effort to win."

Once again Howard did not join in the laughter. In fact, it was along about then that he threatened to walk out. Instead, he stayed and delivered a speech that was pure Cosell, dripping with equal parts of humor and venom. "It must be an extraordinary feeling for you to be finally confronted by a professional," he began. "A guy like Dolson, who goes after sports-casters, remains for ever more the pinnacle of failure. . . . Criticizing me is like shooting spitballs at a battleship."

It was a great speech. The crowd loved it. Later, Howard stood patiently on the platform, signing autographs. Things were going beautifully—until the treasurer of the Philadelphia Sports Writers Association, Bob Kenney of the *Camden Courier-Post*, offered him a check for $300, the rather nominal fee that had been agreed upon in advance. "Fuck the check," Howard told him.

So Kenney offered to pay for the limousine that had rushed the TV personality from an early-evening taping of the "Tonight" show in New York. "Fuck the limousine," Cosell told him. "Where's the door?"

And with that, out the guest speaker marched. Angrily. Defiantly. Imperiously. It was, I've always suspected, all part of a brilliant performance. Anyway, to Howard's credit, he didn't hold a grudge, although nobody had the guts to invite him to another Philadelphia Sports Writers Banquet. No man should be expected to speak there twice. I think the lawyers call it double jeopardy.

Pat Williams put things into perspective at the 1981 banquet. "I knew what kind of group it was," he quipped, "when, during the moment of silence, somebody yelled 'Louder.' "

Come to think of it, what can you expect out of something called the Philadelphia Sports Writers Banquet that's held in Cherry Hill, New Jersey? Only in Philadelphia would the athletes and the sportswriters have to cross state lines to eat together.

To give you an idea how chummy everybody was at the last dinner, the writers presented Mike Schmidt of the Phillies with the "Pro Athlete of the Year" award. Mike sat there through a lengthy introduction that, at times, seemed more like a knock than a boost, then stood up, approached the rostrum, smiled sweetly, and said that he'd been looking forward to the banquet "as much as I would my next appointment for root-canal work. Philadelphia," he added, "is the only city where you can experience the thrill of victory and the agony of reading about it the next morning."

Schmidt didn't go so far as to say that first prize for winning the World Series was a one-year contract to play in Philadelphia, while second prize was two years. Obviously, deep down inside, Mike Schmidt really loves it there.

Actually, it's a unique love-hate relationship that athletes seem to have with the city that has finally lived down its losers image and become a winner—or, at least, a solid championship contender—in every major sport. The fans may boo louder than most when the home team flops, but nobody cheers louder than Philly fans when the home team wins. And, as first the Flyers and then the Phillies found out, nobody puts on better victory parades. Maybe that's because nobody has had more time to prepare for them.

2

Right You Are, Mel

THERE MAY NOT HAVE BEEN THAT *MANY* GREAT TEAMS IN Philadelphia over the years; there may have been a lot more losers than winners, but the city has had its share of sports figures who became, you might say, legends in their time. Look at the names who passed through. Think of the impact they had . . .

For all the last-place finishes, for all the 100–game losers, Philadelphia's baseball teams provided a tremendous number of legendary, or near legendary, figures in the old days. After all, Connie Mack managed there; Eddie Collins, Home Run Baker, Al Simmons, Jimmie Foxx, Mickey Cochrane, Chuck Klein, Ed Delahanty, Nap Lajoie, even Ty Cobb played there; Grover Cleveland Alexander, Lefty Grove, Chief Bender, Eddie Plank, and Robin Roberts pitched there. In football, there were Steve Van Buren, the battering, bruising running back; Norm van Brocklin, the brilliant quarterback; and Chuck Bednarik, the last of the iron men—a center on offense, a linebacker on defense, a terror on all counts. In basketball, there were stars of the stature of Joe Fulks and Hal Greer and Paul Arizin and Tom Gola and, towering above them all, Wilt Chamberlain. And towering even above Wilt, a short, stocky, wonderful man named Eddie Gottlieb, who was the father of pro basketball in Philadelphia . . . and points west.

As great as some of today's big names are, as legendary as the Julius Ervings, the Bobby Clarkes, the Steve Carltons, the Mike Schmidts are sure to become, many of those who preceded them in Philadelphia and became part of the city's sports heritage were giants too. Here then are fond memories of some non-playing

25

Philadelphia "sports legends" of the past and a few of the athletes who played important roles in their careers.

For sheer longevity, Cornelius McGillicuddy, a.k.a. Connie Mack, and Eddie Gottlieb belong at the top of the list. Mack's A's were the best in baseball for a while, and they were the worst in baseball for a longer while, but always Mack himself was somebody special.

*   *   *

Before he arrived on the Philly scene, the city's baseball fans knew what it was to watch the home team get clobbered. In 1876, the year the National League was formed, a Philadelphia franchise known as the Athletics played fifty-nine games, won fourteen of them, and then was expelled for refusing to make the season's last scheduled western trip. Things got better, though. Philadelphia's second National League team, the Phillies, began playing in 1883 and won the grand total of seventeen games. (They also lost eighty-one, but let's not get technical.) Speaking of legends, a pitcher named John Coleman, who was a member of that '83 Phillies team, wasn't far from becoming one. The poor fella lost forty-eight games that year, a record that will live as long as there is baseball. The other regular starter for the '83 Phillies, Art Hagan, also achieved a measure of immortality. He lost a game to Providence, 28-0, a walloping that remains the most one-sided shutout in major-league history.

Connie Mack's A's changed all that—for a while. In one particularly memorable stretch, beginning in 1910, they won four American League pennants in five years and three World Series in four years. And they won back-to-back world championships in 1929–30, an achievement spiced by the greatest rally in World Series history.

The '29 A's trailed the Chicago Cubs, 8-0, in the seventh inning of game four. The game was so hopelessly lost, legend has it, that Mack had made up his mind to remove his regulars in the last two innings and play out the string with the scrubs. He never got the chance.

Held to three hits through the first six innings by Charley Root, one of the Cubs' finest, the A's opened the home seventh with an Al Simmons' homer . . . and the avalanche was on. Before it was over, Mule Haas smashed a three-run, inside-the-park homer that pulled the A's within a run and so excited Jimmy Dykes that he smacked Mack on the back with such vigor that the tall, slender owner-manager went flying off the bench and landed among the bats.

Dykes atoned for it, though, with a long, bases-loaded double to left that knocked in the last two runs of the ten-run explosion that turned the 8–0 Cub romp into a 10–8 A's victory. With a lead to protect, Mack took no chances. He brought in Lefty Grove, who struck out four of the six Cubs he faced.

Greatest Comeback in World Series History
(Oct. 12, 1929 at Philadelphia)

Chicago (N.L.)	AB	R	H	O	A	E	Philadelphia (A.L.)	AB	R	H	O	A	E
McMillan, 3b	4	0	0	1	3	0	Bishop, 2b	5	1	2	2	3	0
English, ss	4	0	0	2	1	0	Haas, cf	4	1	1	2	0	0
Hornsby, 2b	5	2	2	1	1	0	Cochrane, c	4	1	2	9	0	0
Wilson, cf	3	1	2	3	0	1	Simmons, lf	5	2	2	0	0	0
Cuyler, rf	4	2	3	0	0	1	Foxx, 1b	4	2	2	10	0	0
Stephenson, lf	4	1	1	2	1	0	Miller, rf	3	1	2	3	0	1
Grimm, 1b	4	2	2	7	0	0	Dykes, 3b	4	1	3	0	2	0
Taylor, c	3	0	0	8	1	0	Boley, ss	3	1	1	1	5	0
Root, p	3	0	0	0	0	0	Quinn, p	2	0	0	0	0	0
Nehf, p	0	0	0	0	0	0	Walberg, p	0	0	0	0	0	1
Blake, p	0	0	0	0	0	0	Rommel, p	0	0	0	0	0	0
Malone, p	0	0	0	0	0	0	a-Burns	2	0	0	0	0	0
b-Hartnett	1	0	0	0	0	0	Grove, p	0	0	0	0	0	0
Carlson, p	0	0	0	0	1	0							
Totals	35	8	10	24	8	2	Totals	36	10	15	27	10	2

a—Popped out and struck out for Rommel in 7th.
b—Struck out for Malone in 8th.

Chicago (N.L.)	000	205	1 00	—	8
Philadelphia (A.L.)	000	000	(10)0x	—	10

RBI—Cuyler 2, Stephenson, Grimm 2, Taylor, Bishop, Haas 3, Simmons, Foxx, Dykes 3, Boley. 2B—Cochrane, Dykes, 3B—Hornsby. HR—Grimm, Haas, Simmons. SAC—Taylor, Haas, Boley. DP—Dykes, Bishop and Foxx. LEFT—Chicago 4, Philadelphia 6. SO—By Quinn 2, by Walberg 2, by Grove 4, by Root 3, by Malone 2, by Carlson 1.
BB—Off Quinn 2, off Rommel 1, off Nehf 1. HBP—by Malone (Miller). Hits—Off Quinn, 7 in 5 innings (pitched to 4 batters in 6th), off Walberg, 1 in 1, off Rommel, 2 in 1, off Grove, 0 in 2, off Root, 9 in 6 1/3, off Nehf, 1 in 0 (pitched to 2 batters in 7th), off Blake, 2 in 0 (pitched to 2 batters in 7th), off Malone, 1 in 2/3, off Carlson, 2 in 1. Winning Pitcher—Rommel. Losing Pitcher—Blake. U—Van Graftan (A.L.), Klem (N.L.), Dinneen (A.L.), Moran (N.L.). T—2:12, A—29,921.

But the greatness of that A's team merely added to the shock when Mack, for the second time in his career, was forced to unload his top players for financial reasons, thereby turning a baseball juggernaut into a patsy. The first time Mack was forced to do that—following the loss of the 1914 World Series to the Boston Braves—the A's hit rock bottom with a thud that later Philadelphia sports teams would be hard-pressed to equal (although a few of them were up to the challenge). After waving goodbye to such superstars as Eddie Collins, Chief Bender, and Eddie Plank—all Hall of Famers—the A's sank so fast it's a wonder Mack didn't get the bends. Seven straight years the A's finished last, and in most of those years they finished bad lasts. The 1916 team was the world's worst. Its record: 36 wins and 117 defeats, a record of major league baseball futility that stands to this day. Not only were those A's eighth and last, but they finished forty—count 'em, 40—games behind the seventh-place team. Even Connie Mack couldn't win without the horses.

The A's were so bad in that era that *Spalding's Baseball Guide* for 1923 saluted the team's seventh-place finish in '22 as "the big event in baseball in the Quaker City." Civic pride notwithstanding, Philadelphians managed to keep their joy under control. Exhaustive research turned up no evidence of a post-season parade down Broad Street.

In all, the A's finished last eighteen times from 1915 through 1954, when they left Philadelphia and headed west. But if they were bad for long periods of time—and they surely were—the National League Phillies were no pikers when it came to living in the cellar either. The Phillies, in fact, have more last-place finishes to their discredit (twenty-three) than the Philadelphia A's, but they had an unfair advantage: They stayed long after the A's left.

The Phillies never lost 117 games in a single season. They did, however, make several noble efforts in that direction. In one five-year stretch, starting in 1938, Phillie teams lost, in order, 105 games, 106 games, 103 games, 111 games, and 109 games. If only they had played 162–game schedules in those days, instead of a mere 154, there's no telling to what depths those Phillies would have plunged.

There *is* telling to what depths the 1961 Phillies plunged. They established a standard for baseball futility that may never be equalled in the big leagues, losing twenty-three games in a row, three more than Connie Mack's worst A's teams ever lost in a row. On the other hand, the A's reached twenty straight twice.

But along with those bad years, Connie Mack produced some truly great ones, winning nine pennants and five World Series. Until the 1980 Phillies went all the way, Mack had provided this baseball-crazy city with its only world championships.

Even Connie Mack couldn't go on managing forever, and finally the time came for the old man to step down. In his place came Jimmy Dykes —a Philadelphia legend in his own right—but the A's, at least the Philly variety, weren't about to win any more pennants. Dykes, of course, eventually got fired. Years later he explained, in his usual joking manner, how money problems had led to his dismissal. "When they [Connie's sons, Roy and Earl] fired me they said the reason was they couldn't find me," Dykes related one day between card games at the Bala Golf Club, where he spent much of his time in his latter years. "I said, 'You must be in damn bad financial shape. You only needed a dime to call me at Bala.' "

*   *   *

Connie Mack was a tall, almost gaunt figure. Eddie Gottlieb, the man they called "The Mogul," was a stumpy five-foot-seven. Not that his lack of height made any difference. He was a prince among men, a tireless worker for pro basketball who would give his friends—and he had many—the shirt off his back, even if it wouldn't fit most of them.

Gotty was a basketball pioneer who never lost his zest for the pro game. It was this remarkable little man who put together one of the great teams of the sport's early years, the Philadelphia Sphas, whose nickname derived from the initials of the South Philadelphia Hebrew Association. And it was Gotty who formed the Philadelphia Warriors in the old Basketball Association of America, forerunner of today's NBA.

Eddie Gottlieb, in short, did it all. He coached, he general-managed, he owned; he was the heart, the soul, the guts of pro basketball in Philadelphia. He was a throwback to another era, yet a man who was able to change with the times.

Today, a display case stands near the door to the main exhibit room in the Basketball Hall of Fame in Springfield, Massachusetts. That display case—tracing the history of the Sphas—was Gotty's pride and joy. To anyone hooked on basketball lore, it's a treasure chest, worth far more than the $7,500 it cost Gotty to make it a permanent part of the Hall. All the names are there: Doc Newman . . . Davey Banks . . . Chick Passon . . . Cy Kaselman . . . Harry Litwack . . . Inky Lautman . . . Moe Goldman . . . Shikey Gotthoffer . . . Red Wolfe . . . Petey Rosenberg . . . and more. They played in an era when pro basketball was a game, not a get-rich-quick opportunity for a kid who happens to be unusually tall.

"We got paid on a game basis," recalled Harry Litwack, one of Gotty's boys who went on to have a highly successful career as basketball coach at Temple University. "I'd say the average would be $15 to $30 a game."

There was a particularly memorable night in Union City, New Jersey, when the Sphas, on a hot streak and running away with the second half of the American League race, met one of their stiffest tests. If you think it's tough for a visiting basketball team to win at Boston Garden, you should have seen that gym in Union City.

"We had won fourteen straight," Gotty said one day when he was in a reminiscing mood. "Seven home, seven away. In those days to win on the other court, it was murder. They had a player named Paul Adamo. He was their high scorer, and Harry was playing him."

And playing him tough. The fans weren't at all happy.

"We played three fifteen-minute periods," said Litwack, "with a five-to-seven-minute intermission in between for dancing."

That's the way it was in those days. When the basketball teams stopped playing, the band started playing. Anyhow, the intermission at Union City wasn't long enough for Gotty to lead his team to the locker room. So, while the band played and the people danced, the Sphas waited on the bench.

"Suddenly," said Gotty, "I see a crowd gathering. They start clobbering a guy. We couldn't see who they were clobbering. Then the guy stuck his head up. It was Harry."

"A group from Hoboken," Litwack said. "For no reason they hit me over the head with a Coke bottle. I don't know how many stitches I got in my head. I had to go to the hospital. Later on it became infected on me. I had a helluva time . . . but we licked 'em."

There were tougher places to play than Union City, though. Gotty and Litwack used to talk about those visits to Prospect Hall to play a team called the Brooklyn Visitation. "There was a lady in the front row with hat pins," Harry said. "She used to jab you when you went by. Not the home team, though." People always said the Sphas jumped like hell when they played in Prospect Hall.

Then there was Arcadia Hall in Brooklyn, where the Jewels played. "The seats in the front row there used to be occupied by Murder, Inc.," Gotty said, "although we didn't know it at the time. If trouble started, they'd be the first guys out of the hall because they knew the cops would go after them."

Somehow, Eddie Gottlieb and the Philadelphia Sphas survived all that. They even gained a particularly memorable victory in Harlem's Renaissance Casino, home of one of pro basketball's greatest black teams, the Rens.

"We're one of the few, maybe the only team to beat them on their home court," Gotty said. "They were ahead of us by one point with seconds to go. There was a jump ball near our basket. Gotthoffer was 6-1 or 6-2. He was jumping for us. Their guy, Wee Willie Smith, was 6-7 or 6-8. The referee was Frank Forbes. He throws up the ball and Gotthoffer, I don't know what he did to Smitty. . . ."

Whatever he did, Forbes didn't see it. The Sphas got the ball. "One of our guys passed to Red Rosan under the basket," Gotty recalled. Rosan scored; the Sphas won.

Road trips were murder in those days. There was the trip back from Reading, Pennsylvania, on New Year's Day, 1934. "The night before it snowed like hell," Gotty said. "I was driving back in my seven-passenger Ford, in which nine guys rode. I've got the radio tuned in to the Columbia-Stanford [Rose Bowl] game. We're not too far from Norristown when suddenly I hit a patch of ice. Like a schmuck, I apply the brakes. Next thing I know the car's whirling around . . ."

That seven-passenger Ford, with the eight basketball players and their coach inside, wound up sideways in a ditch. There they remained, listening to the football game and waiting for the tow truck to arrive.

The Sphas played a lot of games in a lot of strange places in their twenty-nine year history. No trip, no opponent was too tough to take on. They even played on a basketball court behind a bar in a place called Mauch Chunk, later renamed Jim Thorpe, Pennsylvania.

The Western trips were especially difficult. Cleveland . . . Oshkosh . . . Toledo. Off they'd go, packed into Gotty's car. "Zink [announcer Dave Zinkoff, who handled the PA duties through decades of pro basketball in Philadelphia] would stretch out on the floor in front of the back seat," Gotty said. "The guys would take off their shoes and use him for a foot rest."

Zinkoff, as you can see, was generally pretty easy to get along with. There was one time, though, when he rebelled. The Sphas were filling the ballroom in the old Broadwood Hotel for the weekly Saturday night games and dances, and Zink decided his colorful announcing was a big reason. "He asked for a raise," Gotty said. " 'On the strength of what?' I asked him. 'Look at all the people coming to hear me announce,' he said. If he'd told me, 'I'm working hard; I deserve a raise,' he might've gotten something. But when he said he was drawing the people, he didn't have a chance."

Thus began one of pro basketball's first great holdout sagas. "I was getting five dollars a week," Zinkoff said. "I was holding out for six."

The holdout lasted two, maybe three weeks. Despite his absence, the people kept coming. Finally, the old friends reached a "compromise." Zink went back to work—for five dollars a week. Gotty always did drive a hard bargain. The man just had a way with figures, that's all.

Among his other accomplishments, Eddie Gottlieb was the guy who mapped out that most impossible of monstrosities, the NBA schedule. The gag was that the most sophisticated of computers couldn't do it, so Gotty did . . . almost to his dying day. Only it wasn't a gag. It took an Eddie Gottlieb to schedule the more than 900 regular-season NBA games, somehow arranging it so teams weren't scheduled in Los Angeles and New York on the same night. It was a monumental undertaking trying to fit the demands of NBA teams to arena schedules throughout the country. No big deal, Gotty would shrug. It only took him about four months. Unless, of course, there were complications.

"I had a schedule 95 percent completed before we took in four new clubs," he said in December of 1976. "So I had to start over and do it in six or seven weeks. Otherwise there wouldn't have been a schedule."

There *wouldn't* have been, either. Gotty worked from eight to twelve hours a day to put it together. "I was ready to take all the papers, throw them out, burn them. That's the way I felt."

But he resisted the temptation and completed the awesome job. Gotty took his papers to Montreal during the '76 Olympic Games, worked on them from nine in the morning to six in the evening, then went out and watched an Olympic event at night. That was Eddie Gottlieb; he packed an awful lot into his long life. He did things that far younger men would never attempt.

"I had days," he said, "where fourteen, fifteen, seventeen clubs requested the same date [to play games]. It isn't easy, but it keeps my brain going. Pretty good, eh, for a guy who's past."

Past? Past what? Seventy-five? Eighty?

Gotty smiled. "Just say 'past,' " he replied.

The truth was, Eddie Gottlieb remained youthful until the very end, his years notwithstanding. He bridged the old days of pro basketball with the new. He was the one constant, the one breath of fresh air in a constantly changing world. While others panicked, Gotty sat there, calmly, intelligently surveying the passing scene. Most sports figures have long since retired by the time they are elected to the Hall of Fame; Gotty hadn't even slowed down.

Some of his fondest memories involved Joe Fulks, the man of many shots who did as much as anybody—maybe more—to put pro basketball on the major-league map.

It was May of 1946 when Gotty, trying to build a Philadelphia team for the new Basketball Association of America, first turned his attention to Fulks, who had earned raves while playing in the Philippines as a Marine.

Times were very different then. No pro draft. No multi-million-dollar contracts. The new pro league had set a salary limit of $50,000 for an entire team.

It took time, but Gotty tracked down Fulks, who had been discharged from the Marines and was living in Kentucky. "He didn't know me from a bag of peanuts, the general manager–coach

of the old Philly Warriors said. "I asked him if he'd be interested in
playing."

Fulks was interested, all right—if the price was right. Like
Zinkoff, he drove a hard bargain. Either he got enough money, he
informed Gotty, or he would finish his college career at Murray
State.

"How much can I get?" Joe asked him.

"Five thousand," Gotty told him.

There was silence on the other end of the long-distance
hookup. At first, Gotty thought that Fulks was overwhelmed by
the size of the offer. "Gee," he remembered saying to himself, "I
offered this hillbilly too much."

But the "hillbilly" was nobody's fool. He was twenty-six years
old, and he had a family to support.

"I want $8,000," Joe Fulks told Gottlieb.

This time Gotty was responsible for the silence that followed.
Finally he sputtered, "How can we pay you $8,000? There won't
be anything left."

As far as Fulks was concerned, that was Gotty's problem.
Time passed. The player never budged in his demands. There was
nothing for Gotty to do but meet him face to face. No use. Fulks
still wouldn't sign for less. It was $8,000 or bust.

Gotty conferred with Pete Tyrrell, general manager of the
Philadelphia Arena, which owned the Warriors at the time.
"Pete," he said, "we're not going to move this guy. He wants eight,
and it's eight or nothing. I've never seen him play. I don't know
how good he is, but if he's as good as they say and somebody else
signs him, we'll regret this the rest of our lives."

Tyrrell got the message. "All right," he said, "give it to him."

Gotty did, and a pro basketball superstar was born. Fulks
averaged 23.2 points per game his rookie year, seven points more
than the second-leading scorer in the league. Years later, Gotty
recalled the thrill of seeing his $8,000 wonder in action for the first
time. It was just a workout, but it was enough to convince Gotty
that the money had been well spent.

"I had never seen anything like it," he said. "Here's a guy who
spent the entire pre-game workout taking shots that he would take
in the game—two-hand jump shots, one hand with the right, one
hand with the left, driving shots from the left, driving shots from

the right, set shots from the floor. He's the first guy I ever saw who took a basketball and during the entire practice kept that ball to himself. Nobody else was supposed to touch that ball. He just kept shooting and shooting. My personal opinion is that he was responsible for the league staying in existence. He was the first superstar."

Before Fulks threw in his last field goal, in the early '50s, he had boosted his annual salary close to $20,000. Today, they'd have to float a loan to get him.

For Eddie Gottlieb, the final buzzer sounded in December of 1979. The chapel in the funeral home on North Broad Street was packed. Gotty would have appreciated that. He always like to play to full houses.

The people came from New York, from California, from Florida to pay their last respects to the short, stocky pro-basketball giant. Larry O'Brien, the commissioner of the NBA, was there. So were some of the great old names in the sport—Red Auerbach, Ben Kerner, Danny Biasone. Dolph Schayes was there. And Paul Arizin. And Billy Cunningham. And so many more. Harry Litwack flew up from his home in Miami as a standby passenger when he couldn't get a reservation.

Eddie Gottlieb had been elected to the Hall of Fame for pioneering pro basketball. But the people who crowded into the chapel in the funeral home on North Broad Street were there because Gotty was Gotty, a man who went out of his way to help others, a man who remained young through his 60s and 70s and was still young when he died at 81.

Those weren't all basketball people in the crowd either. Eddie Gottlieb's warmth had touched far more than just the basketball world.

Joey Bishop, the nightclub and TV comic from South Philly, was there. "He gave me my first job," Bishop said. "South Mountain Manor, Wernersville, Pennsylvania, in 1937. We [Bishop and his brothers] were a trio. Gotty said, 'We'll give you $25.' I thought he meant $25 for each of us, so I okayed it, but he meant $25 all together. The first week we get paid $8 apiece. I went to Gotty and I said, 'I don't think that's fair.' He said, 'I'll tell you what. We'll do your laundry too.' " Joey Bishop smiled. "That's the God's honest truth," he said.

Max Patkin, the baseball clown, was also at the funeral. "Gotty got me started," he said. "He booked me in 1948. He's the only reason I'm in this business . . . Eddie Gottlieb was one of the last of the giants [in pro sports]. How many do you have left? The George Halases, the Art Rooneys . . ."

Zach Clayton, who had played for the Renaissance, one of the great pro basketball teams of the early days, and later for the Harlem Globetrotters, was there too. "The second pair of sneakers I ever owned, Gotty gave me," he said.

So many people crowded into that funeral home in North Philadelphia and each, it seemed, brought along a story of how Eddie Gottlieb had provided a helping hand. "He did me one of the biggest favors of my life," Harry Litwack said. "In order to open my basketball camp I needed money. I came to him, and I asked him for a loan of $50,000. He gave it to me. He was such a good-hearted guy, such a charitable man."

He was a little guy whom everybody learned to look up to. As Eddie Gottlieb and Connie Mack demonstrated, a man doesn't have to have a powerful physique, doesn't even have to be a great athlete to attain "legend" status in sports.

Which brings us to By Saam.

*   *   *

Don't laugh. If By Saam isn't a Philadelphia sports legend, then who is? Here's a guy who lasted nearly four decades in one city in one of the world's most insecure businesses: sports broadcasting. Players came and went. Managers came and went. Sponsors came and went. And By Saam kept rolling along. His was the voice that soothed generations of baseball fans each spring and summer. There was something reassuring about the sound of that familiar voice. Philadelphians grew up listening to it. As surely as the A's and the Phillies would finish in the second division, By Saam's dulcet tones would herald the coming of a new season.

But why a legend, you say? Because of his incredible longevity, for one thing. And, above all, because of some of the wildly funny things he said.

"I think By was unique in one way," another veteran Philadelphia sports announcer, Bill Campbell, once said. "He enjoyed what he did. You know the expression he always used—*rolling along*? It didn't matter whether the team was winning or getting killed. By broadcast the way he lived. He rolled along. I had peaks and valleys. Not By. He always treated it like a game. He wasn't upset by wins and losses."

Nor was he upset by some of those marvelous, legendary goofs.

Ah, the goofs. What man can spend that many years describing the daily fortunes of baseball teams without committing an occasional blunder? Not By Saam.

"I used to come on the air every afternoon and say, 'Good afternoon everyone, this is By Saam speaking,' " he recalled one day during spring training late in his broadcasting career.

He could recite that introduction without thinking. Presumably, that was the problem because one day he greeted his public by saying, "Good afternoon By Saam, this is everyone speaking."

Saam laughed good-naturedly as he told the story. "You get your lines messed up once in a while," he said.

When a man ad-libs some 6,500 big-league baseball games, he's bound to put his foot in his mouth occasionally.

"We're in the [Houston] Astrodome the first year it was open," Bill Campbell remembered. "By's sitting there, talking [on the air]. . . ."

And Campbell and Richie Ashburn were sitting in the booth with him, gazing around at baseball's first indoor stadium, listening to By Saam set the stage.

" 'What a beautiful night for baseball,' he said," Campbell recalled. " 'The flags are hanging limp. There's no breeze at all.' Richie and I almost died laughing."

Well, after all, somebody might have left a window open. You know how drafty those Astrodomes can get.

Then there was the time that an enemy batter sent Alex Johnson retreating rapidly toward the left-field wall. By was on top of the play. "Alex Johnson is going back," he crooned. "He's going back . . . back. His head hits the wall. He reaches down, picks it up, and throws it into second base."

Surely a classic befitting the By Saam legend, as was his first World Series announcing assignment, in which he shared a radio booth with Mel Allen. The game rolled into the bottom of the fifth. It was time for Allen to introduce his play-by-play partner for the second half of the ball game. "I was so wrapped up in what I was doing I didn't think about what Mel was saying," Saam said. Allen wasn't holding anything back. He made By sound like a wondrous combination of Edward R. Murrow, Walter Cronkite, and Red Barber, with a touch of Vin Scully thrown in. "Here's the personable, knowledgeable announcer of the Phillies," he told the listeners. And By Saam leaned forward and chirped into the microphone, "Right you are, Mel."

Late in the 1975 season, with the Phillies locked in mortal combat with the Mets, Saam came up with this gem while talking about a young Mets pitcher: "He's not throwing very hard. The ball comes up there looking like a fruitcake." There was a pause, followed by the sound of laughter in the booth, followed by Saam's soothing voice saying, "I mean a grapefruit. Oh well, you get the idea."

No rundown of the best of Saam would be complete without at least a passing reference to his uncanny knack for spouting non sequitors. "Ron Stone is coming out of the dugout to pinch hit," he would say, "but good seats are still available for tomorrow night's game."

The man was, by all standards, the stuff that legends are made of. Above all, though, I'll always remember the day I was interviewing By in his hotel room in Florida one spring training. His golf bag was leaning against the bed as he spoke. Occasionally, Saam would check his watch; he had to be at the first tee pretty soon.

The conversation wandered into a discussion of how some people had the idea that announcing baseball games—even baseball games involving a succession of losing Philadelphia teams—was a ridiculously easy way to make a living. "Even my friends kid and say, 'You're on vacation,' " Saam said, and he shook his head at the folly of anybody actually thinking that. "If you analyze all the time you're away and you spread that out over a year, we work just as hard as the average guy," he protested vigorously.

By leaned forward, letting those words of wisdom sink in. Then he glanced at the big, impressive-looking golf bag leaning against the bed and he added, in all seriousness, "And besides, it isn't easy carrying a golf bag with you on those road trips."

Right you are, By.

3

Good Sightlines, Bad Roof

NOWADAYS IT'S HARD TO TELL ONE STADIUM OR ARENA FROM another without a scorecard. All the new, modern, multi-purpose stadiums—from Riverfront to the Vet, from Three Rivers to Busch Stadium—bear a striking resemblance to inverted hatboxes. The arenas? Mostly, they look like space ships that came in for a landing.

In the old days, however, it was a different story—and in Philadelphia the old days went on and on, years after many other cities had entered the new days. There wasn't a modern indoor arena in town until 1967, when the Spectrum was completed. And Veterans Stadium didn't appear on the South Philly horizon until 1971.

Let's not complain, though. There was something about the old days, and the old places our teams used to play in . . .

The Vet may look a lot like Busch Stadium in St. Louis, or any number of other ball parks, but nothing looked like Baker Bowl except Baker Bowl.

Ah, those (they tell me) were the days. They don't make ball parks like Baker Bowl any more. Allen Lewis, for years one of the country's most respected baseball writers—and now a member of the Hall of Fame Veterans Committee—sat in the first row of the upper deck at Baker Bowl as a boy, watching his beloved Phillies blow game after game. The stands were so close to the playing field, he said, "you felt like you were in the game."

The right-field foul pole was a mere 279 feet away, and the high, tin fence in right was a favorite target area for the National League's lefthanded hitters. Every time a baseball would go crashing off that tin fence, the noise would echo from 15th Street to Broad Street.

One memorable afternoon the Brooklyn Dodgers were in town, and Walter Beck, a pitcher nicknamed "Boom-Boom" for obvious reasons, was facing the Phillies. The artillery fire started early. Boom-Boom was getting bombed. The tin fence was taking an awful beating . . . and so was Hack Wilson, the Brooklyn right fielder. Legend has it, the poor fella had had a big night on the town, and now there he was, chasing down a seemingly non-stop barrage of enemy missiles that were bouncing off that high, tin fence behind him. Hack was downright pooped as Casey Stengel, the Brooklyn manager, came walking out of the Dodger dugout and headed for the mound in the midst of one of the Phillie attacks. While Casey talked to his pitcher, Wilson leaned over, hands on his knees, his body aching and weary, his mind a zillion light years away.

Stengel had seen—and heard—enough. He wanted a new pitcher. Boom-Boom was infuriated. Instead of handing the ball to his manager, as custom dictated, he turned and fired the ball as hard as he could in the direction of right field. That ball, like so many others, crashed against the tin fence and bounced down. The familiar noise snapped Hack Wilson out of his daydream. He whirled, retrieved the ball and pegged it into second base before realizing nobody had hit it.

Baker Bowl, which opened in 1887, must not have been the sturdiest ball park ever built. On August 6, 1903, a fire broke out in a building across the street beyond left field, and the fans, yearning for a better look, began climbing to the top of the stands on the 15th Street side. The crowd of fire-watchers grew so large, and the strain on the stands grew so great that they collapsed. Twelve died in the tragedy, and more than 200 were hurt.

There were many days at Baker Bowl when not enough spectators showed up to put a strain on anything—except the Phillies' financial statement. On one such day the Phillies were locked in a particularly dull ball game that got so tedious the writers, in an effort to amuse themselves, sat there eating peanuts and dropping the shells on the scattered fans below. There must have been some complaints because pretty soon the owner of the club came rushing up to the press box, which was really a part of the stands set off by chicken wire, and told the journalists to cease and desist. "Don't you realize," he bellowed, "there are customers down there?" At which point Warren Brown, a well-known Chicago sportswriter, snapped to attention and exclaimed, "Boy, what a story that is!"

The opening of Shibe Park (renamed Connie Mack Stadium before the start of the 1953 season) was an even bigger story. In its final years, it may have been a decaying, outdated stadium with seats that were too cramped, clubhouses that were too small, and parking lots that simply couldn't handle a big crowd. But in 1909, when it opened, Shibe Park was baseball's showplace. And even in 1970, when it closed, it was a great place to watch a game. The sightlines were super—unless, of course, you happened to wind up behind a post.

The new ball parks may be far more comfortable, far more convenient than the old places. But they'll never really replace them. Maybe the Vet has bright green artificial turf and an electronic scoreboard that provides up-to-the-minute stats, shows cartoons, and even—God help us—commercials. Connie Mack Stadium had the feel of history about it. A man could watch a game there and point to the spot where Al Simmons or Jimmie Foxx or Mickey Mantle or Ted Williams had hit one. He could stare down at the mound in 1970 and imagine seeing Robin Roberts pitching off it in 1950. There was an aura about Connie Mack Stadium, about Ebbets Field, about the Polo Grounds, about all the old big-league parks that can never be recaptured.

The Phillies left Baker Bowl and joined the American League A's in the stadium on 21st Street and Lehigh Avenue on July 4, 1938. The two teams combined to make a lot of baseball history there, even if it wasn't all pleasant history from a Philadelphia standpoint.

It was at Shibe Park that Connie Mack's A's came up with that incredible, ten-run, seventh-inning rally in the 1929 World Series. And it was there that Pat Seerey and Lou Gehrig hit four home runs in a game, and Ted Williams rapped out six hits in eight at-bats in a season-ending doubleheader to raise his 1941 batting average to .406. Also, remarkably enough, it was the park where the Giants' Mel Ott, one of the National League's premier home run hitters, *never* hit a home run. Chances are, though, the left-handed hitter belted quite a few shots off the high right-field wall.

A total of nine no-hitters were pitched in Shibe Park–Connie Mack Stadium, but not a single one by a Phillies pitcher. In fact, no Phillies pitcher has ever pitched a no-hitter in any Philadelphia ball park.

Chief Bender of the A's did it, though, in 1910, as did Bullet Joe Bush in 1916, and Sam Jones of the Yankees and Howard Ehmke of the Red Sox did it to the A's in 1923. There was a twenty-two-year lapse before Dick Fowler of the A's no-hit the St. Louis Browns in '45 and two years later Bill McCahan, another A's righthander, stopped the Washington Senators. After that, the Phillies were victimized three times—by Hall-of-Famer Sandy Koufax in 1964 and by two lesser lights, George Culver of the Reds in 1968 and Bill Stoneman of the Expos in 1969.

The Phillies never had the pleasure of clinching a pennant at Connie Mack Stadium; their 1950 pennant was wrapped up in Brooklyn's Ebbets Field. But Connie Mack Stadium, even in its fading years, could be called—if you didn't mind stretching things a little bit—a home of champions. After all, back-to-back National League pennants *were* clinched there—by the Los Angeles Dodgers in 1966 and the St. Louis Cardinals in 1967. In those days, the only thing the Phillies led the league in was keeping champagne on ice for somebody else. The club's biggest need in that era wasn't more pitching or harder hitting or better defense; it was a bigger visiting clubhouse to handle those pennant-clinching bashes by the opposition.

The Dodger clinching in '66—on the final day of the season—was particularly memorable. The "magic number" to eliminate the Giants was down to one as the Dodgers took on the Phillies in a Sunday double-header, a situation so compelling that Danny Kaye, the entertainer and baseball buff of note, came to Philadelphia to root the Dodgers to victory. The pressure on Kaye was even greater than it was on his heroes. They had two chances to win on this day. He had only one; well before the second game ended, he would have to leave for a television appearance in New York City. Danny, it turned out, was to be the mystery guest on "What's My Line?"

A tan raincoat pulled tightly around him, an old, scrunched-up rain hat covering his red hair, Kaye watched the first game from a vantage point next to the Dodger radio booth under the third base roof at Connie Mack Stadium. Chain-smoking cigarettes, periodically removing his hat to run an anxious hand over his tousled hair, he looked as nervous as a comedian whose option had just been dropped.

The Phillies were the problem. They had the lead, and they kept it. When Tony Gonzalez raced to the right-field foul line for Maury Wills' game-ending fly ball, Kaye put both hands on the top of his head, tugged down viciously on his hat, and muttered, "I had to stay up all night [to fly from the West coast] for this. Can you imagine?"

To make matters worse, the Pirates blew some golden opportunities to knock off the Giants, who finally pulled out the game . . . and now the Dodgers had to beat the Phillies in the nightcap to clinch. Poor Danny Kaye. I'll never forget the crestfallen look on his face. Down below, Sandy Koufax was warming up for one of the biggest games of his career—and it was almost time to leave for "What's My Line?"

Koufax, pitching with two days' rest, won the game, and the Dodgers crammed into that tight, little visiting clubhouse on the first-base side of Connie Mack Stadium and celebrated—without Danny Kaye.

The Cardinals' celebration the following season was wilder, even though the race they won was far more one-sided. By beating the Phillies on this day, the Cards went thirteen games up with eleven to play, then went to town. They screamed. They hollered. They squirted champagne. In general, they went nuts. Finally, with Orlando Cepeda in charge, they carted a succession of innocent victims through the sardine-like mob and tossed their victims into the shower. Jack Buck, the announcer, got hauled away. So did Red Schoendienst, the manager, and Stan Musial, the general manager. Stan the Man wasn't expecting such treatment. He was wearing a dark brown suit and looked horrified when Cepeda and friends closed in. "No . . . no," he pleaded. "Yes . . . yes," they replied, and took him away to his watery fate.

Yessir, visiting teams knew how to have fun at Connie Mack Stadium.

Closing night at the old ball park wasn't much fun, though. Designed as a nostalgic trip down memory lane, it turned into a frightening, bloody orgy.

It seemed like such a clever promotional stunt, handing out slabs of wood stamped with the historic date—October 1, 1970—and the words, "I was there." But Bill Giles, the promotional whiz whose idea it was, made the serious tactical error of handing out those wooden slabs to the fans as they entered the park, not when they left. As a result, instead of the souvenirs they were intended to be, those slabs of wood became weapons.

As the game—a meaningless exercise between the Montreal Expos and the Phillies, the two worst teams in the National League East—progressed, the list of casualties in the stands increased. People had their heads bashed open with those souvenir slabs. Nine of the casualties were rushed to nearby hospitals. More than two dozen were treated in the little medical room behind home plate.

For some fans, the souvenir slabs weren't enough. Eager for something else to remember the old ball park by, they began ripping apart seats while the game was still going on. Perhaps the most terrifying moment of all occurred when hundreds—maybe thousands—of fans began pounding their wooden slabs against the concrete stands late in the game. Sitting there, listening to the racket, you had the feeling the stadium was being torn down while you were still in it.

It was no picnic for the players either. Fans kept running out of the stands, interrupting the game so many times that the public address announcer was ordered to issue a warning that the game might be forfeited to the Expos . . . as if it really mattered.

To make things worse, the game went into extra innings. As the tenth inning began, Montreal manager Gene Mauch—a long-time Phillie —conferred with the umpires along the third-base line. 'Don't you even think of forfeiting,' " Mauch said, "I told them, 'You'll get somebody hurt bad. . . .' They said, 'We were just trying to scare them.' "

Well, there *was* something to be scared about—the sound of wood smashing against wood, of chairs being ripped to pieces, of a stadium being destroyed.

"I'm just glad Montreal wasn't beating us, 10–1," Deron Johnson told his teammates, "or we never would have finished the game."

Instead the Phillies were winning, 1–0, when John Bateman

hit a catchable line drive to left field with one out in the top of the ninth. Phillie left fielder Ron Stone failed to make the catch, but nobody blamed him. It isn't easy catching a line drive when a fan is standing next to you, pulling on your arm.

Last Game at Connie Mack Stadium

(October 1, 1970)

Montreal	ab	r	h	rbi	Philadelphia	ab	r	h	rbi
Gosger, lf	5	0	0	0	Taylor, 2b	5	1	0	0
Sutherland, 2b	4	0	0	0	McCarver, c	5	1	3	1
Staub, rf	2	0	0	0	Gamble, rf	4	0	2	1
Fairly, 1b	5	0	1	0	Johnson, 1b	3	0	0	0
Bailey, 3b	4	0	0	0	Stone, lf	4	0	1	0
Day, cf	4	0	1	0	Money, 3b	4	0	1	0
Bateman, c	4	0	1	0	Browne, cf	4	0	1	0
Phillips, pr	0	1	0	0	Bowa, ss	4	0	0	0
Brand, c	0	0	0	0	Lersch, p	3	0	1	0
Wine, ss	4	0	2	1	Selma, p	1	0	0	0
Morton, p	2	0	0	0					
Jones, ph	0	0	0	0					
Marshall, p	0	0	0	0					
Fairey, ph	1	0	0	0					
Reed, p	0	0	0	0					
Totals	36	1	5	1	Totals	37	2	9	2

Montreal	000	000	001	0 — 1
Philadelphia	001	000	000	1 — 2

E—Money, Bailey, Taylor. LEFT—Montreal 9, Philadelphia 8. 2B—Wine. 3B—McCarver. SB—Bateman. McCarver. SAC—Sutherland.

	IP	H	R	ER	BB	SO
Morton	7	7	1	1	1	3
Marshall	1	0	0	0	1	0
Reed (L, 6-5)	1 2/3	2	1	1	0	1
Lersch	8 1/3	5	1	1	3	7
Selma (W, 8-9)	1 1/3	0	0	0	0	1

T—2:46. A—31,822.

So the season—and the old ball park—lasted one inning more as the noise level mounted and the fans grew more and more impatient. It took Tim McCarver to put the stadium to rest, running home with the winning run in the bottom of the tenth—a signal for the players on both teams to begin running for their lives.

One lady drove 160 miles to see the game. She was walking out of the ball park after the game when an unidentified assailant smacked her on the side of the head with one of those wooden slabs. A sixty-five-year-old man was swept onto the field when the game ended. All around him the lunatics cavorted, brandishing pieces of wood, ripping up clumps of grass, clawing at the bases, running amok. They found the man sitting motionless on what was left of the playing field. He had suffered a stroke.

One fan made a grab for Bill Wilson's cap, raking the Phillies' relief pitcher across the face with his nails in the process. Wilson went after him and brought him to earth with a flying tackle. "I'm trying out for the Eagles tomorrow," he said, and the way the Eagles were going then, he might have made it.

"Mob violence," Coach Billy DeMars termed it. "Some son of a gun hit me in the back, like a karate chop. They were stealing helmets, bats, everything in sight . . ."

And so it was that Philadelphia said goodbye to Connie Mack Stadium. It wasn't the kind of goodbye that Bill Giles had expected. In the eighth inning the Phillies' executive had called the dugout with instructions for the players. DeMars had answered the phone. "When the game's over," Giles told him, "have everybody line up and give out your hats to the people who won them [in a series of drawings held during the game]."

Needless to say, that was one set of instructions that went unheeded.

*   *   *

The Eagles' farewell to Franklin Field wasn't quite as dramatic. Maybe that was because there were really two farewells—the one in December of 1969 that turned into a false alarm when the Vet wasn't ready in time for the 1970 season, and the "final farewell" a year later.

The '69 "farewell" came on a dismal, snowy day that was fit for masochists, not historians. The Eagles, like the Phillies of that era, were bad. And their fans weren't happy about it. The snowballs started flying out of the upper deck of the Ivy League stadium shortly before 1 P.M., pelting the jeep and the snowplows and any humans within range. A man in a raincoat put a red flag in place at the northeast corner of the stadium . . . and ducked as a snowball went sailing past his ear. A linesman, easily identifiable in his striped shirt, ran out of the dressing room and was bombarded as the fans cheered. The poor man sought refuge under the west goal post.

At that point, the public address announcer made his plea. "Please, ladies and gentlemen," he said, "We ask you, please, to refrain from throwing snowballs. . . ." At that very moment, an especially large snowball hit the ground a few feet from the linesman. Finally, the announcer informed the crowd that one man had already been injured and the barrage temporarily stopped. Asked who was hurt, a member of the Eagles' public relations staff said, "Nobody . . . but we thought that was the best way to stop them. I hope you'll forgive a white lie."

With snow falling and snowballs flying, lies weren't the only things white on this day.

The game itself was in keeping with most of the season: awful. The Atlanta Falcons beat the Eagles, 27–3. The best Philadelphia arms on display in Franklin Field that afternoon were throwing snowballs instead of footballs. There were some big plays, however. The best was a superb, clutch catch by the Falcons' trainer, who turned around just in the nick of time and speared a snowball aimed at his head. As the final seconds of what was to have been the final game ticked off, a fan in the north stands stood up and led organized boos.

It was hardly a day to remember. Few of the players had any attachment for the stadium, even though it was the site of the Eagles' last NFL championship game, nine years before. One man was sad at the thought of leaving, however. Chuck Bednarik, one of the heroes of that 1960 title game, had spent this day ducking snowballs on the sidelines and watching the dreary performance. But he loved Franklin Field. As a college player at Penn, this was home to him. As a pro, this had become "home" too.

"People are going to start appreciating this place when they go to the other place," he said that day, looking out over the field. "Let 'em complain about the locker rooms. How much time do you spend in the locker room? This is where you spend your time—on the field. When we came here from Shibe Park, that's when we really felt big league. This is an awe-inspiring stadium. It has atmosphere. It has memories. It has nostalgia. . . ." With that Chuck Bednarik turned and walked slowly out of the ancient, red-brick stadium. "I think," he added, "Franklin Field made pro football in Philadelphia."

He, at least, was not disappointed when the Eagles were

forced to play yet another season in the place. The "second farewell" was a winning effort—a 30–20 victory over the Pittsburgh Steelers that brought the Eagles' final 1970 record to 3–10–1. As head coach Jerry Williams neared the twenty-two concrete steps leading to the cramped locker room with the radiators hanging from the walls and the paint peeling behind his desk, the voice of Matt Guokas, Sr., boomed over the loudspeaker. "Merry, Merry Christmas and a Happy New Year," he told the fans. "And thank you."

The response was loud and clear. The people booed.

                    *   *   *

The new indoor arena wasn't very fancy, but it served the purpose extremely well. You could see the ice, or the court, or whatever you happened to be looking at, from any vantage point in the Spectrum stands, which was more than you could say about New York's new Madison Square Garden. Even if one Philadelphia columnist wrote, with truth on his side, that the place looked very much like a sardine can from the outside, there were no serious complaints—until the roof blew off.

The Flyers were driving for the expansion-division, regular-season championship in their first season of operation when they found themselves suddenly homeless. And to a hockey team, there is no place like home.

A few days after the windstorm whipped through South Philadelphia and part of the Spectrum roof went whipping away with it, Bud Poile, then the general manager of the Flyers, stood behind the players' bench, his hands jammed deep into his pockets, and stared at the roof for what seemed like a very long time. Finally, he shrugged and looked away. "Doesn't look like it's going to fall down to me," he said.

But others weren't so sure . . . and before the Spectrum could be reopened for business, repairs would have to be made. And that left the Flyers, and the 76ers, out in the cold.

You had to feel sorry for Bud Poile. A career hockey man, he had always wanted to wind up in the big leagues. Now here he was, general manager of the only big-league team with a topless rink. "After twenty-six years in hockey, I thought I'd seen everything," he muttered, "but this is a new one."

Jack Ramsay, general manager of the 76ers at the time, wasn't too thrilled about the sudden ventilation either. The 76ers had 15,000 tickets sold for a game that Friday night, and now it would have to be played in Civic Center Convention Hall, which had only about 10,000 seats. Still, the 76ers had a reasonable Philadelphia alternative to the Spectrum. The Flyers didn't.

It was a mess. The stretch drive was on, and Poile had to look for available rinks in such faraway places as Montreal, Toronto, Quebec, even Winnipeg. He had tried New York as a site for one "home" game, and been considerably less than satisfied. "I'll never play another [home] game in New York," Bud said. "The hell with that. Not after what happened."

What happened was they put thousands of kids in the place . . . and they cheered wildly for the other team. Let's face it, you couldn't expect New York kids to cheer for Philadelphia.

"The president of the Rangers told us, 'Don't worry. Our fans will cheer for you,' " Poile said.

Oh well. Live and learn.

"Do you know something?" asked Bill Putnam, then president of the Flyers. "This is the first time in the fifty-one-year history of the National Hockey League that a game has been played on neutral ice."

All in all, the homeless waifs didn't fare that badly. They held on to finish first in their division, although it only took a 31–32–11 record to do it.

*   *   *

It was April 4, 1971. The Phillies had arrived from Clearwater, Florida, ready to stake their claim on last place in the National League East. Ah, but the cellar had never looked like this. It was the beginning of a new era—an era of plush, carpeted clubhouses, of synthetic turf, of giant, electronic scoreboards, of huge crowds. Another six days would pass before the Phillies would play their first game at the Vet, but this final, pre-season workout provided them with their first look at their new home. Connie Mack Stadium it wasn't.

Don Money sat on the dugout steps and took in the scene—the distant rows of multi-colored seats, that animated scoreboard in deep right-center field, the sparkling green of the rug that covered the playing field. It was, to be sure, a different world than he had known.

First Game at Veterans Stadium

(April 10, 1971)

Montreal	ab	r	h	rbi	Philadelphia	ab	r	h	rbi
Day, cf	4	0	0	0	Bowa, ss	4	1	2	0
Raymond, p	0	0	0	0	Money, 3b	3	1	1	2
Reed, p	0	0	0	0	Montanez, cf	2	1	1	0
Brand, ph	1	0	0	0	Johnson, 1b	3	1	1	0
Hunt, 2b	3	1	1	0	Briggs, lf	3	0	0	0
Staub, rf	4	0	1	0	Freed, rf	3	0	2	1
Bailey, 3b	4	0	1	1	McCarver, c	3	0	1	1
Fairly, lf	2	0	1	0	Doyle, 2b	2	0	0	0
Jones, rf	4	0	0	0	Taylor, ph, 2b	2	0	0	0
Bateman, c	4	0	2	0	Bunning, p	2	0	0	0
Wine, ss	1	0	0	0	Hoerner, p	0	0	0	0
Fairey, ph	1	0	0	0					
Laboy, ph	1	0	0	0					
Stoneman, p	2	0	0	0					
O'Donoghue, p	0	0	0	0					
Marshall, p	0	0	0	0					
Sutherland, ph	0	0	0	0					
Totals	31	1	6	1	Totals	27	4	8	4

Montreal	000	001	000 — 1
Philadelphia	000	003	10x — 4

E—Jones, Money. DP—Montreal 1, Philadelphia 1. LEFT—Montreal 10, Philadelphia 7. 2B—Hunt, Bailey, 3B—Bowa, HR—Money. SB—Hunt, Bowa. SAC—Bunning. SF—McCarver, Money.

	IP	H	R	ER	BB	SO
Stoneman (L, 0-1)	5	7	3	3	3	1
O'Donoghue	1/3	0	0	0	0	0
Marshall	1/3	0	0	0	0	0
Raymond	2/3	1	1	1	2	1
Bunning (W, 1-0)	7 1/3	6	1	1	3	4
Hoerner (S, 1)	1 2/3	0	0	0	1	2

HBP—By Bunning (Hunt). T—2:43. A—55,352.

"This is Philadelphia," the third baseman said, and he shook his head. "I don't believe it."

A crowd of about 25,000 turned out for the pre-opening ceremonies that day. The people seemed determined to let everybody know that they hadn't changed, even if the site of Phillie and Eagles games had. When Phillies general manager John Quinn was introduced, they booed. When Eagles GM Pete Retzlaff was introduced, they booed some more. When Mayor James Tate put in an appearance, they saluted him with the loudest boo of all. Don Money didn't have to worry. This *was* Philadelphia.

Ah, but it was a new, bright Philadelphia, a Philadelphia where the fans could boo in comfort, where a team could finish last in style . . . and, somewhere down the road, win championships in style.

"What a difference a year makes," Phillies manager Frank Lucchesi murmured as he entered his new office for the first time. "Now it's a pleasure to get out of your car, to walk in, to step on the red carpet. It's a palace."

And the palace was in readiness. Somebody had even stocked the manager's office with all the necessities of Philadelphia baseball life. On the shelf were a couple of dozen packages of aspirin, a big jar of vitamins, an even bigger jar of antacid tablets, everything a Phillies manager of that era could possibly want, with the possible exception of fast-acting poison. "If this won't take care of you," Lucchesi's benefactor suggested on the neatly-printed sign above the shelf, "call a doctor."

It took a while to get there, but the Phillies—and the Eagles too—had entered the twentieth century. They finally had a fancy, new place to play. Now all they needed were some fancy, new players to play there.

4

Days of Greatness

EVERY SO OFTEN A FINE ATHLETE PERFORMS TO THE ABSOLUTE LIMIT of his ability. A Joe DiMaggio, a Mickey Mantle, an O.J. Simpson, an Earl Campbell, a Jerry West, an Elgin Baylor, a Gordie Howe, a Maurice Richard reaches heights that seems staggering even for him. It's a dream that comes true, the day in which everything falls into place.

Considering all the superb athletes who played for Philadelphia teams over the years, there were bound to be days—and nights—when the stars glowed brighter than ever before, when a great athlete put together a once-in-a-lifetime performance.

Joe Fulks had such a night at the Philadelphia Arena, pumping in the then unheard-of total of sixty-three points for the old Warriors, but it took Wilt Chamberlain to produce a truly monumental point total. He was 7 feet, 2 inches tall, this product of Philadelphia's Overbrook High School who honed his talents while playing for the University of Kansas and the Harlem Globetrotters. "I know the Trotters haven't lost a game since you joined them," Eddie Gottlieb kidded the big man one night before a Globetrotter game at the Camden, New Jersey, Convention Hall, "but don't let that bother you. They didn't lose any before you joined them either."

Later, when Wilt played in the NBA, some people acted as if his teams should never lose there either. When they did lose—particularly in playoff games to the Boston Celtics—Chamberlain had to bear the brunt of the criticism, and it bothered him.

"Bill Russell's been given credit for being an unselfish ball player," Wilt said a few months before leading the 1967

Philadelphia 76ers to the NBA title. "Wilt Chamberlain is given credit for being selfish. 'Bill Russell does what's best for his club. Wilt Chamberlain does what's best for himself.' That's the most asinine statement in the world."

In all probability, it came about as a result of Wilt's fantastic scoring prowess, and the way he was used—particularly in his early pro years when Gottlieb encouraged him to pour in points at a record-breaking clip. But not even Gotty could have imagined the game Wilt would come up with at the Hershey Arena on March 2, 1962.

Joe Fulks' 63-Point Game (1st Pro to Top 50)
(February 10, 1949, at Philadelphia Arena)

Indianapolis Jets	G-ST	F-FT	Pts.	A	PF
Kirk, f	4-15	3-3	11	2	3
Mogus, f	5-13	4-8	14	4	2
Hamilton, f	4-14	2-2	10	3	2
Towery, c	3-9	0-0	6	0	1
Mandic, c	3-4	0-0	6	2	3
Eskridge, c	1-2	1-1	3	0	3
Byrnes, g	4-16	5-5	13	1	0
Malamed, g	4-10	2-3	10	1	1
Brookfield, g	5-17	3-3	13	0	4
Nagy, g	0-3	1-1	1	1	0
Totals	33-103	21-26	87	14	19

Philadelphia Warriors	G-ST	F-FT	Pts.	A	PF
Fulks, f	27-56	9-14	63	0	3
Musi, f	2-9	1-1	5	0	2
Fleishman, f	3-7	0-0	6	2	2
Sadowski, c	1-8	2-3	4	3	1
Bornheimer, c	2-4	0-1	4	2	6
Bishop, g	3-10	1-1	7	1	0
Senesky, g	4-6	3-4	11	3	3
Dallmar, g	1-3	0-0	2	2	0
Crossin, g	0-3	0-0	0	1	2
Torgoff, g	1-2	1-1	3	1	2
Morgenthaler, g	1-1	1-2	3	1	0
Totals	45-109	18-27	108	16	21

Indianapolis Jets	14	24	22	27	—	87
Philadelphia Warriors	23	26	28	31	—	108

Officials—Sid Borgia and Hagan Anderson. A—1,500.

There wasn't much of a crowd that night in Hershey, where the old Warriors used to play several of their "home" games in the course of the regular season. Playoff time was approaching. This tussle with the New York Knicks hardly figured to be a classic. Ah, but little did the people know. Wilt scored twenty-three points in the first twelve-minute period and eighteen in the second. Then he got serious. In the third period this man mountain of a basketball player poured in the astonishing total of twenty-eight points. Now he had sixty-nine . . . and each time he scored the public address announcer kept the fans advised of his rapidly growing total.

The name of the game in the fourth quarter was "get the ball to Wilt." Guy Rodgers, an outstanding guard from Philadelphia's Temple University, kept doing precisely that, and Chamberlain kept throwing it at the basket. He took twenty-one shots in the final period and made twelve of them. His last bucket—with forty-two seconds to go—combined with the seven free throws he made down the stretch sent him soaring to the magic number: 100.

The final score was Warriors 169, Knicks 147. Chamberlain, who played the entire forty-eight minutes, wound up making thirty-six of sixty-three shots from the floor and twenty-eight of thirty-two from the foul line. In addition, he pulled down twenty-five rebounds and, somewhere along the way, actually found time to dish out two assists. Trivia buffs might be interested to know that the poor souls assigned the impossible task of stopping Wilt on that historic night were Darrell Imhoff and, for a while, Dave Budd.

In retrospect, the most amazing thing about Wilt's performance was his 87.5 percent foul shooting because, if there was one thing the giant couldn't do through most of his career, it was sink free throws. The idea of Chamberlain making twenty-eight and missing only four was so preposterous to those who spent years observing Wilt's struggles at the foul line that one cynic actually suggested the Hershey game was a figment of some joker's imagination.

"A guy in New York," recalled long-time Philly pro basketball statistician and public relations man Harvey Pollack, "wrote a tongue-in-cheek story that the game never happened. He wrote that Wilt never made twenty-eight of thirty-two fouls in his life, and that *The Inquirer* didn't have a reporter there."

Also, there were no news photographers present in the second half to record Chamberlain's drive for the century mark. But hold it. Don't get suspicious. The game really was played. Wilt

Chamberlain really did make all those free throws and score all those points. Harvey Pollack, for one, will testify to it under oath—and Harvey, who towers over pro basketball statisticians the way Wilt towers over most mere mortals, was the man who made up the official box that night. Not only that, but he was covering for *The Inquirer*, the Associated Press, and United Press International. Come to think of it, if not for Harvey the world may never have found out about those 100 points.

Wilt Chamberlain's 100-Point Game
(March 2, 1962, at Hershey, Pennsylvania)

PHILADELPHIA (169)

Player	Pos.	Min.	FGA	FGM	FTA	FTM	Reb.	Ast.	PF	Pts.
Arizin	F	31	18	7	2	2	5	4	0	16
Conlin		14	4	0	0	0	4	1	1	0
Ruklik		8	1	0	2	0	2	1	2	0
Meschery	F	40	12	7	2	2	7	3	4	16
Luckenbill		3	0	0	0	0	1	0	2	0
Chamberlain	C	48	63	36	32	28	25	2	2	100
Rodgers	G	48	4	1	12	9	7	20	5	11
Attles	G	34	8	8	1	1	5	6	4	17
Larese		14	5	4	1	1	1	2	5	9
Totals		240	115	63	52	43	60	39	25	169

Team Rebounds—3.

NEW YORK (147)

Player	Pos.	Min.	FGA	FGM	FTA	FTM	Reb.	Ast.	PF	Pts.
Naulls	F	43	22	9	15	13	7	2	5	31
Green	F	21	7	3	0	0	7	1	5	6
Buckner		33	26	16	1	1	8	0	4	33
Imhoff	C	20	7	3	1	1	6	0	6	7
Budd		27	8	6	1	1	10	1	1	13
Guerin	G	46	29	13	17	13	8	6	5	39
Butler	G	32	13	4	0	0	7	3	1	8
Butcher		18	6	3	6	4	3	4	5	10
Totals		240	118	57	41	33	60	17	32	147

Team Rebounds—4.

Score by Periods:	1st	2nd	3rd	4th	Totals
Philadelphia	42	37	46	44—	169
New York	26	42	38	41—	147

CHAMBERLAIN'S SCORING BY PERIODS:

	Min.	FGA	FGM	FTA	FTM	Reb.	Ast.	PF	Pts.
First Quarter	12	14	7	9	9	10	0	0	23
Second Quarter	12	12	7	5	4	4	1	1	18
Third Quarter	12	16	10	8	8	6	1	0	28
Fourth Quarter	12	21	12	10	7	5	0	1	31
Totals	48	63	36	32	28	25	2	2	100

Referees—Willie Smith and David D'Ambrosio.

As brilliant as Wilt Chamberlain was that night in Hershey, he wasn't perfect. After all, he *did* miss twenty-seven field-goal attempts and four foul shots.

But Jim Bunning was perfect.

It happened on Father's Day, 1964, at New York's Shea Stadium, in the first game of a Phillies-Mets double header . . . the first regular-season perfect game in the big leagues in forty-two years.

"I never thought about pitching a no-hitter," Bunning, now a State Senator in Kentucky, said recently. "I would think that Nolan Ryan thinks about it every time he pitches; he's somebody who can overmatch hitters. I never overmatched that many hitters. I mean, *completely* over-matched a whole lineup."

Maybe not, but Bunning got his first no-hitter while pitching for the Detroit Tigers on July 20, 1958, against one of the hardest hitting teams in one of the toughest pitching parks. The Boston Red Sox have never been easy to hold in check in Fenway Park, and when Bunning did it a guy named Ted Williams was playing.

Williams, as luck would have it, was the game's final batter, the man Bunning had to get to preserve his no-hitter. "It never entered my mind to walk him," Jim would say later. "I didn't pitch around anybody then."

He got the man many consider the finest pure hitter in baseball history on a routine fly ball to right field, the fourth one Williams hit that day. "The most perfect cans of corn you've ever seen in your life," Bunning said.

That first no-hitter drained Jim. "It didn't sink in until after I did it," said this fiercest of competitors. "I got into the locker room and almost collapsed. I was totally exhausted."

His second big-league no-hitter—the perfect one—was an entirely different sort of experience. In Boston it may have taken time for the significance of his feat to hit home. In New York, on that unforgettable Sunday afternoon, Bunning realized what he was doing while he was doing it.

"I think I was totally aware of what was happening," he said, "which makes it much more interesting. From the fifth inning on, I knew what I had and I wasn't going to let it get away. That's the way I felt."

It takes a little luck to pitch a perfect game, and Bunning's came in the fifth inning when Jesse Gonder ripped a one-out shot that looked like a hit. Phillies' second baseman Tony Taylor broke to his left, knocked the ball down with a diving stop and got Gonder at first. There was also a good stop by rookie third-baseman Richie Allen on a seventh-inning smash by Ron Hunt, but most of the time Bunning was in total command of the expansion team.

"I made some bad pitches early," he said. "I threw some high sliders and got away with them. [They were] ticked back, ticked back. And then everything just started to go."

It was an exhilarating experience to be so completely in charge of a ball game, to be closing in on a pitching feat of such magnitude.

Six outs to go. Joe Christopher, leading off the eighth for the Mets, went down swinging, and now there were five.

Jesse Gonder was next, and Bunning got him on one pitch—a routine grounder to second, and now there were four.

Bob Taylor, the Mets' left fielder, fell behind in the count, one ball and two strikes. Then came an outside pitch for ball two, a foul out of play, and another outside pitch. The count was full; one more ball and the perfect game would be ruined. Phillie catcher Gus Triandos signaled for a slider, and Bunning aimed it for the outside corner. Taylor took it, and plate umpire Ed Sudol shot up the right arm. Strike three, and now there were three outs to go.

"The only concern I had was [George] Altman," Bunning said. "He was on the bench, and I knew Casey [Stengel] was going to use him to pinch hit."

The only question was when. Bunning hoped fervently that the Mets' manager wouldn't save Altman for last; Jim much preferred to have Casey's other lefthanded pinch hitter, John Stephenson, represent the twenty-seventh out.

"I knew if I got Stephenson up there with two out, I had it," Bunning said. "I knew I could get him out on curve balls, no matter what. I could throw him five, seven, eight curve balls and get him out. Altman, I wasn't so sure of. I didn't know if I could still jam him with the ball."

Jim got his wish. George Altman was in the on-deck circle as Bunning faced Charley Smith in the bottom of the ninth. The count on the New York shortshop went to 2–and–1 before he popped a foul beyond third base. Shortstop Bobby Wine made the catch, and now there were two outs to go . . . and Altman was at the plate.

Bunning tried to pitch him inside, but didn't get the ball as far in as he would have liked. Altman sent a long, high foul to right, and Jim drew a deep breath. "I was aware," he said. "I knew what I had to do."

Altman fouled off the next pitch, missed the one after that. The Shea fans were screaming now. Bunning had his ninth strikeout.

And now there was one out to go.

Jim Bunning's Perfect Game

(June 21, 1964, at New York)

Philadelphia	AB	R	H	RBI	O	A		New York	AB	R	H	RBI	O	A
Briggs, cf	4	1	0	0	2	0		Hickman, lf	3	0	0	0	2	0
Herrnstein, 1b	4	0	0	0	6	0		Hunt, 2b	3	0	0	0	3	2
Callison, rf	4	1	2	1	1	0		Kranepool, 1b	3	0	0	0	8	1
Allen, 3b	3	0	1	1	0	2		Christopher, rf	3	0	0	0	4	0
Covington, lf	2	0	0	0	1	0		Gonder, c	3	0	0	0	7	2
a-Wine, ss	1	1	0	0	2	1		R. Taylor, lf	3	0	0	0	1	0
T. Taylor, 2b	3	2	1	0	0	3		C. Smith, ss	3	0	0	0	1	1
Rojas, ss, lf	3	0	1	0	3	0		Samuel, 3b	2	0	0	0	0	1
Triandos, c	4	1	2	2	12	0		c-Altman	1	0	0	0	0	0
								Stallard, p	1	0	0	0	0	2
								Wakefield, p	0	0	0	0	0	0
								b-Kanehl	1	0	0	0	0	0
								Sturdivant, p	0	0	0	0	1	0
								d-Stephenson	1	0	0	0	0	0
Totals	32	6	8	6	27	6		Totals	27	0	0	0	27	0

a-Ran for Covington in 6th.
b-Grounded out for Wakefield in 6th.
c-Struck out for Samuel in 9th.
d-Struck out for Sturdivant in 9th.

Philadelphia	110	004	000 —	6
New York	000	000	000 —	0

2B—Triandos, Bunning. HR—Callison. SAO—Herrnstein, Rojas.
LEFT—Philadelphia 5, New York 0.

	IP	H	R	ER	BB	SO
Bunning (W, 7-2)	9	0	0	0	0	10
Stallard (L, 4-9)	5 2/3	7	6	6	4	3
Wakefield	1/3	0	0	0	0	0
Sturdivant	3	1	0	0	0	3

T— 2:19. A—32,026.

You never can tell in baseball. Even a guy with an average of .047 might get a hit off a tough pitcher. Accidents did happen. But John Stephenson would have to get that hit off a curve ball, and Bunning knew the odds were greatly against that happening.

Stephenson swung at the first breaking ball. Strike one. He looked at the second one. Strike two. The big Sunday crowd was standing now as Jim Bunning went to the resin bag, popped the ball in his glove, looked in for the curve-ball sign he knew was coming.

Curve balls. Nothing but curve balls. Stephenson watched this one break outside. Ball one. Another curve ball. Again it missed outside. Ball two. And yet another. This time it was Stephenson who missed. Jim Bunning pounded his fist into his glove in a rare show of jubilation. "I knew what I had done," he said. "I was completely in control of myself."

He was, on that afternoon, the perfect pitcher.

*   *   *

The teenager who pitched—and won—the second game of the double-header at Shea that day in '64 never quite reached perfection on the mound. But what he did on a June night in Cincinnati in 1971 was almost as noteworthy. Not only did Rick Wise pitch a no-hitter for the Phillies against the Reds, he slugged two home runs.

That was, far and away, the highlight of a dismal season for the Phillies, who finished last in the National League East that year, and it made Wise something of a Philadelphia folk hero. Eight months later, to the shock of many, Rick was shipped to St. Louis in the trade that made Steve Carlton a Phillie. But even today Wise has a special place in his heart for Philadelphia, its fans, and its baseball team.

"The people say hi to me," he said. "They're friendly. I can't say anything bad about Philly. I can say only good things about it, have only good memories. It was my first team, and you never forget that no matter how many teams you've been on since.

"It's just been a great baseball town, Philly, a great sports town. Those are the impressions I remember. . . . They're fanatics there. They have a great heritage in sports, and particularly in baseball."

And Rick Wise added something to it, especially on that night in Cincinnati.

Philadelphians who turned on their radios in the bottom of the ninth must have been a bit confused by By Saam's efforts *not* to defy baseball superstition. Long-standing tradition had it that no-hitters were never to be discussed, and By wasn't about to be the guy who ruined Rick's no-hitter.

Rick Wise's No-Hitter
(June 23, 1971, at Cincinnati)

Philadelphia	ab	r	h	rbi	Cincinnati	ab	r	h	rbi
Harmon, 2b	4	0	0	0	Rose, rf	4	0	0	0
Bowa, ss	4	0	0	0	Foster, cf	3	0	0	0
McCarver, c	3	0	2	0	May, 1b	3	0	0	0
Johnson, 1b	2	0	0	0	Bench, c	3	0	0	0
Lis, lf	2	1	0	0	Perez, 3b	3	0	0	0
Stone, lf	1	0	0	0	McRae, lf	3	0	0	0
Montanez, cf	4	0	1	0	Helms, 2b	3	0	0	0
Freed, rf	4	1	1	1	Concepcion, ss	1	0	0	0
Vukovich, 3b	4	0	1	0	Stewart, ph	1	0	0	0
Wise, p	4	2	2	3	Grimsley, p	1	0	0	0
					Carbo, ph	1	0	0	0
					Carroll, p	0	0	0	0
					Granger, p	0	0	0	0
					Cline, ph	1	0	0	0
Totals	32	4	7	4	Totals	27	0	0	0

Philadelphia	010 020 010	— 4
Cincinnati	000 000 000	— 0

DP—Cincinnati 2. LEFT—Philadelphia 5, Cincinnati 1. 2B—Montanez, Freed. HR—Wise 2.

	IP	H	R	ER	BB	SO
Wise (W, 8-4)	9	0	0	0	1	2
Grimsley (L, 4-3)	6	4	3	3	2	1
Carroll	2	2	1	1	1	1
Granger	1	1	0	0	0	1

HBP—By Grimsley (Lis). T— 1:53. A—13,392.

"Everybody in this ball park knows what's going on," he beat around the bush. "It's right up on the scoreboard. . . . The Phillies are ahead, 4–0, but people aren't too concerned with the score now."

On the TV side, though, Harry Kalas took a different approach. Let's tune in . . .

"We move on to the bottom half of the ninth inning, Rick Wise with a no-hit, no-run game going. . . . Jimmy Stewart to be followed by pinch-hitter Ty Cline and then Pete Rose. Three left-handed hitters for Wise to get out in the ninth. . . . Last Phillie to pitch as no-hitter was Jim Bunning, a perfect game at Shea Stadium in 1964. . . . Three and two to Jimmy Stewart. *Strike three called!* That's one of 'em. Wise with one out in the ninth inning of a no-hit, no-run game. . . .

"Tension mounting here in the bottom half of the ninth inning. . . . Well, I wonder what's going through the minds of the Phillies fielders. . . . Cline, a ground ball hit to [Terry] Harmon. Harmon to Wise covering. Two of 'em. Here's one out away from a no-hitter. . . .

"Cincinnati fans are pulling for a no-hitter. Standing between Rick and a no-hit, no-run game is one of the best hitters in the National League, Pete Rose. . . .

"One ball and two strikes to Pete Rose. Wise is out in front of him with two out in the ninth inning and a no-hit, no-run game on the line. . . . The one-two pitch, fast ball low. It's two and two. . . . Rick gets the sign. Here's the pitch. High. Ball three. Full count to Pete Rose. Well, it's going down to the wire. . . . Here's the three-two pitch. Swing, a line drive. *He did it!* [Third baseman John] Vukovich made the grab and Wise has done it, a no-hit, no-run game."

In an era when memorable Philadelphia sports performances were few and far between, Rick Wise's pitching and slugging achievements that night at Riverfront Stadium gave the city's downtrodden fans something to shout about.

*   *   *

If a no-hitter is a pitcher's dream, then four home runs in a game is a hitter's. The first Philadelphia slugger to accomplish that rather extra-ordinary feat was Chuck Klein, who only recently was elected to baseball's Hall of Fame. The lefthanded power hitter boomed four balls out of Pittsburgh's Forbes Field on July 10, 1936, the last leaving the premises in the tenth inning to trigger a 9–6 Phillie victory.

The last Philadelphia slugger to hit the one-game, home-run jackpot was the remarkable Michael Jack Schmidt.

Even when he was batting .211 as a first-year pro for the

Chuck Klein's 4-Homer Game
(July 10, 1936, at Pittsburgh)

Philadelphia	AB	R	H	Pittsburgh	AB	E	H
Sulik, cf	5	1	1	Jensen, lf	4	1	1
J. Moore, lf	5	1	1	L. Waner, cf	4	1	1
Klein, rf	5	4	4	P. Waner, rf	4	2	2
Camilli, 1b	4	2	1	Vaughan, ss	5	0	1
Atwood, c	4	0	1	Suhr, 1b	4	0	2
Wilson, c	0	1	0	Brubaker, 3b	5	0	0
Chiozza, 3b	5	0	2	Young, 2b	3	0	1
Norris, ss	4	0	1	Lavagetto, 2b	1	1	0
Gomez, 2b	5	0	0	Todd, c	2	0	0
Passeau, p	4	0	1	Padden, c	2	1	0
Walters, p	0	0	0	Weaver, p	1	0	0
				Lucas, ph	1	0	0
				Brown, p	1	0	0
				Schulte, ph	1	0	1
				Finney, pr	0	0	0
				Swift, p	0	0	0
Totals	41	9	12	Totals	38	6	9

Philadelphia	400	010	100	3 — 9
Pittsburgh	000	103	002	0 — 6

E—Norris 2, L. Waner, Vaughan 2, Young. RBI—Klein 6, Norris 2, Suhr, P. Waner, Vaughan, Schulte, L. Waner, Chiozza. 2B—Camilli. 3B—Suhr. HR—Klein 4. SAC—Atwood, Norris. DP—Philadelphia 3, Pittsburgh 1. LEFT—Philadelphia 5, Pittsburgh 7.

BB—Off Weaver 1, off Passeau 1, off Brown 1. Hits—Off Weaver, 6 in 5, off Passeau, 8 in 8 2/3, off Swift, 4 in 1, off Brown, 2 in 4, off Walters, 1 in 1 1/3. WP—Walters. LP—Swift. U—Sears, Klem, Ballanfant. T— 2:15.

Eastern League's Reading Phillies in 1971, even when his average dropped to an embarrassing .196 in 367 at-bats with the Philadelphia Phillies in 1973, there was something about Mike Schmidt that told you to be patient, that hinted of marvelous things to come. The young man was simply a natural-born athlete. He had all the tools. It was just a matter of learning to use them.

"I just come to the ball park with the idea I'm going to play as hard as I can because I love to play hard," Schmidt said not long ago. "I get high on going out on a baseball field. It may not look like it. I may look nonchalant from time to time and unemotional from time to time, but I really get a thrill out of it . . . whether I get four hits, whether I go 0 for four. I think that's enabled me to enjoy the success I've had in my career. I respect the game. I respect the challenge of trying to hit more line drives, trying to strike out less, trying to become a better hitter. I guess until the day I retire—and hopefully that's going to be a long way away—the challenge of the game of baseball to me is fun."

And seldom has a man risen to the challenge the way Schmidt

did at Chicago's Wrigley Field—his favorite target area—on the afternoon of April 17, 1976. Richie Allen was a Phillie then—on his second tour of duty with the club—and Schmidt has always credited him with putting him in the proper frame of mind just prior to that four-home-run binge.

"He used to be a helluva leader," Schmidt said about the most controversial of all Phillies, "but he never, ever said a word until he was asked or really felt an impulse to say something to the team in a meeting. I'll tell you what, I'd just sit and listen to Dick talk about some of his experiences."

On that April day in Chicago, Allen was in a playful mood. "He made me stay in the clubhouse with him after everybody'd gone on the field," Schmidt recalled. "He said, 'Let's go out and have some fun today. Let's jack around in the infield when we throw the ball around.' "

Schmidt thought that was a fine idea. "We used to play like he was a quarterback and we'd run out on the field and he'd throw passes to us between innings," Mike said. " 'Don't make this like it's work,' he told me. 'Let's enjoy it.' And then wham-bam-bam, I had the greatest game in my career; the whole team did."

As comebacks go, what the Phillies did that day would be hard to top. After four innings the score was Cubs 13, Phillies 2. Enter fun-loving Mike Schmidt. Exit four National League baseballs. He hit a two-run blast in the fifth, a solo shot in the seventh, a three-run job in the eighth, and, to cap the day, a two-run game-winner in the tenth. Final score: Phillies 18, Cubs 16.

Billy DeMars, the Phillies' hitting instructor, remembered watching those balls jump out of the park . . . and he also remembered working with Schmidt the day before at Wrigley Field to help him get in the groove.

"We had an off-day in Chicago, and he worked off the batting tee," DeMars said. "I remember I had it on the field behind home plate, and he came over and hit some off of it, and then the next day . . ."

Pow! Pow! Pow! Pow! DeMars, who was also coaching at third then, got a sore arm from patting Schmidt on the back.

"When Mike has it going," said Billy, "He's awesome. Awesome. I mean, he can hit for average and tremendous power, and he's got a great eye."

DeMars had seen another big-league slugger erupt for four

homers in one game. He was with the Philadelphia A's when Pat Seerey did it against them. So Schmidt's barrage brought back memories.

Mike Schmidt's 4–Homer Game
(April 17, 1976, at Chicago)

Philadelphia	ab	r	h	rbi	Chicago	ab	r	h	rbi
Cash, 2b	6	1	2	2	Monday, cf	6	3	4	4
Bowa, ss	6	3	3	1	Cardenal, lf	5	1	1	0
Johnstone, rf	5	2	4	2	Summers, lf	0	0	0	0
Luzinski, lf	5	0	1	1	d-Mitterwald	1	0	0	0
Brown, lf	0	0	0	0	Wallis, lf	1	0	0	0
Allen, 1b	5	2	1	2	Madlock, 3b	7	2	3	3
Schmidt, 3b	6	4	5	8	Morales, rf	5	2	1	0
Maddox, cf	5	2	2	1	Thornton, 1b	4	3	1	1
McGraw, p	0	0	0	0	Trillo, 2b	5	0	2	3
e-McCarver	1	1	1	0	Swisher, c	6	1	3	4
Underwood, p	0	0	0	0	Rosello, ss	4	1	2	1
Lonborg, p	0	0	0	0	Kelleher, ss	2	0	1	0
Boone, c	6	1	3	1	R. Reuschel, p	1	2	0	0
Carlton, p	1	0	0	0	Garman, p	0	0	0	0
Schueler, p	0	0	0	0	Knowles, p	0	0	0	0
Garber, p	0	0	0	0	P. Reuschel, p	0	0	0	0
a-Hutton	0	0	0	0	Schultz, p	0	0	0	0
Reed, p	0	0	0	0	f-Adams	1	1	1	0
b-Martin	1	0	0	0					
Twitchell, p	0	0	0	0					
c-Tolan,	3	2	2	0					
Totals	**50**	**18**	**24**	**18**	**Totals**	**48**	**16**	**19**	**16**

a—Walked for Garber in 4th.
b—Grounded out for Reed in 6th.
c—Singled for Twitchell in 8th.
d—Struck out for Summers in 8th.
e—Singled for McGraw in 10th.
f—Doubled for Schultz in 10th.

Philadelphia	010	120	353	3 — 18
Chicago	075	100	002	1 — 16

DP—Philadelphia 1, Chicago 1. LEFT—Philadelphia 8, Chicago 12. 2B—Cardenal, Madlock 2, Thornton, Boone, Adama. 3B—Johnstone, Bowa. HR—Maddox, Swisher, Monday 2, Schmidt 4, Boone. SAC—R. Reuschel, Johnstone, SF—Luzinski, Cash.

	IP	H	R	ER	BB	SO
Carlton	1 2/3	7	7	7	2	1
Schueler	2/3	3	3	3	0	0
Garber	2/3	2	2	2	1	1
Reed	2	1	1	1	1	1
Twitchell	2	0	0	0	1	1
McGraw (W, 1-1)	2	4	2	2	1	2
Underwood	2/3	2	1	1	0	1
Lonborg	1/3	0	0	0	0	0
R. Reuschel	7	14	7	7	1	4
Garman	2/3	4	5	5	1	1
Knowles (L, 1-1)	1 1/3	3	4	4	1	0
P. Reuschel	0	3	2	2	1	0
Schultz	1	0	0	0	0	0

HBP—By Scheuler (R. Reuschel), by Garber (Thornton), by Twitchell (Monday). BALK-Schultz. U—Olsen, Davidson, Rennert, Vargo. T— 3:42. A—28,287.

"When Pat Seerey did it and when Mike Schmidt did it, you almost got the feeling that one guy was playing them by himself," Billy said. "It was like a one-man show. When you're the hitting coach, it's a tremendous thrill to watch a guy go up there, the way Mike did, and look so good and make it look so easy. I mean, one of them was right over that center-field fence—into the green tarp. He's just awesome."

5

The Kids Who Played Like Men

THEY WENT DOWN IN BASEBALL HISTORY AS THE WHIZ KIDS. IN keeping with their heritage, however, they almost went down as the Fizz Kids.

It was an exciting, young team that gave Philadelphia its first National League pennant in thirty-five years and its second in history. Robin Roberts and Curt Simmons, the top two starters on the 1950 Phillies—they won thirty-seven between them—were both "bonus babies" enjoying their first outstanding big-league seasons. Only two years before Robbie had started the season pitching in the minors; in '50 he became the Phillies' first twenty-game winner since Grover Cleveland Alexander in 1917. Simmons, who didn't graduate from high school until June of 1947, was even younger. But after struggling with his control and losing considerably more games than he won as a budding big leaguer in 1948-49, the lefthander suddenly emerged as a winning pitcher in '50.

Robbie and Simmons weren't the only "kids" who played like men under Eddie Sawyer that year. When the season started, Mike Goliat, the second baseman, was twenty-four; Granny Hamner, the shortstop, was twenty-two; Willie (Puddinhead) Jones, the third baseman, was twenty-four; Richie Ashburn, the center fielder, was twenty-three; and Del Ennis, the local-boy-made-good who was the top home-run and RBI man on the team, was twenty-four. In addition, two rookie pitchers, Bob Miller and Bubba Church, combined to win nineteen games. So it was fitting that the Philadelphia press borrowed a nickname originally tagged on a youthful University of Illinois basketball team . . . and baseball's Whiz Kids were born.

Before the season ended, though, they almost died.

Think the 1964 Phillies, six-and-a-half games up with twelve to go, went down in flames? The '50 Phillies came within a deep breath of blowing an even bigger lead in the last week and a half of the season. In fact, the entire final month was a wild roller-coaster ride.

On Sunday, September 3, the Whiz Kids returned from a highly successful, two-week road trip with a seven-game lead . . . and a huge mob waited for hours on a rainy night to greet them at the airport. The heroes were many that evening—Robbie and Curt, Del and Granny—but perhaps the single biggest hero of all was a man in his 30s who didn't look anything like a kid. Make no mistake about it, though; Jim Konstanty was a whiz in 1950. No more than a mediocre minor-league pitcher, he became a brilliant reliever in Philadelphia, appearing in 74 of the Phillies' 154 games that year, winning 16 of them and protecting leads in 24 more. So there was no reason for the Philly faithful to be anything less than ecstatic when the Phillies came home to play the New York Giants in a Labor Day double-header. Then came the first shock: two shutout defeats.

The Phillies careened on from there. Their lead went down to four and a half, then back up to seven and a half by September 15. With eleven days to go, they still had a seven-and-a-half game cushion on the Brooklyn Dodgers.

There were danger signs, to be sure. Simmons had been called up for reserve duty. Miller, winner of his first eight decisions in '50, had a bad back. Church was out for a while after getting hit by a batted ball. Still, pennant fever was sweeping Philadelphia. Why not? With nine days to go, the lead was still seven.

Then came the gut-wrenching near collapse. The Dodgers came to Shibe Park and swept a two-game series, and the margin was down to five. Momentarily, the Phillies stiffened, winning two out of three in Boston. But back-to-back doubleheaders in New York loomed . . . and those four games threatened to turn the Whiz Kids into the Fizz Kids for keeps.

Gene Kelly was in his first year as the radio voice of the Phillies then, and a quarter of a century later—when the Phillies reunited the Whiz Kids and presented them with World Series rings—he recalled those desperate, final days of the '50 season, and how Gene's broadcasting partner had gone down to the clubhouse, day after day, to get ready for a clinching party that kept getting delayed. "Finally," Kelly said, "Eddie Sawyer told us, 'Throw that stuff [the radio equipment] out. It isn't bringing us any luck.' "

Not in the Polo Grounds, it wasn't. The Phillies nearly pulled out the first of those four games, rallying for five runs in the top of the eighth to tie the game at five-all, but the Giants won it in the tenth . . . and the panic was on. The Phillies scored only a total of two runs in the next three games, and their lead was down to three games, two in the "loss column."

There was still a chance they could clinch the pennant before meeting the Dodgers in a season-closing, two-game series at Ebbets Field. While the Phillies tried to pull themselves together on an off-day, the Dodgers had to play a doubleheader against the Braves. One Dodger loss, and it would be over. The champagne could finally be opened; the party could finally begin.

"We're in the hotel," Granny Hamner remembered, "watching the Dodgers play the Braves on TV. Boston's ahead both games. We thought we had it won."

Gene Kelly thought so too. He was at Ebbets Field that day doing the play-by-play back to Philadelphia. In the opening game, Boston was leading, 5–2, in the eighth . . . and lost, 7–5. In the second game, Boston was leading, 6–3, after five and a half innings . . . and lost, 7–6. Now the Phillies' lead was down to two games, and the Dodgers could catch them —and force a best-of-three playoff—by sweeping the weekend series in Brooklyn.

The Saturday afternoon game was all Brooklyn. Roy Campanella hit a three-run homer, Duke Snider hit a two-run homer, and the Dodgers won, 7–3. So it came down to this: the two aces, Robin Roberts and Don Newcombe, each going for his twentieth victory, on a Sunday afternoon with a packed house of 34,000–plus ready to scream themselves hoarse at Ebbets Field. For Robbie, it was, amazingly enough, his third start in five days. But Sawyer had no choice. Simmons was doing reserve duty. It *hat* to be Robbie.

The game was a classic. Robbie had made five unsuccessful tries for no. 20, and now he had to face the red-hot Dodgers—Snider and Campy and PeeWee Reese and Jackie Robinson and Gil Hodges and the rest of those bombers—in that band-

box of a ball park. It was the single biggest game of Robin Roberts'
career, and he performed brilliantly. The only run the Dodgers
scored against him came on a fluke home run by Reese, who lofted
a fly ball against the short right-field screen in the bottom of the
sixth. Instead of bouncing back onto the playing field, the ball
landed on a ledge between the top of the wall and the
screen . . . and it stayed there as the Dodger shortstop circled the
bases with the run that matched the one the Phillies scored on a
Willie Jones single in the top half of the inning.

Into the bottom of the ninth they went, still tied at a run
apiece. If the Dodgers scored now, the game would be over; the
pennant race would be tied. Robbie opened the inning by walking
Cal Abrams. Reese singled him to second. The batter was Duke
Snider.

Fortunately, the tape of Gene Kelly's play-by-play description
of the final innings of that game was saved. Let him tell it in that
staccato delivery of his, as he did to a breathless Philadelphia
audience on October 1, 1950:

"Last half of the ninth, score tied, 1-1, and what represents
the winning run is on second base in Abrams . . . Infield moves in
to look for the bunt. Duke steps in. Roberts stretches,
throws . . . Snider takes a full cut. Line drive to center field.
Ashburn races in for the ball. Here comes the throw . . . He is *out!*
A beautiful throw by Richie Ashburn and [catcher Stan] Lopata
had Abrams standing up. He didn't even go to a slide."

That play would be second-guessed and third-guessed in the
days and weeks and years to follow. Dodger third-base coach Milt
Stock had waved Abrams on to the plate on Snider's sharp single
although there was nobody out at the time and big hitters—Jackie
Robinson, Carl Furillo, and Gil Hodges—were coming up. It was
the coaching blunder that saved the Whiz Kids . . . but Robbie
was still in deep trouble. Reese and Snider had moved up on
Ashburn's throw to the plate. The potential winning run was on
third with one out.

Sawyer did what he had to do—order an intentional walk to
Robinson, filling the bases. Then Roberts did what he had to
do—stop Furillo from hitting the ball out of the infield. The
Dodger right fielder popped to first baseman Eddie Waitkus, and
that left it up to Hodges. Here's Gene Kelly . . .

"Reese at third, Snider at second, Robinson at first . . . Roberts in the big motion, throwing . . . Strike one called . . . The nothing-and-one pitch . . . Inside, high. Ball one . . . Roberts facing Hodges, youthful veteran against youthful veteran. [Roberts] throwing, [Hodges] swinging . . . a fly ball toward right field. Ennis moving way, way back . . . under . . . makes it! What an inning by Roberts! Listen to that crowd."

So the game went into the 10th, and now it was Newcombe's turn to try to tiptoe through a mine field. Robbie opened the inning with a single up the middle, and Waitkus got him to second with a soft single to center. Newcombe earned a temporary reprieve, turning Ashburn's attempted sacrifice bunt into a force at third. Up stepped Dick Sisler, who had already punched out three singles off the big righthander. Gene Kelly would remember this moment until his dying day . . .

Phillies' Pennant Clincher

(October 1, 1950, at Brooklyn)

Philadelphia	ab	r	h	o	a	Brooklyn	ab	r	h	o	a
Waitkus, 1b	5	1	1	18	0	Abrams, lf	2	0	0	2	0
Ashburn, cf	5	1	0	2	1	Reese, ss	4	1	3	3	3
Sisler, lf	5	2	4	0	1	Snider, cf	4	0	1	3	0
Mayo, lf	0	0	0	1	0	Robinson, 2b	3	0	0	4	3
Ennis, rf	5	0	2	2	0	Furillo, rf	4	0	0	3	0
Jones, 3b	5	0	1	0	3	Hodges, 1b	4	0	0	9	3
Hamner, ss	4	0	0	1	2	Campanella, c	4	0	1	2	4
Seminick, c	3	0	1	3	1	Cox, 3b	3	0	0	1	2
a-Caballero	0	0	0	0	0	b-Russell	1	0	0	0	0
Lopata, c	0	0	0	1	0	Newcombe, p	3	0	0	3	2
Goliat, 2b	4	0	1	1	3	c-Brown	1	0	0	0	0
Roberts, p	2	0	1	1	6						
Totals	38	4	11	30	16	Totals	33	1	5	30	17

a—Ran for Seminick in 9th.
b—Struck out for Cox in 10th.
c—Fouled out for Newcombe in 10th.

Philadelphia	000	001	000	3 — 4
Brooklyn	000	001	000	0 — 1

E—None. RBI—Jones, Reese, Sisler 3. 2B—Reese. HR—Reese, Sisler. SAC—Roberts. DP—Philadelphia 1, Brooklyn 1. LEDFT—Philadelphia 7, Brooklyn 5. BB—Roberts 3, Newcombe 2. SO—Roberts 2, Newcombe 3. U—Goetz, Dascoli, Jorda, Donatelli. T—2:35. A—35,073.

"Now Newcombe is set in the stretch . . . Swinging, a fly . . . very, very deep to left field . . . Moving back, Al Abrams . . . Way, way back. [His voice was rising now, even as Sisler's fly ball kept rising toward the left-field stands.] He can't get it! A home run!"

At that moment somebody had screamed into the microphone. It was a wild, bloodcurdling cry. "E-e-e-e-yowp!" Gene Kelly's dad had been in the broadcasting booth with him. It was he who had been unable to hold back.

"My father, rest his soul," Gene would say twenty-five years later as he listened to the tape in the living room of his Merion, Pennsylvania, home. "It sounds like me. They all thought it was me. But it wasn't."

Sisler's opposite-field homer dramatically and emphatically pulled the Phillies out of their late-season skid. Robbie breezed through the last of the 10th, and the Kids had officially become Whizzes, not Fizzes.

The World Series against the Yankees was another story. Vic Raschi barely outpitched Konstanty, 1–0, in the first game as the Phillies' relief ace, who had come out of the bullpen in all 133 of his previous major-league appearances, pitched brilliantly as a starter. And Robbie somehow found the strength to start game no. 2 at Shibe Park, duelling Yankee flame-thrower Allie Reynolds to a 1–1 standoff after nine innings. Then Joe DiMaggio, who had popped up four straight times against the Phillie righthander, lined the ball into the upper left-hand seats . . . and the Yankees were on their way to four in a row.

Still, for three decades the Whiz Kids of 1950 would represent the ultimate achievement by a Philadelphia National League baseball team. Twenty-six years later, in August 1976, the brilliant pitcher who contributed twenty victories to the 1950 pennant march was elected to baseball's Hall of Fame. Before he was through pitching in the big leagues, Robin Roberts, now coach of the University of South Florida's baseball team in Tampa, won 286 games. But to understand the real secret of Robbie's greatness, to find the real reason why he was able to excel in this kids' game and enjoy it for so many years, you had to be in Williamsport, Pennsylvania, on a cold—very, very cold—April night in 1967 when Robin Roberts, forty years young, returned to the Class AA Eastern League for a final fling.

Imagine. Here was a pitcher who had attained greatness in the majors, starting a game for the Reading Phillies. It seemed unbelievable then; in retrospect, it seems unbelievable now. But Robbie loved the game too much to quit playing it without a fight.

Of all the games I saw him pitch, that one somehow stands out because it told you so much about the man. There aren't many former big leaguers who would have subjected themselves to the ordeal Robbie did that night. Shibe Park, Ebbets Field, all the places where he had pitched and won during his big-league days seemed a million miles away that night. This was a different world, a world that supposedly only kids trying to get to the big leagues for the first time could tolerate.

The visiting clubhouse in Williamsport's Bowman Field was small. Wooden lockers lined one side. Across the room, beyond the oil heater and the soft-drink machine, there were no lockers, just nails pounded into the wall. Above each nail was a strip of tape with a name scrawled on it. One of the names that night was *Roberts.*

Robbie hung his jacket on the nail and sat down on an old, green folding chair. "When you've been in the league longer, you'll get a locker," a friend kidded him, and Robbie smiled—a brief, mechanical smile. His mind was on the game.

On this cold, quiet night in northcentral Pennsylvania, Hall-of-Famer-to-be Robin Roberts was about to face the Williamsport Mets. He was there because no big-league club had been willing to take a chance on his aging right arm. "I wrote to most of the first-division teams," he said. "After that I called a lot of clubs. I didn't miss many."

Most men would have given up then, but Robbie didn't win all those major-league games being like most men. So at forty, a year and a half after undergoing an elbow operation, he made a decision that shocked many of his old friends. He became a minor leaguer—"as a last resort," he said.

"The people who criticize, they don't understand," Robbie told the two writers who cared enough to travel to Williamsport for the game that night.

The people of Williamsport didn't seem to understand either. Or care. A Robin Roberts doesn't pitch against the Williamsport Mets every day. Or every decade. But despite the pre-game publicity, only 391 fans were scattered around the 6,000-seat ball park when Robbie walked to the mound.

It was a strange, almost eerie setting—the near-empty stands, the frozen ball players huddled in the dugouts, the kids playing softball beyond the outfield fences, oblivious to the drama about to unfold in Bowman Field, and Robbie on the mound, wearing the familiar gray uniform with red trim and the name "Phillies" across the chest. You had to look closely to notice there was an R, not a P on the red cap, or that the uniform was one of those hand-me-downs minor-league players so often have to wear.

All the old mannerisms were there. He brushed his right pants leg between pitches, tugged at the peak of his cap, kicked at the dirt. His opponent, a twenty-four-year-old future big leaguer named Jerry Johnson, matched him, inning after inning. Watching Robbie's face as the pitching duel went on, you knew that could have been Don Newcombe pitching for the other team, and the ball park could have been Ebbets Field in Brooklyn; the intense look, the determination he showed would have been no different.

There was, I suppose, something a little sad about it all. But there was also something noble and inspiring. How many men would have been willing to do what Robin Roberts did that night?

The game was still scoreless with two on and two out in the Williamsport half of the fifth. Then John Gonsalves smacked the ball back at Robbie. The ball hit him on the right calf and caromed into short left field, a run-scoring single. Robbie finished strong, getting three of his nine strikeouts in the last inning, but that run beat him. "Nothing has changed," said Reading pitching coach Dallas Green, Philadelphia's big-league manager-to-be. "The Phillies still don't get him any runs."

Robin Roberts lost that game, but his enthusiasm remained. Here was a man who loved baseball, who loved it enough to endure the unpleasantness of a freezing night in Williamsport on the long-shot—and, as it turned out, unrealized—hope that it might lead to another chance in the big leagues.

"I remember that nail in the locker room," Robbie said on the day he was inducted into the Cooperstown Hall of Fame. "I saw that nail, and I had a hunch I might be ready to quit."

But he didn't quit. At least, not right away. He kept pitching long enough to win five games for the Reading Phillies, long enough to experience conditions you wouldn't expect a man who had put together six consecutive twenty-victory seasons in the big leagues to endure.

"I walked out to pitch at York," he said in Cooperstown, "and I looked around, and there were dandelions blooming all over the infield. But the killer was Pawtucket. They had a hole in front of the rubber, a hole this deep"—and he held his hands a foot apart. "I started to warm up and I said, 'No way.' "

So he asked for the "ground crew," and an old fella with a shovel sauntered out. Robbie took a look at him, took the shovel, and fixed the mound himself.

"A lot of guys have gone through that [the experience of pitching under nearly impossible conditions in the minors]," Dallas Green would say a number of years later, "but not when they're Hall of Famers."

Robin Roberts wasn't like "a lot of guys." He was as different, as unique as the teams, the fans, the tradition of the city in which he won most of those 286 big-league games.

*   *   *

Three members of the 1950 Whiz Kids were still part of the Phillies organization when the 1980 team hit the jackpot. Richie Ashburn was in the broadcasting booth. Andy Seminick was scouting. And Granny Hamner, the clutch-hitting shortstop, was still putting on a uniform as a special instructor in the farm system.

That Granny is still around today remains one of the stirring stories of our time. The man, you see, lives dangerously.

What's that? You didn't think being an instructor in the farm system was all that dangerous? Listen, pal, compared to what Hamner has gone through in the last five or six years, standing at home plate with a bat in your hands facing Don Newcombe was a breeze.

First, there was that trip to Peninsula to work with some of the infielders on the Phillies' Class A Club there—"about five years ago, I guess," Granny said recently. Everything was going just great . . . until one day Hamner, with his love of the great outdoors, decided to go fishing in the Chesapeake Bay.

"I went with my brother's son-in-law," he said, "and a big

storm came up. He was trying to get in too fast, and the boat sank. I was in the water for like three hours. Only thing I could grab hold of was a little kid's life jacket. It wouldn't hold me up, so I had to kick my legs to stay afloat."

Grasping that tiny life jacket, he kept kicking, somehow managing to keep his head above water. Since Hamner couldn't swim a stroke, that was no small achievement.

"My legs were getting awfully tired," he said. "I didn't know how much longer I could last."

Fortunately for Granny, his brother's son-in-law *could* swim. "He swam probably 500 yards ahead of me and an oil tanker came by and saw him," Hamner recalled. "The tanker picked him up, and he told them I was back there. I thought I was a goner because I couldn't kick my legs a helluva lot longer. It was close."

But then, so was the incident that occurred in the spring of 1980.

Granny was working with some of the Phillies kids in Sarasota, Florida—an extended spring training, they called it. "The night before," he said, "I drove up to St. Pete and played poker all night. Then I had to rush back to Sarasota in the morning."

It was about 7 A.M., and the weather was brutal. The rain was pelting down so hard that visibility was near zero. And to make matters worse, the direct route from St. Petersburg to Sarasota was over an engineering marvel known as the Sunshine Skyway, which spans Tampa Bay. At its highest point, the Sunshine Skyway bridge rises 150 feet above the water.

That bridge was so high that I can recall one Phillie ballplayer, a second baseman named Freddie Andrews, who would clench his fists and close his eyes and break out in a cold sweat whenever the bus carrying him to that day's spring training game would cross Sunshine Skyway.

Anyhow, Granny Hamner harbored no such fears of high bridges. Through the driving rain he pushed his station wagon . . . until the storm got so bad and the visibility so low that he pulled off the road for a short time. "A bus passed me while I was sitting on the side," he said. "I thought, 'What the hell, if he can go, I can go.' But Granny waited perhaps another thirty seconds before resuming his journey. That delay probably saved his life.

"There were eighty-mile-an-hour winds," he said. "You couldn't see nothin'. But then, all of a sudden, it looked like it cleared up a little bit, so I got back on the road."

Onto the bridge he drove, and up . . . up . . . up . . . up, through the rain and the wind. He didn't know it at the time but a freighter, its pilot unable to see where he was, had crashed into the Skyway a short time before and a quarter-mile section of the towering bridge fell into Tampa Bay. The bus Hamner had seen go by—the one he almost followed—plunged 150 feet into the water below. In all, thirty-five people died as their vehicles fell through the gaping hole in the Skyway, unable to see what had happened until it was too late.

Granny had no idea what had happened either. But luckily for him the visibility had improved to the point that he could make out the red of the brake lights in front of him. "Otherwise," he said, "I'd have run into the guy. There were three cars in front of me when I stopped, and the first one was half over the edge."

In a short time a police car drove up behind Granny. "The guy didn't know what happened," Hamner said. "All he knew was we'd all stopped."

The policeman stuck his head out the window and shouted something to the drivers up ahead. Granny Hamner said he will never forget the words as long as he lives.

"You know what he said?" Granny asked. "He said, 'Let's keep this traffic moving.' "

Let no man say that the life of an old Whiz Kid is without its memorable moments.

6

The Pennant That Flew Away

IN 1961 THE PHILLIES WEREN'T MERELY A BAD TEAM; THEY WERE terrible. Oh sure, Art Mahaffey could beat anybody on a given day. And the intense, young guy with the penetrating stare and the razorsharp mind stalking the dugout could manage with anybody practically any day. But it would take more baseball expertise than even Gene Mauch possessed, more than the burning desire to win that flamed inside his body to make this Phillies team competitive.

"We knew factually that we were just overmatched," recalled Ruben Amaro, now a Phillies coach, then a young Phillies shortstop. "We were in the wrong league. We should've been in another league—not the National League—with that ball club. We tried. I thought we played as good as we could play in many games. But it was just a matter of being too young and too new and not strong enough . . ."

The 1961 Phillies, in their first full season under Gene Mauch, lost 107 games. They would have lost more, but they were lucky in a way. That was the last of the National League's 154–game seasons.

One of their forty-seven victories came in the second game of a doubleheader at Connie Mack Stadium against the San Francisco Giants on Friday night, July 28. A righthander named John Buzhardt boosted his record to 3-and-10 by beating the Giants, 4–3, a victory that made the Phillies 30–64 on the year, twenty-nine games out of first place and—most discouraging of all—ten games out of seventh in the eight-team National League.

Still, it was a rather notable victory for the '61 Phillies, who didn't win another game until John Buzhardt beat the Milwaukee

Braves, 7–4, in the second game of a doubleheader at Milwaukee's County Stadium on Sunday, August 20. Between those two Buzhardt wins the Phillies conspired to lose twenty-three consecutive games, establishing a modern major-league record. They did it strictly on merit.

The losing streak started on July 29 when Orlando Cepeda's first career grand slam gave the Giants a 4–3 victory. It included eight one-run defeats, eleven straight games in which the opposing pitcher went all the way, eight straight games in which the Phillies never so much as held a lead, four shutouts—three of them in succession—and sixteen games in which our heroes scored two or less runs. The Phillies were rotten all over; they lost six games in Philadelphia, three in Cincinnati, four in St. Louis, three in Pittsburgh, three in Chicago, and four in Milwaukee. It may have been just a coincidence, but in the midst of the streak—on Monday night, August 7—beer was sold at Connie Mack Stadium for the first time. If ever there was a major-league baseball team capable of driving an entire city to drink, it was those '61 Phillies.

One thing you had to say about them—they lost to some good pitchers along the way—as well as an occasional turkey. Among their conquerors were the likes of Curt Simmons, Bob Friend (twice), Bob Gibson, Lew Burdette, and, in loss no. 23, the great lefthander, Warren Spahn. The 5–2 loss to Spahn, who pitched a five-hitter in the first game of a Sunday double-header, was not only the Phillies' twenty-third loss in a row but their twenty-eighth in twenty-nine games, dropping their record to 30–87.

Then came Buzhardt's epic victory in Milwaukee, and the Phillies came winging home, a mere fifty-six games under .500, a trifling forty-two games behind the first-place Cincinnati Reds, a paltry nineteen-and-a-half behind the seventh-place Chicago Cubs. The city was so turned on by their accomplishments that a crowd awaited the team's arrival at the Philadelphia airport. Estimates as to the size of that crowd vary widely. Allen Lewis, who covered the Phillies for *The Inquirer* at the time, recalled that "several hundred" turned out. Ruben Amaro talked in terms of a few thousand. But whatever the actual count, the fact that people would turn out on a Sunday night to welcome them home had to come as a shock to most of the '61 Phillies.

Frank Sullivan, a towering righthanded pitcher who possessed a good sense of humor—something that certainly came in handy for anybody who played for that team—spotted the waiting throng and announced solemnly to his teammates, "Go out in twos and threes, men. They're selling rocks at a dollar a pail, and that way they won't get us in one burst."

"They told us on the plane there were maybe 3-4-5,000 people waiting for us," Ruben Amaro recalled. "Tony Gonzalez came over to me before we got off the plane, and he said, 'Are those guys coming to cheer us or lynch us?' "

Gonzalez was unduly concerned. The people had come to cheer their record-breaking Phillies. "I think the first two or three guys that got off the plane were a little bit apprehensive," Amaro said, "but then after we knew the people were really serious about supporting our efforts, it was beautiful, beautiful. We had a great time that night."

Chances are, no Philadelphia team was ever cheered more for accomplishing less. Still, it was a sign the people understood the problem. It wasn't a lack of trying, it was a lack of talent, and a lack of experience. Even while they lost, Gene Mauch kept seeing a vision of brighter days ahead. "He led us to believe, 'Hey, you guys aren't going to be down too long,' " Amaro said. "He told us that we've got to make less mistakes on the field than those guys we're playing, and that was the greatest foundation for being the kind of ball club we were in 1964."

Ah, 1964. You knew it had to come, didn't you? You knew there couldn't be a book about professional sports in Philadelphia without somebody bringing up 1964, the year the National League pennant flew away.

"The most fun I ever had was 150 games that you all saw," Gene Mauch told a couple of Philadelphia sports writers before a 1980 spring training game in Tampa. "That was the most fun that anybody ever had."

But some damn fool had to go and expand the baseball schedule to 162 games . . . and Gene Mauch's brilliant managing job with the '64 Phillies went down the drain.

The '64 Phillies, after all, weren't supposed to win the National League pennant. They only had two hitters who played against all pitching—rookie third-baseman Richie Allen and right fielder Johnny Callison. And they had two consistently solid starters—righthander Jim Bunning and lefthander Chris Short. But they had a tough bullpen headed by Jack Baldschun, who would keep wriggling out of jams despite running those 3–and–1 and 3–and–2 counts. And they had Mauch, the fiery leader, the little general, platooning up a storm, always seeking an edge here, an advantage there, somehow fitting all the pieces together.

The success of the '64 Phillies through those first 150 or so games didn't come as a complete surprise, mind you. By '63, Mauch and John Quinn had put together a respectable, fourth-place club that finished twelve games over .500. "I remember somebody asking [Dodger pitcher] Johnny Padres on our last trip into Los Angeles in '63, 'Do you think the Phillies are a coming team?' He said, 'No, they're not coming. They're here.' "

By 1964, it was clear to all that the Phillies had arrived. On paper there might have been two or three better teams in the National League. But on the field, where it mattered, Mauch had them playing the game the way it was meant to be played. The '64 Phillies did all the little things that show up only in the victory column. They hit the cutoff men. They sacrificed and they squeezed and they played hit and run and they moved up the runners.

"We didn't have the talent of this club [the Phillies of the early '80s] or the talent that some other clubs have had in the past," said Bobby Wine, like Amaro a part-time shortstop then, a coach now. "But we each did the little things to help us win. We bunted a guy over, we'd hit and run when we had to, little things like that. There weren't many guys that weren't part of the team. We just ran a little short at the end."

After 150 games, there seemed to be no way the '64 Phillies could lose. They had just completed their final West Coast swing of the season by winning two out of three against the Dodgers, and they came home to start a seven-game Connie Mack Stadium stand leading by six-and-a-half games with twelve to go.

When you stop to think about it, it's amazing that the tattered, battered, ragamuffin 1961 Phillies could evolve into a winning (81–80) team by 1962, a team capable of winning eighty-seven games by 1963, and a team that had the National League pennant all but wrapped up with two weeks to go in 1964. Sadly, the 1964 Phillies would not be remembered for the tremendous strides they made and for the pennant they almost won, but for the late-season collapse that remains, to this day, baseball's most shocking. Here, after all, was a team that had two legitimate "stoppers" in Bunning and Short. It seemed inconceivable, as the Phillies returned home from Los Angeles, that a long losing streak awaited them.

Perhaps there was a clue that weird things were about to happen to the club in the one loss at Los Angeles. Short pitched brilliantly that night and carried a lead into the late innings before huge Dodger slugger Frank Howard, always a Chris Short nemesis, unloaded a long, game-tying home run. The Saturday night game went on and on, pushing into Sunday morning. Along the way the Phillies were hit by one of several injuries that were very much a part of the '64 collapse. "About the tenth inning or so," Ruben Amaro recalled, "I got on base and [catcher Clay] Dalrymple had the hit and run on, and he missed the pitch, so I came back to first base. I was safe, but I slid too close to first base, and I pulled my shoulder out of place."

From then on, Amaro was of practically no use to the club. It wasn't until June of the following year that he could really throw again.

Much of the pain that Saturday night in Los Angeles, however, was caused by the way the Phillies lost the game. The end came in the bottom of the sixteenth inning. The Dodgers had two out, Willie Davis on third and Ron Fairly, a lefthanded batter, at the plate. Mauch played the percentages and brought in a left-hander named Morrie Steevens to face Fairly. Steevens had just joined the club after a brief, undistinguished career with the Cubs.

The kid got two strikes on Fairly, and then a crazy thing happened: Willie Davis broke for the plate. There's no way a runner can try to steal home with two out and two strikes on the batter; all the pitcher has to do is throw the ball over the plate for strike three and the inning's over. The batter can't swing with that runner bearing down on him; he might kill his teammate with a line drive. No matter. Davis got the bright idea to make a dash for it . . . and Steevens panicked. The ball went flying to the backstop. Willie Davis' steal of home beat the Phillies, 4–3.

At the time it didn't seem like that big a deal, though—especially when the Phillies recorded their ninetieth victory of the season the following afternoon in Dodger Stadium. Jim Bunning got it for them, surviving a ninth-inning scare to nail down a 3–2 win that cut the Phillies' "magic number" to seven. It was an exhilarating victory. Who could have known it was also the last victory for more than a week and a half?

"I had to get one more guy out [after an error had kept the Dodgers alive in the bottom of the ninth], and I did," Bunning said. "And we celebrated."

The man Bunning had to get was John Roseboro, who went down swinging on a 2–2 pitch. Nothing but cheerful thoughts danced through Phillie heads on the trip home that night. "We had it all," Bunning said. "All we had to do was hold it."

The pennant was theirs. They could feel it. They could taste it.

Ruben Amaro placed a long-distance telephone call to his father in Mexico. The elder Amaro had been a baseball star in Cuba. He loved the game as much as his son did. Ruben wanted him to be a part of the victory drive.

"We come back from the road," Ruben said, "and I call him and I say, 'Father, it looks like we're in and I really want you to come here and enjoy the World Series and I want you to come early.' I remember my father saying, 'I don't like to sound pessimistic or anything, but I wouldn't really be sure of playing [in the World Series] until I know you have clinched the pennant.' "

Ruben's father had been through some wild finishes himself in Cuba. "There was one [pennant race]," his son recalled, "all they had to do was win one game out of the last three, and they lost the three games, and the guy that beat them the last game was a guy that wasn't even a regular. With two strikes, they threw him a waste pitch, a pitch over his head, and that was the pitch he hit for a home run."

And then the following year Ruben's father's team went into the final three games of the season needing a sweep to win the pennant. Max Lanier, of St. Louis Cardinal fame, won the Friday game. Somebody else won the Saturday game. Back came Lanier on Sunday, and he won that game . . . and the pennant. When Ruben's dad related those stories, the message was clear: Don't count your pennants before they're clinched.

But even if Ruben Amaro's father decided to play it safe and wait in Mexico until clinching day, Philadelphia braced itself for a pennant party. With a good home stand and a little luck, the clincher could have come the next weekend before the team took off on its final road trip of the season. But the home stand . . . and the luck . . . was all bad.

On Monday night, September 21, Art Mahaffey and John Tsitouris were locked in a scoreless tie through five innings. Then came trouble. With one out in the sixth, Chico Ruiz singled to right, and Vada Pinson hit one off Tony Taylor's glove into right field for another hit. Ruiz sprinted to third, but Johnny Callison gunned down Pinson at second. Now there were two out, and Frank Robinson, the Reds' most dangerous hitter, was at bat.

If you don't try to steal home with two out and two strikes on the hitter, you also don't try to steal home with Frank Robinson at the plate. Trouble was, somebody forgot to explain that to Ruiz. As Cincinnati's acting manager, Dick Sisler, looked on in amazement, Ruiz made his break for home . . . and as Gene Mauch stared in horror from the Phillies dugout, Mahaffey threw the ball to the backstop. That was the only run of the ball game. For the second time in three days, the Phillies had been beaten on steals of home. Nobody knew it at the time, but the ten-game losing streak had started.

The next night, the Reds bombarded Chris Short and beat the Phillies, 9–2, as Robinson hit a two-run homer. The night after that, Vada Pinson hit two homers, and Dennis Bennett, a sore-armed lefty, was beaten, 6–4.

Already there was some criticism in the press of the way Mauch had handled his pitchers, using Bunning and Short with two days rest. Maybe they were worn out now.

Surely, Bunning didn't feel that way. "I was perfectly confident we weren't going to blow it," he said. "I couldn't see how we could blow it and have two teams go by us."

And yet that's what happened as the Phillie skid gained momentum. The Braves followed the Reds into Connie Mack Stadium, and they brought their bats with them. Bunning lost the Thursday night game, 5–3, and the losing streak had reached four, equaling the club's longest of the season. The next game was a killer. The Phillies kept rallying and rallying, and still they lost. Callison boomed a game-tying, two-run homer in the eighth.

Richie Allen came up in the home tenth with a runner on base and the Phillies trailing by two runs . . . and hit an inside-the-park homer, and again it was tied. But an infield hit, two walks, an RBI single by Eddie Mathews, and an error made John Boozer a 7–5 loser in the twelfth. Next day was almost as bad. The Phillies carried a 4–3 lead into the ninth when Bobby Shantz, who had pitched the club out of deep eighth-inning trouble, gave up a bases-loaded triple to Rico Carty that gave the Braves a 6–4 win.

Things were getting desperate now, so desperate that Jim Bunning volunteered to pitch again Sunday afternoon. The spirit was willing; the arm wasn't. The Braves clobbered the great righthander and won, 14–8. Not even three home runs by Johnny Callison could halt the Great Collapse.

On to St. Louis the Phillies went, clinging to the shaky remains of what had been a seemingly safe lead only a week before. Chris Short pitched the Monday night game . . . and lost it, 5–1. The skid was at eight and counting; Mauch called a team meeting in an effort to pull things together.

"He just tried to enrage us," Bunning said. " 'You're letting it slip away,' he told us. 'Let's go.' But he didn't put it in quite those nice terms. I remember him saying, 'Go start a fight. Do something.' You could see it was getting to him inside."

It was getting to most of them. Next night the Phillies lost their ninth in a row as lefthander Ray Sadecki became a twenty-game winner, beating Dennis Bennett, 4–2. Then it was Bunning's turn—again with only two days' rest. Curt Simmons beat him, 8–5. The losing streak had reached ten; the team that had hoped to clinch the pennant at home the week before was now on the brink of elimination. But even as the club headed for the season-ending, two-game series in Cincinnati, trailing both the Reds and the Cards in the standings, there was a lingering hope.

"I really didn't feel like we were going to lose it," Bobby Wine said. "I thought, 'Tomorrow we'll win a game, and we'll be OK.' I really felt that way, and most of the guys did. And that was all we had to do; we had to win just one game out of that streak."

"We made more mistakes [in those ten games] than we made in 150 games before that," Ruben Amaro said. "I remember Alex Johnson overran the bases twice [to kill rallies]. It was just a nagging conglomeration of little things."

Now it was anybody's pennant—the Reds', the Cards', and still possibly the Phillies.' That last weekend in Cincinnati remains etched in Jim Bunning's mind. Just when it seemed to be all over for the Phillies they rallied from a 3–0 deficit, beating the Reds with four runs in the top of the eighth—two on a right-field double by Allen. A triple play, started by left fielder Alex Johnson, who ran up the left-field terrace at Crosley Field to spear a long line drive, had prevented the Reds from opening up a huge early lead. Still, the Phillies needed help from the goshawful New York Mets to stay alive—and they got it. The Mets knocked off the Cardinals in St. Louis on that Friday night and, wonder of wonders, they tore the Cardinals into shreds on Saturday afternoon, an off day for the Phillies and Reds.

"I heard [on the radio] Alvin Jackson beat the Cardinals," Jim Bunning said. "I thought, 'All we have to do is beat the Reds tomorrow and have the Mets win again and we have a three-way tie.'"

In light of what had occurred in the past two weeks, that combination of events didn't seem all that far-fetched. So Bunning got ready to pitch against John Tsitouris on the final Sunday of the 1964 season at Crosley Field. It was either the biggest game of his life or the most meaningless. He had no way of knowing.

"I was perfectly calm," Jim said. "I knew I could beat Cincinnati. I knew the club was in a much better frame of mind than it had been."

Bunning's most vivid recollection of that day involved an incident that happened before the game. He was stretched out on the rubbing table with Joe Liscio, the Phillies' trainer, working on him, getting him loose. Just then, Freddie Hutchinson entered the room. Hutchinson, dying of cancer, had turned over the Reds' managerial job to Dick Sisler. Once a fine big-league pitcher, and always a highly respected man, it was pathetic to see him now in his final days. He walked bent slightly from the waist; his face looked terribly drawn and tired. Two days before, when the Phillies arrived in town with their ten-game losing streak, Hutch had placed a phone call to Gene Mauch in the Phillies' clubhouse.

"The phone rang," Mauch recalled, "and I picked it up, and it was Hutch. He said, 'I wish there was something I could say to help.' Imagine him saying that to me."

That was the type of person Freddie Hutchinson was. Bunning knew. He had played for him briefly, and then only in spring training, as a member of the Detroit Tigers. But even that brief encounter was enough to leave a mark.

"He affected me," Bunning would say years later. "He was the straightest guy who ever was. He's the only manager who sent me out of the major league camp who had the courtesy to call me in and tell me what he thought I needed to do to get back in the major leagues, one on one."

In a game filled with double-talkers, Hutchinson—like Jim Bunning—was a straight-talker. That Sunday afternoon glimpse of Hutch before the final game jolted Bunning.

"He was looking for Gene," the pitcher remembered. "He was just about done. You could tell. He couldn't control one of his eyelids. He . . ." And with that, Bunning's voice trailed off. Even now, the memory was painful.

"Hutch said, 'Where is that little bastard?'," Bunning said.

" 'Fred,' I told him, 'you just missed him. He's out on the field.' "

Hutchinson nodded. "I want to say goodbye to him," he told Bunning, and then he left.

If that scene was unforgettable, the game wasn't. Tsitouris had nothing; Bunning had everything. The Phillies won, 10¢0, and yet they, like the Cincinnati Reds, wound up as losers.

The Cardinals and the Mets were still playing when Jim Bunning retired the final batter, but St. Louis had opened up a big lead. The pennant race was as good as over.

"I'll tell you one thing that sticks in my mind," Ruben Amaro said, seventeen years later. "I remember the atmosphere in the clubhouse in Cincinnati when we finally heard the results of the [St. Louis] game with New York. It was like everybody sat stunned. I mean, for an endless time. I can't tell you for twenty minutes, a half an hour, an hour—I don't know how long we sat there. But I know what I was praying for on the bench during the game. 'Please God, give us a shot. Give us one more game.' That, I think, was the desperate prayer of most everybody involved. It [not winning the pennant] was really hard to swallow. Position by position, talentwise, I think we were maybe the third, fourth best club in the league, but as far as the way we played, we were beautiful."

For 150 games, anyway.

It was, to be sure, a grim scene in the Phillies' clubhouse as the finality of the thing struck home. The pennant race was over, really over. And they had lost. No manager ever had more difficulty accepting defeat than Gene Mauch did that day. "When you manage the way I want to manage, you don't miss something by a game or two," he said in a voice so low writers standing near him strained to hear his words.

And when you pitch the way Jim Bunning wants to pitch, you don't come that close to a World Series—and come up one game short—without an enormous sense of disappointment and frustration. "I didn't say anything to anybody," he said. "Nobody said anything to anybody. It was a total blah. We were out of it. We were let down. We were completely gone. We had it; it was ours, and we let it go."

For Jim Bunning, that was the single most miserable moment he had ever experienced in baseball. He dressed quickly and dashed to the airport; there was a Players Association meeting in New York City that he had to attend. Jim's wife, Mary, still remembers running into Carolyn Rose, Pete's wife, in the ladies room after the game that dashed the hopes of both their husbands' teams. The two girls threw their arms around each other and cried.

The pain didn't disappear quickly. If anything, it intensified when the Cardinals began playing the Yankees in the World Series a few days later. "That's when it really started to sink in," Bunning said. "I didn't turn on one game. I don't even know who did what in that Series, and that's the only Series I don't know what happened. I just didn't have any desire to watch it. All I could think was, 'I should've opened the Series.'

"Everybody blamed Gene [Mauch] for what happened, but to this day and until I die I will never blame him."

It didn't really matter whose fault it was. It had happened. The six-and-a-half-game lead and the National League pennant had vanished in two weeks. The St. Louis Cardinals, not the Philadelphia Phillies, were in the World Series. Bob Gibson, not Jim Bunning, was pitching—and winning—the big games, the really big games, on national television. "The most frustrating part of baseball," Jim Bunning called it.

For him, and for Mauch, that sense of frustration never entirely disappeared. The saddest part of the Great Collapse of '64 is that one of the most highly respected managers in the game and one of the finest pitchers in the game lost their big opportunities to be part of a World Series.

If Mauch deserved criticism for overworking Bunning and Short down the stretch, then he also deserved tremendous credit for the job he did through the first 150 games. Bunning, Wine, Amaro, most of those '64 Phillies still consider him somebody special, a manager without peer when it came to running a ball game.

"I don't think there's anybody that has ever come close to him, of the managers I played with in baseball," Ruben Amaro said. "To me, he was really instrumental in opening up my mind as far as the game was concerned. I played for Ralph Houk and I played for Johnny Keane and I played with Fred Hutchinson and Bill Rigney, but that man was beyond those people."

"I think Gene Mauch is one of the best managers in baseball," Bobby Wine said. "He taught more people how to play baseball than people will give him credit for. I'll tell you what . . . he told me when he got this job [when Eddie Sawyer quit following the opening game of the 1960 season] that he was scared to death. He said, 'Here I am in the big leagues. I'm the youngest manager in the big leagues. I've got to do something.' So he came in like a lion, and he kept that up pretty much of his managing career. A lot of people say, 'I don't like that guy.' But when they played for him it was the opposite. Talk to Dick Groat or Larry Jackson, talk to any players that were with other ball clubs. They'll tell you, when you're playing against him, yeah, you want to beat him because he's so intense. He intimidates you. He tries to do things that'll help you win. He'll think up something to try to throw the other team off, a lot of little things. OK, some you don't agree with, some of 'em you don't like, but like I say, he taught more guys how to play baseball than anybody else."

He did everything, in fact, in two decades as a big-league manager except win a pennant. In 1964 he had both hands firmly on it, and it got away.

Ruben Amaro still has some of the tickets that were printed for the 1964 Phillies World Series that was never played. "I bought them for all the people in Mexico," he said, "for my family and some of my friends that were coming to the World Series. I had bought exactly $1,800 worth of tickets. It so happens, we never gave the tickets back [because] they never cashed the check."

For Ruben Amaro, winning the 1964 pennant would have had special meaning. After all, he had been a Phillie in 1961. He had been there for the 23-game losing streak, for the 107 losses.

"It was really depressing to lose in '64," he said. "It lingered for a long time. I'd say, 'We didn't win the darn thing. We didn't even finish second by ourselves.' Just looking back, it was a disastrous thing—moreso because I had been there in '61 when we had the worst ball club, and it really would have given me a tremendous amount of pride to say, 'Hey, we finally are here.' "

To Amaro, the injuries were the real reason the Phillies lost the 1964 pennant. There was the injury to Ruben's shoulder and the injury to Dalrymple's knee and the injury to Vic Power's thumb and, perhaps most disastrous of all, the injured thumb that cost the Phillies the services of Frank Thomas at first base.

"It just wasn't meant to be," Bobby Wine said. "We played as good as we could—until that one stretch of time."

And that one stretch of time, those ten losing games, hurt infinitely more than the twenty-three losses three years before. Just how much it hurt was evident the following spring when Gene Mauch, arriving at the team's Clearwater, Florida, training camp, made it clear that he didn't want to talk about 1964. Unfortunately, some of the media types who showed up in camp that spring did.

One of them was Howard Cosell. He showed up with a film crew and asked Mauch if he could interview him on camera. Mauch said he could—on one condition: no questions about the collapse of 1964.

It was time for the interview. Camera . . . action . . .

Cosell wasn't about to pass up an opportunity to press Gene Mauch on the subject that all America—with the possible exception of Philadelphia—wanted to hear explored. He looked the Philies' fearless leader squarely in the eye and asked him the one question Mauch didn't want to answer: What had happened in the stretch drive of '64?

Gene Mauch didn't flinch. He didn't hesitate. He stared right back and he said, in a way that only Gene Mauch could, "Fuck you, Howard."

Come to think of it, that's as good a way as any to wind up the story of the '64 Phillies.

7

The 9 and 73ers

NINE AND SEVENTY THREE. THINK ABOUT THAT, SPORTS FANS. The only pro basketball teams to do worse were the Washington Generals, the Boston Shamrocks, and the Atlantic City Seagulls. And they were playing the Harlem Globetrotters. The Generals, the Shamrocks, and the Seagulls had an excuse. They were paid to lose. The 1972–73 Philadelphia 76ers played in the National Basketball Association. They were descendents, for crying out loud, of the 1967–68 Philadelphia 76ers, who won the NBA title and were hailed as the greatest team in the history of the league.

What in the world, you ask, could turn the best into the worst, the all-time winners into the all-time losers? Well, for starters check out the first-round draft choices that the 76ers plucked out of the college ranks beginning in 1967. In order they were: Craig Raymond, draft of '67; Shaler Halimon, draft of '68; Bud Odgen, draft of '69; Al Henry, draft of '70; and Dana Lewis, draft of '71. You've heard of professional teams that chose to build with draft choices; here was the first pro team that destroyed itself with draft choices. Philly was the only town where, when you heard people hollering, "Abolish the Draft," you couldn't be sure whether they were talking about the armed forces or the NBA.

Part of the problem, quite clearly, was that Jack Ramsay, a superb coach, didn't have the time to be a superb coach *and* a superb general manager. So, showing a rare sense of timing, Ramsay left Philadelphia at the end of 1971–72, the first losing season of his coaching career. At least it was a respectable losing season compared to what was to follow.

"See that statue?" Ramsay would say a year later while driving past Philadelphia City Hall, at the top of which the figure of

William Penn attracted tourists and pigeons. "If I was still coaching in Philadelphia, I'd be hanging up there."

Instead, the dubious honor went to a man named Roy Rubin.

First, however, the 76ers tried to land a "name" coach, and with that in mind they approached two of the biggest names in the business. The big effort went into trying to sign Al McGuire, then a highly successful —and colorful—college coach at Marquette. Don DeJardin, who followed Ramsay as 76ers' general manager, met with McGuire's attorney and, Don thought, "finalized an agreement."

"Terms, dollars were agreeable," DeJardin said, "but there was one hangup that eventually fouled up the whole thing. That was the method of payments. McGuire wanted to receive a large advance. The manner of payment was unacceptable to Koz [76ers' owner Irv Kosloff] and his accountant. They wouldn't agree, and we had to go on to the next choice. It's been written four or five times since that I was the reason McGuire didn't take the 76ers' job. That's not the case."

DeJardin, in fact, met with McGuire's attorney in Milwaukee in May of '72. Marquette was notified, and tentative agreement was reached on a five-year deal—a deal that, unfortunately for the 76ers and fortunately for McGuire, fell through.

The other big name was—now take a deep breath—Adolph Rupp.

It was Rupp himself, the legendary, one-time University of Kentucky coach, who told the story one April while attending Basketball Hall of Fame ceremonies in Springfield, Massachusetts. Rupp was seventy years old when the idea was broached by Irv Kosloff in a Springfield hotel room during the 1972 induction ceremonies. Showing the same sage basketball sense that helped him win twenty-four Southeastern Conference championships and four national titles, Rupp said no. Or, as he put it a year later, "After the year they had, thank God I didn't go."

Rupp did think about it for four days before making his decision known, however. "He made the offer right here," he said on the first anniversary of the smartest decision of his illustrious career. "Haskell Cohen [former NBA publicist] got us together. He said, 'I recommended you to Mr. Kosloff, and I certainly recommend Mr. Kosloff to you. You're both high grade.' He told us, 'Gentlemen, I'd certainly like to see you work together.' "

With friends like that, Adolph Rupp didn't need any enemies. But his wife came to the rescue. "She said no," Rupp said. "She wouldn't consider going to Philadelphia."

So Rupp took a job as president of the Memphis team in the American Basketball Association. "My wife likes Memphis," he explained. "It isn't too big. The people know you. You go down the street in Philadelphia, who the hell do you know?"

On the other hand, if you walked down the street in Philadelphia as the coach of the 1972–73 76ers, who the hell would you want to know?

Speaking of walking down the street, the 76ers' losing 1971–72 season was such agony for Ramsay that he got in the habit of taking long walks by himself in the wee hours of the morning, replaying in his mind the previous night's excruciating defeat. One night in Chicago Ramsay's 76ers blew one at the buzzer, and the intense, emotional coach was so upset that he embarked on one of his solo, post-midnight walks and wound up in a neighborhood that wasn't safe at high noon.

"I was steaming," Ramsay recalled much later. He was so steaming, so eager to take out his anger and frustration on somebody or something that he actually found himself thinking, "I'd like to see someone try to mug me."

And then, said Ramsay, he saw the figure through the darkness on the other side of the street. If ever Jack had seen a potential mugger, this guy was it. And then, sure enough, the figure crossed the street and came toward him.

"I took my gloves off," said Ramsay, who was itching for a good fight. "The guy came up to me. 'Hey, brother,' he said, 'got a match?' I said, 'No, I don't have a match. I don't even smoke.' "

There was an awkward moment or two of silence. Jack Ramsay braced himself for the onslaught he felt sure was about to come. He'd show this no-good so-and-so, this man who went through the Chicago streets in the middle of night preying on innocent, if losing, coaches. Seldom has a muggee been so prepared for a mugger.

"You know what happened?" Jack said. "The guy said, 'Thanks, anyway,' and he walked away. Things were going so bad I couldn't even get mugged."

If that had been Roy Rubin, the guy would have been a real mugger, and he would have had two dozen friends waiting around the corner. Poor Roy Rubin. Poor, *poor* Roy Rubin. Al McGuire and Adolph Rupp should have been ashamed of themselves for subjecting him to his fifty-one game career as coach of the Philadelphia 9–and–73ers.

Rubin took the job because he wanted to try the "big time" after a successful tour of duty as coach of Long Island University. The 76ers team he inherited provided him with the damndest initiation into the "big time" any man ever had. Getting initiated into this fraternity, Roy discovered, was tantamount to facing "hell night" three or four times a week.

He was a pleasant, decent man too. The face was Phil Foster. The voice was Rodney Dangerfield. The paunch was Jackie Gleason. The mission was impossible.

Poor, poor, *poor* Roy Rubin. At Long Island University he had basketball players. He had tenure. He had friends. "I could have spent the rest of my life like Mr. Chips," he said in that outgoing, humorous way of his.

Instead, he answered the call of the "big time." Mr. Chips became Mr. Schnook, and he did it with his eyes at least part-way open. Not that anybody could have foreseen the disaster that awaited him. No NBA team had a right to be *that* bad.

"I'm giving up a lot," he said that day, and his voice was cheerful. "Another guy might say, 'Gee . . . he's got to be out of his skull.' "

And that guy, Rubin went on to learn the hard way, would be right. But you can't blame a man for trying, even if the 76ers *had* come up with an incredible succession of virtually useless first-round draft choices . . . even if their best player, Billy Cunningham, *had* jumped to the other league . . . even if Jack Ramsay *had* seen the handwriting on the wall and escaped to Buffalo. Let's face it; people don't generally go to Buffalo unless things are pretty bad where they are.

"I know what I'm getting into," Rubin kept insisting between bites of lunch at the Sheraton Hotel in midtown Philly, not far from that statue of William Penn, where even now the rope was being placed in readiness. "I may lose more games in two weeks than I lost in two years, or four years. I dunno. That's part of the game. I'm not a magician. I'm not a genius."

But he was smart enough to sign a three-year contract.

"There's no way I would take this job without a long-term contract," he said. "No way."

After meeting with the Philly press that day, Roy Rubin had to be more certain than ever that he was smart in getting a multiyear contract. All he heard was how lousy the 76ers were. "You need a horse in the middle," he finally concluded. "That's pretty obvious. And you need guards as well as a center. You need everybody. After what I heard today, maybe I should quit."

Truer words were never spoken in jest. The 76ers didn't have a prayer that season. Among other things, they couldn't handle the press. Any kind of press—the man-to-man press, the zone press, the half-court press, the Philly press. The writers came up with more funny lines than the team came up with field goals. Poor Roy Rubin could be excused for not laughing.

"I'll tell you the truth," he said one day early in the season, "I'm tired of hearing myself called 'Poor Roy Rubin.' Even at the newsstand near where I live [in center city], the guy calls me 'Poor Roy Rubin.' "

The name stuck. The more games the 76ers lost, the more people got in the habit of referring to Rubin as "Poor Roy." And, boy, did they lose games! The season opened with a fifteen-game losing streak, followed by a victory, followed by six more losses, followed by a victory, followed by three more losses, followed by . . . oh well, what's the use? Even writing about this team is painful.

"I didn't want to be a celebrity this way," Rubin sighed after the 76ers had lost their fifteenth straight. "I'm suffering. My stomach hurts. My chest hurts. I hurt all over."

The pain must have been especially severe the night the 76ers ran their record to 1–21. With ten minutes to go, they were actually five points up and the Spectrum crowd—less than 4,000—was making so much noise that Rubin said, "Dammit, a lousy five-point lead, and it sounded like 30,000 people in there."

Then the 76ers reverted to form, getting outscored, 20–2, in the next six minutes. Rubin called three time-outs in a futile attempt to stop the avalanche of enemy points. No use.

"I'll look anywhere for a player," Poor Roy said. "I'll look in a schoolyard, anywhere. I don't expect anything, but I'm not leaving any stones unturned." And with that, the desperate coach took off for an Eastern League game in Trenton, New Jersey, in the hope of finding somebody there. "With my luck," he said, "I'll probably get up to Trenton and find out they've got the night off."

If you want to know how bad Roy Rubin's luck was, try this on for size. The night he got his first NBA victory, breaking that season-opening, fifteen-game losing streak against the Houston Rockets in San Antonio, he started to jump up to dispute a call . . . and pulled a muscle in his leg. "After the game," reported Don DeJardin, "when everybody was celebrating, Roy had to take off his pants and put ice on his leg."

Now *that's* when you're going bad.

Rubin, at least, got through the first home victory without suffering a serious injury. The historic date was December 1, 1972. The unsuspecting victims were the Kansas City Kings. Needless to say, it wasn't easy. The 76ers blew a thirteen-point lead. Then they put on a spurt and pulled ahead by fourteen. And then they blew *that*. But the law of averages was on their side. No NBA team had ever gone through an entire season without winning a home game.

With twenty seconds to go, the 76ers were up by four, and they had Freddie (Mad Dog) Carter at the foul line. (If you're wondering where he got the nickname, you'd be mad too if you had to play on this team.)

Victory for our heroes seemed so certain at this point that John Block turned to Roy Rubin on the bench and said, "Looks like we've got it." The coach recoiled in horror at the outrageous, thoroughly uncalled-for display of confidence. "Not yet," he warned Block. "There's still too much time." With this team, any time was too much time, but Block, it turned out, knew whereof he spoke. The 76ers won. They were now 1–10 at home. On the Spectrum message board the lights spelled out, "We had 'em all the way." Nothing could spoil this night. Roy Rubin was even able to celebrate with his pants on.

That celebration, like the previous one, was cut short by the next game, which the 76ers lost. Never did this joke of a team put together back-to-back victories under their beleaguered, befuddled coach. For the 1972–73 Philadelphia 76ers, a hot streak consisted of back-to-back off days.

In mid-January of 1973, their record had dipped to an almost unbelievable 4–45. (If you'd seen them play, you wouldn't believe they could win four games either.) Defeat no. 45 was a brutal walloping in Milwaukee that left coaches and players alike shaking their heads in despair. "I never thought it would be this bad," John Block said. "The players are trying to get through the season as soon as possible. It's just a nightmare we hope will end."

Poor Roy Rubin, looking as thoroughly miserable as a human being could, sat in the Milwaukee Airport the next morning, waiting for the early flight home. If his players couldn't wait for the nightmare to end, think how he must have felt.

"People ask me, 'Would you do it again?' " he said. "I give them a stock answer. I tell them, 'I never look back.' Well, that's a lot of bull. If I knew what it was going to be like, how I would feel day after day, how I would toss and turn in bed with the TV on, waking up every few minutes. . . . I've lost forty-five pounds since I took this job. That's the one good thing that's happened. But I lost it the wrong way."

He lost it by worrying, not by dieting. He lost it by squirming on the bench through an avalanche of defeats.

It was 6:40 A.M. Poor Roy Rubin sat in that airport waiting room, fitfully dozing, waiting for the flight to be called. Outside, it was still dark. Just another typical NBA road trip.

The silence was broken by an airline representative. He was walking through the waiting areas in search of a passenger.

"Mr. Weindelberger," the man called out. "Mr. Weindelberger. . . "

There was no answer, so he kept walking, kept looking. Finally, he approached the dozing man on the waiting room chair.

"You Mr. Weindelberger?" the airline rep asked.

Poor Roy Rubin awoke with a start.

"No," he said when the question was repeated, "but I wish I was."

Two defeats later, the coach of the worst team in NBA history was fired. GM DeJardin promptly put through another call to Milwaukee, on the off chance that Al McGuire had temporarily taken leave of his senses and would consider taking a seat on the bench of this 4–47 ball club. No such luck. McGuire's sanity was intact. This time it was more than the financial arrangements that prompted him to say no.

Thus it was left to Kevin Loughery to have the dubious

distinction of coaching the 9–and–73ers through the last thirty-one games of their misery. Ah, but Kevin got even. In late April of '73, on the eve of the NBA draft—the annual event that had made the 76ers what they were—Don DeJardin sat in the office, waiting for his coach to arrive. A meeting had been set up for 2 P.M., but 2 P.M. came and went with no sign of Loughery. So did 3 P.M. And 4 P.M. And 5 P.M. DeJardin grew understandably worried. Something must have happened to Loughery—something even worse than coaching the 76ers.

"Don was concerned that Kevin was late because he'd had an automobile accident," club owner Irv Kosloff said.

So you can imagine DeJardin's relief when the office phone rang at about 6 o'clock and he heard Kevin Loughery's voice telling him that everything was fine. That is, almost everything. Seems Kevin, who had agreed verbally to coach the 76ers for two more seasons, had just signed to coach the ABA's New York Nets.

It was a fitting climax to a season when absolutely nothing went right, a season that brought Roy Rubin's coaching career to a sudden, jolting halt after two decades of success in high school and college. What happens to a man who goes through an experience like that? What does a coach do when his shot at the "big time" winds up with four victories, forty-seven defeats, and a public firing? Roy Rubin went to Florida to lick his wounds in 1973. They were deep wounds, and the healing process took time.

"I was sort of dejected," he said. "I didn't know what to do. I really hadn't met failure before."

For a month and a half he "goofed around Florida, trying to get my head on straight." There were some college offers, he said, but those fifty-one games with the 76ers had given him his fill of basketball for a while. And besides, the thought of returning to the recruiting "rat race" turned him off.

So Roy Rubin, the coach of the worst team in NBA history, did what you might have expected him to do. He switched careers, leaving basketball . . . and the 76ers . . . and Philadelphia way behind. Today, Rubin—his warm personality, his sense of humor fully restored—is in the restaurant business, owner of the International House of Pancakes on busy Biscayne Boulevard and 24th Street in Miami. At least now when the product he produces turns out flat, nobody complains.

"I don't have any regrets," he said recently about the Philadelphia experience that changed his life. "The best thing I have to say about the [76ers] job was it got me to Florida. I miss basketball, but I don't miss the climate. There's something peculiar about the weather down here. Even though you're working you feel like you're on vacation."

At no time did coaching that 76ers' team seem like a vacation. Even now, talking about those bad, old days can be painful. "I had coached twenty years before that," Roy said, "but I don't think anybody is prepared to take those kind of losses."

Maybe a Dick Motta, with a successful pro coaching career already established, could walk into an expansion situation—as coach of the Dallas Mavericks in 1980–81—and prepare himself mentally for the losses that were sure to come. Rubin couldn't. "He can forget losses," Roy said. "I could never do that. Still, there were certain things I liked about the life. I can understand why some of these guys [in the pros] never want to give it up. They enjoy getting away from the house. They enjoy traveling around the country. They enjoy the adoration—if they're winning."

Rubin, of course, never really had a chance to win. "At the college level," he said, "the rules are different. You can steal a game once in a while. You can hold the ball. On the pro level, it's a different ball game. You've got to have the talent. If you took twenty-three coaches in the pros and threw them up in the air and they fell in different places, probably all twenty-three teams would end up the same."

That might be stretching it a bit, but Rubin's point is well taken. Without the material Jack Ramsay lost in Philadelphia. With the material —and particularly with Bill Walton—Ramsay won a championship in Portland. It's the same in baseball. Casey Stengel won five straight world championships as manager of the Yankees; he landed in the cellar as manager of the expansion Mets.

"Dick Motta is a perfect example," Rubin said of the man who did so much winning in Chicago and Washington . . . and so much losing in Dallas.

There wasn't a man alive who could better relate to what Dick Motta went through in Dallas that season than Roy Rubin. Nor was there a man alive—at least outside of Dallas—who followed the fortunes of the Mavericks with more interest. The Mavs, after all, had a fighting chance to break the record of the 1972–73 76ers. "It's funny," said Rubin, "for a while early in the season I was hoping they'd do it."

Roy's too nice a guy to wish bad luck to a basketball team or its coach. He wanted the Mavs and Motta to have as pleasant a season as was humanly possible—so long as they didn't win more than eight games. think of it: 8 and 74. Or maybe even 7 and 75. No longer would the NBA record book list Roy Rubin's team as the worst in league history. No longer would the phone in the International House of Pancakes on Biscayne Boulevard start ringing every time an NBA club went into a tailspin.

"Seems like every time a team comes in with a long losing streak, somebody calls me," Roy said. "A guy even called me from a paper in San Jose [California]. You know how it is, a team goes on a bad streak and right away they start comparing. They find out I own a restaurant. First thing you know, they're down here or they're on the phone." He laughed. Nothing bitter about that laugh. He had learned to live with that, even to enjoy it in a way. If his 76ers were to be forever held up as a standard by which all rotten pro basketball teams were measured, so be it. Roy Rubin had survived 4 and 47. He could surely handle this.

Rubin, you see, liked people, and he liked to talk basketball, and in the normal course of events the owner of a pancake restaurant on Biscayne Boulevard in Miami would be out of touch with the sport. In a weird sort of way, that 9–and–73 76ers' team kept him in touch.

"I'm sort of living off this 'fame,' " he said. "It's a reverse type of fame, but I'm telling you, it's hysterical. I keep waiting for somebody to call me up to do a light-beer commercial. Maybe I should get an agent."

He was Rodney Dangerfield again, ripping off the one-liners with that beautiful, dead-pan expression. It was good to hear him laugh, good to know that those fifty-one games as coach of the Philadelphia 76ers hadn't scarred him for life, merely turned him from basketball to pancakes, from ace bandages to maple syrup.

"So I reversed it," he said. "I started rooting for Dallas to win so our record could stand up."

Let the record show that on Sunday, February 22, 1981, the Dallas Mavericks won their ninth game against a mere fifty-five defeats. A week later they won their tenth. Roy Rubin could rest easily.

8

The Cup Runneth Over

PROFESSIONAL ICE HOCKEY DIDN'T SUDDENLY APPEAR IN Philadelphia after the Spectrum went up; it just seemed that way. Actually, there was a parade of hockey teams in Philly, carrying such names as the Falcons, the Arrows, the Quakers, the Ramblers. Mostly, they were minor-league teams. The only rink in town—at the Arena in West Philadelphia—simply wasn't big enough to support a big-league franchise. But minor-league hockey can be fun too, assuming of course that you have a highly developed sense of humor.

One of the best-known names in the early years of Philadelphia hockey was Herb Gardiner, a standout defenseman with the Montreal Canadiens in the '20s who was named the National Hockey League's most valuable player in 1926–27 over such fabled stars as Howie Morenz, Frank Bouchard, Eddie Shore, and Aurel Joliat. A Hall of Famer, Gardiner was to hockey what Bednarik was to football: an iron man who played sixty minutes a game, and sometimes overtime, as well. "I was only thirty-five years old at the time," Herb would say, as if that explained everything.

The suspicion grows, however, that playing every minute of every game in Montreal was no more difficult—and maybe a darned sight easier—than coaching a variety of Philly minor-league teams for fourteen years. "At least," Gardiner joked, "I used to get a lot of help coaching [in Philadelphia]. There was one guy who sat up in the balcony at the Arena and never missed a game. Any time he didn't like the way I was running things, he'd send down a sketch of a play he wanted me to use."

As far as can be determined, there's absolutely no truth to the rumor that Freddie Shero found those sketches in an Arena wastebasket a few decades later and turned them into his heralded "system" that brought Philadelphia back-to-back Stanley Cups. But that's getting ahead of the story.

If the "system" didn't arrive before Shero, the roughhouse style of play certainly did. Back in Herb Gardiner's coaching days, Philly had a defenseman named Joe Desson who pulled some stunts that even Dave Schultz, at his worst, never tried. One in particular . . .

Gardiner's outfit was playing a game in Carling's Rink in Baltimore, an ancient building that burned to the ground—to the betterment of hockey—in 1956. "We had an argument going on," Gardiner recalled, "and Carling, the owner of the place, was leaning out over the boards. So Joe punched him right in the nose and sent him flying."

Mr. Carling, apparently, didn't have a highly developed sense of humor. Or maybe he just had a highly developed nose. At any rate, the owner of Carling's Rink stopped the flow of blood long enough to order his arena security force to arrest his assailant. Down to rinkside the cops came. Something had to be done to save Joe Desson from a night in a "penalty box" that had bars on the windows. Herb Gardiner was equal to the occasion. "I just told Joe to keep playing," the old-time iron man said. "As long as he was on the ice, they couldn't get to him."

Or, if they did get to him, it would have to be by putting on ice skates, leaping over the boards, and skating after him. Presumably, Carling couldn't risk having his men do that; his hockey team might get penalized for having too many men on the ice. So Gardiner's strategy worked beautifully . . . for a while.

All good things come to an end, even periods of a hockey game. Eventually Joe Desson got carted off to the hoosegow. "I had to go to the jail and bail him out for $100 after the game," Herb Gardiner said.

Hockey, as you can plainly see, was kind of a nutty sport then too. Take the time Gardiner and his Philadelphia skaters were attacked with soap at the Hershey (Pennsylvania) Arena. "They'd given all the fans samples of soap before the game," Herb said. "Then a decision went against Hershey, and the barrage started. It was coming down so hard my goal-tender hid in the net so he wouldn't be hit. It didn't bother one of my boys, though. He picked it up as fast as they threw it. Told me he hated to see all that good soap go to waste."

Unfortunately, nobody can remember the identity of that player. What a shame that the man who must have been the cleanest hockey player in Philadelphia history has been forgotten. Dave Schultz we remember. Mr. Clean we forget. That's the way it goes.

The Ramblers arrived in Philadelphia in the mid-'50s, playing in something called the Eastern Hockey League. If you saw the Paul Newman movie, *Slap Shot*, you know all about the Eastern Hockey League. There are people who thought *Slap Shot* was a satire on minor-league hockey and the lust for violence; they assumed it was a gross exaggeration. Those of us who watched the EHL in those years didn't think it was exaggerated very much at all.

The Ramblers never gained the notoriety of the latter-day Flyers, who became known far and wide as the "Broad Street Bullies." But then, the "Market Street Menaces" didn't have quite the same ring. They *were* fighters, though. In that league, if you weren't a fighter it was even money you wouldn't be a survivor.

There were people who looked down at the brawling then, even as there are now. Some even suspected the fights were "put on" to build up the gate, a charge guaranteed to infuriate any hockey nut who had ever screamed obscenities at a referee.

In those days, I qualified as a "hockey nut," frequently driving great distances—to Montreal, Quebec, you name it—to watch hockey games in a variety of leagues. So, when Leo Riordan, the executive sports editor of *The Inquirer*, a wonderful man but not a hockey lover, suggested that I write a feature about the phony fights, I argued strenuously. I would gladly write the feature, I told him, but in no way would I suggest that any of those crowd-pleasing brawls was staged.

Off to the Arena I went that night, together with a photographer whose assignment was to catch some of the bloodier, *Slap Shot*-type battles. Before the game I stopped by the locker room and talked to a young winger named Moe Bartoli, a prince of a kid off the ice but practically a non-stop brawler on the ice. In the course of our conversation, I mentioned that a photographer was there to get shots of any fights that might break out. Moe nodded pleasantly and asked me where the photographer would be stationed. I laughed and said, "Hey, yeah, that's a good idea. Start a fight in front of him. It'll make a great picture." Good old Moe wasn't one to let down a friend. He started a whale of a fight directly in front of that photographer. "How'd I do?" he asked me later. "Uh, fine," I said. But I never brought up the subject of hockey fights to Leo Riordan again.

Not that hockey fights are phony; they most certainly aren't. Premeditated? Occasionally. But phony, never. Still, they represent an unfortunate side to the game—especially when carried to extremes. And the Ramblers of the '50s, like the Flyers of the '70s, did get carried away at times. No matter what you say about the Eastern Hockey League, though, it was fun. That is, looking back on it now is fun.

Nobody ever accused the EHL of being big league in any way. The first year, the Ramblers traveled to road games in cars. The seccond year, or maybe it was the third, they stepped up in class: The club provided a pair of station wagons and jammed the players in them. That worked just fine until one of the wagons was sideswiped on the way to Clinton, New York, and went up in smoke. After that, the Ramblers switched to buses. I'll never forget Chuck Stuart, a high-scoring forward who had just come to the club in a trade from another EHL team, seeing the Ramblers' bus for the first time and saying, "Gee, this club travels in style." And he was serious.

Well, the buses were better than the station wagons and infinitely better than the cars. The miracle is the club always made it to the road games in those early years. The trip to Johnstown, Pennsylvania, for example, could be—and often was—exceptionally treacherous during the winter. The ride along the Pennsylvania Turnpike was fine, barring a snowstorm; it was that thirty-six mile stretch of road that wound through the mountains after you left the turnpike that caused problems.

One Friday night the Ramblers played the Johnstown Jets in a post-season playoff game in the Philly Arena, had their usual nightcap at a tavern called The Brown Jug next door, and then hopped in their cars for the post-midnight run to Johnstown, where the teams were scheduled to play again Saturday night. The fog on that mountain road was so bad that one of the players, a winger named Gil MacNeill, had to get out of the car and walk in front, leading the way, so the driver—it happened to be me—wouldn't go over the side. *That* was life in the Eastern Hockey League.

To be honest about it, though, some of the road trips were great. One immediately comes to mind. The Ramblers were scheduled to play a two-game series in Charlotte, North Carolina, and the prospect of a day-long bus ride didn't exactly thrill them. Then came the wonderful news; it was almost too good to be true. Doug Adam, their coach—and a rather strict coach he was—had some business to conduct before going to Charlotte and would fly down the day of the first game. The players couldn't have been happier if they'd just won the Stanley Cup.

That was a resourceful team, those Philadelphia Ramblers. As soon as Adam's plans were confirmed, the players leaped into action. As I recall, Ivan Walmsley, their veteran goaltender, was in charge, but just about everybody had a hand in making that trip to Charlotte something special.

Under ordinary circumstances, Adam didn't even want the players drinking beer on the team bus, but these weren't ordinary circumstances. The players got their hands on all the beer and liquor they could, carted the stuff onto the bus, and turned it into a traveling bar. I don't think Doug Adam knows it until this day, but the team that arrived in Charlotte that night had to be one of the drunkest in sports history. And the crazy thing is, they slept it off, got up the next day and went out and beat Charlotte on their way to a two-game sweep. It was a rather notable achievement; home teams didn't lose very often in the EHL—and Charlotte was probably the toughest home team of all. If only Adam had known the secret of those two rousing, upset victories, the Ramblers might have gone the rest of the season without losing another road game. But, alas, things returned to normal, and no sober team could handle those trips.

There was the time, for instance, that the team was cruising along the New York State Thruway on the way to Utica for a playoff game. Everything was peachy—until the wisps of smoke began to curl up from underneath the hood. Pretty soon, the wisps became billows. The bus driver slammed on the brakes, opened the hood, and saw the flames. So did the players, who evacuated in record time. If they could have skated that fast they'd have been in the NHL. Anyway, the motor burned, and the players did a slow burn, reduced to standing along the highway with their hockey equipment, trying to hitchhike to Utica. They all made it too, even if their performance that night lacked the sparkle and intensity of the fire drill.

Things have really changed, of course. Philadelphia hockey is big-time now. Sellout crowds . . . championship teams . . . major-league salaries. It isn't at all uncommon these inflationary days for a hockey player to earn well up in six figures. In the heyday of the Ramblers, about a quarter of a century ago, the salaries of the top two drawing cards—a pint-sized winger named Rocky Rukavina and a towering defenseman named Ray Crew—were measured in four figures. And there was a decimal point after the second one, as in $75.00 a week. It's hard to believe in this age of whopping salaries, but Ray Crew finally left the Philadelphia Ramblers in a salary dispute that raged over the grand amount of five dollars per week. Crew said he wouldn't play unless they gave him the extra five bucks. Management said no way. Crew left. Management didn't seem to really care—until the amount was published in a local newspaper. The general manager didn't deny that they were fighting over a paltry five dollars; he simply requested that the figure not be used. He thought it might be embarrassing. Well, he was right. It was.

Then up went the Spectrum . . . and along came the Flyers. Philadelphia was ready for hockey's big league. But were hockey people ready for Philadelphia?

Bud Poile, the man chosen to build this expansion team, must have asked himself that question. "There was an article in *Sports Illustrated* giving Philadelphia a hard time," Poile—it rhymes with *oil*—recalled. "The punch line was, 'They even boo at funerals.' I said, 'Holy Geez, Philadelphia is the end of the world.' "

But whatever part of the world it occupied, Philadelphia was now a National Hockey League city, and so Bud Poile, whose ambition was to become an NHL general manager, came. His stay was stormy but productive. Even if he has long since left the Philly scene, some of the men he hired—Keith Allen, for example—are still there.

Poile's introduction to Philadelphia was less than auspicious. He was, after all, a career hockey man, and Philadelphia wasn't a hockey town. Not yet, anyway.

"I remember the first time I spoke at a banquet there," Poile said. "I'm following Curt Simmons, Robin Roberts, all the local heroes." There was a burst of applause for Simmons, a rousing ovation for Robbie. Then the emcee prepared to introduce the new general manager of the Philadelphia Flyers. He glanced at the name on the sheet of paper in front of him. He cleared his throat. He adjusted his glasses. And then, bravely, he charged ahead. "He introduced me as Bud *Pooley*," Bud Poile said. " 'Here's Bud Pooley of the, uh, local hockey team,' he said."

Things got better, though. Maybe because he was prepared for the worst, Poile found Philadelphia not to be all that bad. "Joe Kuharich [then coach of the Eagles] was very good to me when I got there," Bud said. "He told me what to expect. He said I'd get a lot of press, and that all of it wouldn't be good."

Kuharich spoke from experience, and he was right. Poile did have his share of problems with the press, but there were good times too. The truth is, the Philadelphia press—with its generally deserved reputation of being exceptionally tough and hard-hitting—turned into pussycats in the early years of the Flyers. A couple of the writers assigned to the club on a regular basis went so far as to wear the orange-colored blazers with the Flyers' logo on the pocket while covering games. Somehow, it wasn't in keeping with the city's journalistic reputation, but hockey does that to some people. Maybe it's all the hitting . . . and all the fights. Maybe it's the fact that a lot of people who went out to watch the Flyers in the early years of their existence—and that includes some of the writers—didn't know an awful lot about the sport. Whatever the reasons, there's a pronounced "we against them" feeling in hockey that seems stronger than in any other sport. You can feel it in the front office, in the stands, and even in the pressbox. By and large, it seems, hockey people expect the writers to double as rooters. But the Philly approach has changed somewhat over the years. Writers *are* critical of the home team at times. And if they still own Flyers' blazers, they no longer put them on at the drop of a puck. It's enough that the radio-TV people have carried on the tradition of wearing those flaming orange blazers; the Flyers' broadcasting booth is one of the few in sports where visitors are advised to put on sunglasses before entering.

On the subject of broadcasting booths, one of Bud Poile's early problems as GM of the Flyers involved a broadcasting booth. Actually, *booth* was a misnomer. The visiting radio announcers at the Spectrum worked in an area at the top of the lower stands that was originally designed as a second press box and has long since been turned into a deluxe "super box." There was no real privacy there; a visitor could walk directly behind the announcers and, if so inclined, listen to what they were saying. One night, Poile was so inclined.

The Flyers were playing the St. Louis Blues, the team that became their arch rivals in the early expansion years. Then, the Blues—and not the Flyers—were the roughhouse gang, and this particular night Noel Picard, one of the St. Louis toughies, and Pat Hannigan of the Flyers got into a brawl. Picard dropped his stick; Hannigan swung his . . . and the St. Louis announcer, giving the gory details to the Blues' fans back home, took Picard's side. Or so it seemed to Bud Poile, who happened to be eavesdropping at the time.

"He said on the air that Hannigán attacked poor, defenseless Picard," Poile said angrily. "I told him, 'You better get your eyes fixed. You're watching the wrong game.' "

Poile, of course, was entitled to his opinion. But said opinion, sprinkled with words that weren't designed for use on the airwaves, happened to be picked up by the microphone. The ungrateful St. Louis announcers, rather than thank Poile for providing free expert color commentary—and it *was* colorful—complained bitterly. If Bud had a future in broadcasting, it presumably ended there.

Poile wasn't around to experience the glory years, but he chose some good people—on the ice, as well as in the front office. One of the best was Joe Watson, an earnest, hard-working, young defenseman who was Bud's no. 2 pick in the Flyers' expansion draft. Joe didn't have the natural ability of a Bobby Orr, his close friend when both were owned by the Boston Bruins, but he had the attitude, the character, the love of the game that makes an athlete something special. Joe Watson personified the work ethic that was to become the trademark of the championship Flyer teams.

"You have all these dreams when you're a kid," he explained early in his Flyer career. "Most of them don't come true. This one [playing in the National Hockey League] did."

If you knew Joe Watson, you realized that he meant every word of that. To this personable, young man from Smithers, British Columbia, a town 150 miles from Alaska, playing three or four major league ice hockey games a week, getting slammed into the boards—and slamming in return—getting knocked to the ice and battered and sometimes bloodied for the sake of the team was heaven, the fulfillment of a lifelong dream.

"It's a great life," he said one day. "To me, there is no other life. Where else is a guy gonna make $15–20,000 a year, travel all over, meet a lot of people?"

Joe's salary increased significantly from the time he made those remarks, but Joe himself never changed. And his love of the game never waned—not even when he shattered his leg crashing into the boards in St. Louis as a member of the Colorado Rockies, an injury that ended his playing career.

"If not for hockey, I'd be stuck where I came from," Joe said. "I know people there who will never get out of the town. That's the way it is sometimes. A Canadian kid never gets away. When I go home in the summertime I talk to the kids. We sit around, and I tell them about the places I've been, the people I've met. They can't believe it. They go to Vancouver [about 750 miles from Smithers], and they think that's the big city. That's the way it could have been with me too."

When Joe Watson was fifteen, his dad wanted him to go into the priesthood. "That's just not my life," the young man said, flashing that big, infectious grin of his. "No way."

So, instead of becoming a priest, he became a professional hockey player, which is a long step in the other direction. Joe's first year as a pro, Bud Poile invited him to the San Francisco camp, took a long look at him, and said, "You'll be a good minor leaguer, but you'll never make the NHL." Joe Watson worked his butt off to prove Poile wrong, and a few years later it was Poile who made Watson his no. 2 draft pick.

"You've got to sacrifice in this game," Joe Watson would say.

"I remember when I was young, the guys would be out fooling around. Not me. I was a goodie goodie, I was in bed at 9:30–10 o'clock. They were laughing then. Now I'm laughing. They're still in Smithers working with a pick and shovel in a garbage dump or something. I'm here enjoying myself."

At the end of his first full year in the NHL, the people in Smithers had a night for Joe Watson, but perhaps the greatest tribute of all came after he'd left the Flyers. Returning as a member of the Colorado Rockies, Joe skated onto the Spectrum ice in an enemy uniform for the first time—and the place erupted. They cheered, and they got to their feet, and they cheered some more. Philadelphia sports fans have always appreciated the Joe Watsons of the world.

They also appreciated the Bernie Parents and, of course, the Bobby Clarkes. The year the Flyers won their first Stanley Cup, Parent was simply one of the greatest goaltenders who ever put on the pads and the mask and guarded that four-foot-high, six-foot-wide cage in the National Hockey League. Clarke? He merely became the heart, the soul, the driving force behind the Flyers. But for all the big nights, for all the playoff success that the Watsons (Joe and his brother Jimmy), the Parents, the Clarkes, the Rick MacLeishes, and the rest of them provided, the Flyers had their share of growing pains . . . and bitter disappointments. There was the season, mentioned earlier, when the Flyers were just seconds away from clinching a playoff berth. In the broadcasting booth, announcer Gene Hart was counting down those final ticks of the clock—and then, when the countdown had reached four, it suddenly stopped, Buffalo's Gerry Meehan shot, and the red light flashed on above the Flyers' cage signaling a goal that ended the 1972 playoff plans.

Then there was that day in early April 1970 when the Flyers closed out the regular season at the Spectrum against the Minnesota North Stars with a playoff berth the prize for the winner. Neither team was very good that season, but in the NHL you don't have to be very good to make it to the playoffs. So there they were, two losing teams meeting in a crucial, late-season game, with an excited crowd looking on and the scoreboard flashing a reminder, "Playoff tickets go on sale at 9 A.M. Monday."

The playoff tickets never did go on sale, though. Not in

Philly, anyway. The North Stars won the game on a shot that wasn't even supposed to be a shot. Barry Gibbs was merely trying to dump the puck into the Philly zone from just inside the center-ice red line . . . and the darn fool thing went in, past a startled Bernie Parent.

"He flipped it in [toward the Flyers' goal] just before going off the ice," Parent recalled recently, the memory still vivid. "I never saw it. I had my head down, clearing the crease . . . and then I heard *bing!*" The puck was behind him—in the net.

It wasn't bad enough that Flyer playoff hopes had been dashed by the funkiest, the cheapest of goals. That very night, a few hours after the game, the Flyers' Fan Club was holding its annual party. "Appreciation Night for the Flyers," it said on the tickets. "Dinner . . . Dancing . . . Door Prizes . . . Fun."

Fun! The body was still warm. The local heroes had just blown a playoff spot by losing six straight games, the last when its star goalie fell asleep in what had been a scoreless tie. And yet here they were, barely three hours later, partying at a riverside restaurant called Walber's on the Delaware.

They're a unique breed, hockey fans. There aren't nearly as many of them as there are, say, baseball fans or football fans in a city like Philadelphia, but the people who do care about the sport care a lot. And they're somehow quicker to forgive and forget. Let the Phillies fall apart down the stretch the way the Flyers did that year, and the players might need a police escort to go to the neighborhood supermarket. Let the Eagles lose six in a row, and you wouldn't find their coach straightening his tie, combing his hair, and rushing off to hob-nob with the fans on "Appreciation Night." But this was a hockey team that had folded . . . and collapse or no collapse, the party must go on.

So it was that on this rather bizarre occasion, some 300 of the faithful turned out to mingle with their fallen heroes. If the guard at the door came to work wondering if his job was to check for tickets or weapons, his fears were soon erased. This was an overwhelmingly friendly crowd. Also a considerate one. I mean, what better place to hold this affair than next to a river. Every time you heard a splash outside, you couldn't help wondering whether it was a fish, a Flyers' stockholder, a coach, or a player. Must have been all fish. Nobody was reported missing in the course of the evening. Even Vic Stasiuk, the coach of that ill-fated Flyers' team, appeared at the party. (Can you imagine Gene Mauch showing up at a fan club party the night the Phillies lost the 1964 National League pennant?)

A stranger walking in the door that night would never have guessed what had happened at the Spectrum in the afternoon. There was noise, applause, prizes, even laughter.

Stasiuk was a rookie NHL coach in 1969–70. He didn't last very long in Philadelphia. He didn't win any championships there. But he left his mark, just the same. A throwback to the "old school," a man who believed in living, breathing, talking ice hockey at all hours of the day or night, Stasiuk—a fine big-league hockey player in his day—alienated some players with his gung-ho, never-slow-down approach to the game. But there wasn't a phony bone in Vic Stasiuk's body.

They call men who play the game hard all the time "honest hockey players." Well, Vic Stasiuk was an honest hockey coach. And he was an emotional hockey coach. One time, while coaching the minor-league Quebec Aces, he reached over the boards in Rochester and threw a punch at a rival player just to fire up his team. "I hit Jim Pappin," Stasiuk readily admitted. "I owed him a few, anyway. He swung his stick at me and broke it over my arm. All hell broke loose. You got to get 'em involved. This is a game of emotion."

The modern pro athlete was a mystery to Stasiuk at times. "When we were playing," he would say, "we were concerned about playing, about keeping our jobs. Nothing else. Now players are interested in stock-market reports."

So you can imagine how difficult it had to be for Stasiuk to attend that fan-club party on the banks of the Delaware River. He had taken defeat so hard that, after talking briefly to his players in the locker room, he took a solitary walk around the Spectrum, trying to collect his thoughts. "Then I sat in the stands," he said, "and watched all the seat cleaners sweep up. I thought, 'For what?' The 76ers aren't there [in the playoffs]. The Flyers aren't there."

And now here he was, surrounded by noisy, animated, partying people. The music played and the guests drank and danced and had a good time. And Vic Stasiuk sat there and rehashed the last half dozen games of the season, and particularly the final, crushing defeat. He was a compulsive talker, a non-stop storyteller.

"You know the worst thing?" he said. "You can get over losing the bonuses, the monetary rewards, but the worst thing is what's in the record book. There's no *playoff* next to your name. It's in there for all time that way. You can say my rookie season as a National Hockey League coach was not too successful."

You didn't have to say it. Vic was saying it himself, over and over again. Finally, the coach of the 1969–70 Philadelphia Flyers glanced at his watch. It was 10:30 p.m. The party was in high gear now. The music was loud. The line at the bar was long.

Vic Stasiuk looked around the room and stood up. "I'm not in the mood for a party," he said. And he went home.

*   *   *

In February of 1971, the Flyers traded Bernie Parent. Keith Allen, who succeeded Bud Poile as general manager, called it "a very tough decision . . . the toughest thing I've ever done in hockey from an emotional point of view."

Who could have guessed then that Bernie Parent would return as a Flyer, and that he would be a human Rock of Gibraltar in the nets three years later when they got their names inscribed on the Stanley Cup for the first time?

But then, who could have guessed that a strange character who answered to the name of *Freddie Shero* would flash across the Philadelphia sports scene? Or that a diabetic named Bobby Clarke would reach for —and attain—such incredible heights?

It's hard to explain Freddie Shero. You come to realize that even Freddie Shero has trouble explaining Freddie Shero. But he was a fascinating man from the first day he walked into the Spectrum and began saying those strange things and writing those weird sayings on the blackboard in the Flyers' locker room.

"Fame is a vapor," he wrote when the Flyers were closing in on their second Stanley Cup in 1975, "Popularity an accident, Riches take wings, Only one thing endures, And that is character."

Make no mistake about it. Freddie Shero was a character.

The love affair between Shero and the Flyers faithful wasn't exactly an overnight happening. Freddie made his debut stalking behind the Philly bench in October of 1971. Word of his "system" had already been passed along to the Philadelphia public, but on this night, at least the system wasn't all that it had been cracked up to be. Late in the third period the Los Angeles Kings had a 7–0 lead over Freddie's Flyers, and a Spectrum fan bellowed, "C'mon, even Kuharich had a better system." Welcome to Philly, Freddie.

Ah, but he won them over. And he won those two Stanley Cups. And, with Bobby Clarke, he became a symbol of those championship years. It didn't matter that nobody really understood Freddie. All that mattered was, he won. And his players believed in him. The fact that he talked in riddles merely added to his charm.

One thing about Freddie. He was his own man. If anything, he seemed to delight in waging his own private war on the front office. With Freddie, the "them" in "we against them" was management. He seemed to delight in building on that "we against them" theme, using it to create a togetherness among his hockey players and coaches.

It was typical of Shero that when Ed Snider, the majority owner of the team and its rooter-in-chief, got on television in May of 1975, while the Flyers were zeroing in on their second title, and accused the Philadelphia press of being too negative toward his team, he promptly took the other side and defended the press.

"I think it's only natural," pontificated Freddie, "for an owner who never played the game to want nothing but positive things written about his team and to get uptight about things that aren't important. But the press has a right to say what it wants to say, and we've got to take it. I don't see where anybody is above criticism."

That was vintage Freddie Shero. He marched to his own music. And, for a couple of years in Philadelphia, that music played loud and clear, even if the man who arranged it was nicknamed "Freddie the Fog."

Shero was a prime example of the old saying, "Truth is stranger than fiction." Ian Fleming wrote stories that were easier to believe than some of Freddie's real-life adventures. For example, on a recent trip to Philadelphia—he was invited back by the Flyers to participate in an old-timers' game—Shero related how he wound up a "loser" in the mammoth victory parade that followed the Flyers' first Stanley Cup victory.

"We're in this parade," he said, "and I'm shaking hands, and I end up with a broken finger."

Ah, but that was only part of it. One of Freddie's proudest possessions at that time was a championship ring from his American Hockey League days in Buffalo. "Somebody stole my Buffalo ring off my finger," he explained. "It's gone. Then, two years later, the ring comes back. This guy says 'I stole your ring when I was shaking your hand in Philadelphia in the parade. I'm sorry. The ring belongs to you.' He didn't leave a name or anything."

So Freddie had his ring back. And by that time his broken finger was mended. All's well that ends well.

The parade *was* on the wild side. "There was this story," said Freddie. "I don't know if it was true. But there was supposed to be this Englishman visiting Philadelphia. He was staying in a downtown hotel, and it was noon when he got out of bed. He looks out the window, and he sees this parade [and those swarms of people] and he calls the desk and says, 'What's going on?' And the guy at the desk says, 'Oh, Philadelphia's like this every Monday.' "

OK, so the fella at the desk was exaggerating. Philadelphia isn't like that every Monday. But Freddie the Fog never seemed to change. He was like that every Monday and Tuesday and Wednesday and—oh well, you get the idea.

Fired as coach-general manager of the New York Rangers, Shero showed up in Philadelphia during the summer of 1981 wearing his two Stanley Cup rings. The precious Buffalo ring presumably was under lock and key at home; Freddie, after all, has a terrible time hanging onto championship rings. But let him tell it. You'll never believe me.

"I don't like to wear them," he began. "I've had so much bad luck. This ring [and he pointed to the first Stanley Cup ring], a week after I got it I lost it in a garbage can. My wife found it. After I lost it, she started to think. She thinks well. 'What could Freddie have done with it? He took out the garbage. Oh yeah. Maybe it fell off his finger.' So I think she unloaded half the garbage truck and found it.

"This one [and he indicated Stanley Cup ring no 2], I'm building a fire in the fireplace, and I lose my ring. I said, 'Mary, what am I going to do?' So she started thinking again. 'What did he do yesterday? All day long he had the ring. I saw it on his finger. What happened? Uh-oh, he was making a fire.' She goes to the fireplace. Nothing there but ashes. It's completely burned—all fallen apart, the diamonds, everything. I must've gone to twenty jewelers. They said they can't fix it. Finally, I found somebody to fix it. It still doesn't seem quite right. It looks different."

What's that you say? Freddie doesn't seem quite right either? Hey, the guy won two Stanley Cup championships at a time when Philadelphia was starving for championships. He's entitled to be—shall we say?—a little eccentric.

If any one man was responsible for the Flyers' emergence as the best team in the NHL in the mid-'70s, it was Bobby Clarke. He was Shero's kind of hockey player. Come to think of it, he was any coach's kind of hockey player. Bobby Clarke plays hockey the way John Havlicek played basketball, the way Chuck Bednarik played football, the way Pete Rose plays baseball. Clarke knew only one speed, and that was full speed ahead. He was a terror in the corners, digging out the puck time after time, setting up plays. In fact, he was a terror all over the ice. Don't let that stillyouthful-looking, toothless grin fool you; Bobby Clarke can be a menace on skates. He would elbow. He would high stick. He would do whatever he had to do to gain the upper hand. If he played "dirty hockey"—and he surely did—well, so did Gordie Howe in his hey-day. Bobby Clarke's peers respected him for the way he played, for the effort he put into the game. And Freddie Shero, and everybody else who coached him, loved him for it.

Even opposing coaches and general managers made no effort to hide their admiration of the Philly center. "He gives more of himself than anybody I ever saw," Punch Imlach said. "He gets caught behind the net, he doesn't give up. He comes back as hard as he can. Most guys get caught, they save their strength for the next time. Clarke, he gives everything he's got all the time.

And if some of the things he gave weren't exactly legal—well, that's hockey. Dave Schultz may have served most of the penalty time and been involved in most of the brawls the year the Flyers won their first Stanley Cup, but you can bet it was Bobby Clarke who did most of the damage.

There was a game against Montreal that season at the Spectrum. Two and a half hours after it was over, Murray Wilson, who had scored Montreal's only goal against the victorious Flyers, was sitting on a table in the visiting locker room. He was in his street clothes with his shirt open and an ice pack pressed against the left side of his neck. The Montreal winger had paid for that first-period goal. His left arm was hanging limp at his side. One look at him, and you knew he was in pain.

"How'd you do it?" Scotty Bowman, who was coaching the Canadiens at the time, inquired.

Wilson looked at him. "Clarke," he said. "A two-hander. After the first goal . . ."

Bowman was hardly surprised. It was Bobby Clarke, after all, who cracked star Soviet forward Valeriy Kharlamov's ankle and put him out of the first major NHL-Soviet confrontation.

"I say the guy [Clarke] is a mean hockey player," Scotty Bowman said the night Wilson was injured, but he meant that as praise, not condemnation. "I think the guy tries every way to win for his team," Bowman added.

He tried legal ways, and he tried illegal ways. He tried clean ways, and he tried dirty ways. But always, Bobby Clarke tried.

"Bobby's like a leech," Freddie Shero said. "Check, check, check. What Bowman is trying to say, Bobby's the ultimate in a competitor. . . . He walks in the corner against somebody, and I say to myself, 'He got the puck again. How did he do it?' Generally his stick is a little higher than it should be. But he's working, always working."

And that work paid off as the Flyers made it to the Stanley Cup finals in 1974 . . . and then whipped the Boston Bruins, led by the incomparable Bobby Orr, in six games. "Somebody said, 'How do you beat Boston?'" Shero said before the series. "To beat Boston you do the same thing to Orr that Clarke did to Kharlamov. Break his ankle."

Orr got off lucky. His team lost the series, but he was able to walk to the locker room when it ended.

Getting to the finals against the Bruins took a lot of doing. In the semis, the Flyers took on Freddie Shero's former—and future—team, the New York Rangers. The series went seven games. It was home-team-take-all, and game no. 7 was in Philly.

The third game, at Madison Square Garden, had been a war, typical of the Shero-Schultz Flyers of that season. Trailing by two goals with five and a half minutes to go, Freddie sent his tough guys into action. Dave Schultz, Don Saleski, and Bob Kelly took it from there. If the Flyers couldn't win this game, at least they were going to soften up the opposition. When the sorry spectacle ended, there were five Flyers in the penalty box and three more in the locker room with misconduct penalties. What did Dave Schultz think of all this? "I think we didn't play rough enough," he said. "We let up. We should have challenged 'em more."

The seventh game, predictably, opened with a fight. It was Schultz (who else?) against the Rangers' Dale Rolfe. Schultz battered him unmercifully, kept belting him, again and again, until the blood was flowing. Naturally, Freddie Shero thought it was great. The turning point of the game, he called it. "We fought 'em man to man," he crowed. "In other words, we didn't jump 'em from behind. We proved our class. . . . It took something out of New York. They didn't do as much hitting after that."

Schultz, a real Jekyll-Hyde type—off the ice, like so many hockey tough guys, he was a real charmer—thought it was great too. "I knew I hadn't had a good fight all series," he said. "Just a bunch of stupid stuff, misconducts. Today was the kind of fight I should've been getting in all the time."

Once the intimidation was out of the way, the hockey game commenced—and it turned into a beauty. After two periods, the Flyers led, 3–1, and if not for the goaltending of the Rangers' Eddie Giacomin, it easily could have been a five- or six-goal spread. Then the more experienced Rangers put on a last-ditch drive, and it was Philly on the defensive, desperately hanging on. "You've got to attack," Dave Schultz said. "You want to attack. But you're thinking, 'Don't let them score,' and all of a sudden they're zooming by you."

Shero needed his best hockey players, not his toughest intimidators on the ice in the face of this Ranger attack; Schultz was relegated to a seat on the bench in the third period.

The pressure grew as the seconds ticked away, and the Rangers closed to within a goal. Here were the Flyers—the *seven-year-old* Flyers—one period away from a berth in the Stanley Cup finals. And there were the Rangers coming at them, time after time, mounting rush after rush.

"You work for this all your life," Joe Watson said. "Like

American boys want to be in a World Series, or a Super Bowl maybe. Or the basketball finals. A Canadian boy wants this."

These Canadian boys wanted it so badly that they pulled themselves together in the final, frantic five minutes, holding the Rangers to only two shots in that span. They had done it. They had become the first expansion team to knock off an established team in the playoffs.

You could argue with the tactics they employed—as indeed many hockey purists did—but you couldn't argue with the results. Nor could you help but appreciate the post-game scene as the winners and the losers of this seven-game playoff series that, at times, looked more like war than sport lined up at center ice and, in keeping with hockey tradition, shook hands. At a glance, it all seemed so hypocritical, so absurd. And yet there's something about the hockey mentality that accepts this, that makes it possible for two men who have been throwing punches twenty minutes earlier to shake hands—and mean it.

The scene after that seventh game was genuinely touching. Bernie Parent and Eddie Giacomin, the rival goalies, locked eyes for a moment, and then embraced. Then Terry Crisp of the Flyers grasped Giacomin's hand and playfully mussed the goalie's hair. "What more can a goaltender do?" Crisp said later. "He takes the team seven games; he loses, 4–3, in your building. What more can you ask of a man?"

Not much. But Giacomin's willingness to stand there, with the Spectrum mob looking on, and to congratulate his conquerors at a time like that was a rather touching display of the other side of a sport that too often forgets what sportsmanship is all about.

"When a man [Giacomin] gives you that extra squeeze," Terry Crisp said, "when he looks you in the eyes and says, 'Good luck next series,' and means it, that's a man."

Crisp meant what he was saying too. Crazy game, professional ice hockey. It can start with a brutally one-sided fight and end with a handshake and an embrace.

These Stanley Cup series are often like high-caliber tennis matches. You keep sitting there, waiting for somebody to "break serve" and win on the road. It never happened in the semis that year, but it happened in game two of the finals at old Boston Garden, and it paved the way for Philadelphia's first Stanley Cup.

The Bruins had won the first game, and they were leading by a goal late in the second game. With just over a minute to go, Bernie Parent started his dash out of the Flyers' net; it was time for a sixth skater, an all-or-nothing bid to get the equalizer. And, by God, the Flyers got it. Moose Dupont scored with fifty-two seconds to go . . . and then it was sudden death.

At the ten-minute mark in the overtime, the Boston crowd rose and let out an expectant roar. Johnny Bucyk seemed to have the winning goal on his stick, Parent at his mercy. But no . . . Bernie stopped him the way Bernie was stopping practically everybody in that series. The game, and the Flyers, were still alive. And then Dave Schultz, of all people, set up the game-winner, digging the puck out of the corner and throwing out a blind pass to Bobby Clarke. "I didn't look," Schultz would say later. "I knew somebody had to be there."

For the Flyers, it was the perfect somebody. Clarke took the pass on his backhand and shot. Gil Gilbert, the Boston goalie, sprawled on the ice and batted it away. But there was Clarke, in position to get his stick on the rebound, to lift it over the body of the fallen goaltender. As the puck went in and the red light flashed, Bobby Clarke, who had to be dog-tired, leaped so high he might have erased the Boston Garden high jump record. No wonder. The Flyers had won in Boston for the first time since 1967. Now the Cup was in their grasp.

They weren't about to let it get away. They won the third game at the Spectrum, and the fourth. There they were, one game away from winning the Stanley Cup, and in the locker room after that fourth game they seemed almost awed by what they were on the verge of doing.

The Bruins had applied tremendous pressure in an effort to regain the "home-ice advantage," but Bernie Parent kept coming up with the big saves. And then, with 5:35 to go in regulation, Bill Barber scored the goal that turned the Spectrum into a madhouse . . . and put the Flyers one victory away from the Cup.

This was no time for premature celebration, and they all knew it. If they didn't, Shero would have reminded them. The last time Freddie had been involved in a Stanley Cup championship series, twenty-four years earlier, he was playing for a Ranger team that won the first three games from the Detroit Red Wings and had a two-goal lead with ten minutes to go in the fifth game. It wasn't enough. Detroit rallied and won the series.

"I'm lucky," Shero said. "Those guys [his teammates on the 1950 Rangers] never came back. I came back. I've got another chance. Sometimes there's only one chance for a person in his lifetime, but I've got a second chance . . ."

He was so wrapped up in this hockey team; it was so much a part of him and he so much a part of it that it seemed inconceivable in those exciting May days of 1974 to think of the Flyers without Freddie Shero behind the bench. "I told Eddie [owner Ed Snider] a long time ago I would never leave," Freddie said the day before the fifth game of the series. "I don't think I *could* leave here. Not when it took me twenty years to get a team like this."

No question that he meant every word of it then. Freddie and the Flyers were as one in the mid-'70s. The players believed completely in him; he knew precisely what he had to do to motivate the players.

They hardly needed a pep talk now, of course, although game no. 5 in Boston was a horror. The Flyers played badly. The fans, encouraged by the actions of the players on the ice, acted badly. The players threw fists; the fans threw bottles. It was awful. "I think the pressure of winning the Cup made our guys stay back," Bernie Parent suggested. "Instead of our regular game, we play too much defense."

"If we don't win [the sixth game in Philadelphia], we're going to be in a lot of trouble," Bobby Clarke warned. "I would say we have to shoot our whole wad on Sunday."

And they did.

"The pressure's more on them today than anytime in the season," Boston coach Bep Guidolin was saying a couple of hours before the sixth game as he paced the corridor outside the visiting hockey locker room at the Spectrum. "They lose today, no way they're going to beat us in Boston. We'll be higher than any hockey club that ever played in Boston Garden. Play a seventh game there, they'll be demoralized."

But this was game six at the Spectrum, not game seven at Boston Garden.

The minutes dragged by, the pressure built up. Even Bernie

Parent felt it on this day. Three-hundred-and-sixty-four days a year he smokes cigars; now, as he waited to walk in the locker room and climb into his gear, he was chain-smoking cigarettes.

Forty-five minutes to the opening faceoff. Joe Watson felt the pain shooting through his back and the butterflies in his stomach. "I told [brother] Jimmy, 'Geez, my back is sore,' " he said. "But you get in the game, you forget all about it. You want to win. That's all there is to it."

Fifteen minutes to game time. The seconds seemed to be crawling by now. On both sides, the players were eager to get started, to hit somebody, to play hockey. The waiting was the worst part.

Bep Guidolin sought out Scotty Morrison, the NHL's referee-in-chief, to check out a report the Boston coach had heard. "What's this about Kate Smith coming out on ice with a piano?" Guidolin asked.

"I dunno," Morrison told him.

"Well, you should know," Guidolin snapped. "If a piano's out there, I want a two-minute delay-of-game penalty. And I want to pick the player [to be penalized] . . ." Guidolin paused, and the barest hint of a smile crossed his face. "And I want her [Kate Smith] to sit with the player."

Only then did Scotty Morrison realize that Guidolin was kidding. They both threw back their heads and laughed.

Kate, of course, was there. In those days, whenever a crisis loomed, whenever the Flyers faced a must game, "the Star-Spangled Banner" was replaced by Kate's stirring rendition of "God Bless America" and on very special occasions the singer herself made a personal appearance. This was the most special occasion of all. Rick MacLeish scored the goal. Bernie Parent did the rest. At precisely 5:30 P.M. on Sunday afternoon, May 19, 1974, the City of Losers had itself a winner. As the final seconds were being counted down, Kate Smith stood up in the super box across the way from the team benches and waved a Flyers pennant. Black and orange streamers and confetti floated down to the ice and the organist, unable to wait until the final buzzer, began playing "God Bless America."

The scene in the locker room was as wild—maybe even wilder—than the post-game scene on the ice as Clarke and Parent lugged that big, beautiful, battered, old Cup with some fans providing an escort. Some of the winners guzzled champagne, or sent it shooting across the locker room. For others, beer was fine. "Champagne's too much for me," said MacLeish. "I'm from a small town."

"I'm gonna get so drunk I'm not going to be able to see," rookie Orest Kindrachuk promised, but for now he was drinking water. "Last time, when we clinched first place, I drank a bottle of this"—he indicated the champagne in his locker—"and I was sick all night."

This time, nobody got sick. It was all too joyful, too wonderful. Don Saleski was running around in the orange-colored, "Kate Lives" T-shirt he wore under his Flyers' jersey. Tom Bladon was spraying champagne on Ed Snider. Tom Dempsey, the Eagles' place-kicker, was hugging Moose Dupont, the defenseman whose shot had been deflected past Bruin goalie Gil Gilbert by MacLeish in the first period.

"Drink from the cup," Snider kept yelling. "Drink from the cup." With some difficulty the owner tipped it so Bobby Clarke could taste the liquid—mostly champagne with a touch of beer—inside. Bobby took a gulp and spit it out. "Not very cold," he said diplomatically.

It would be quite a while before they'd yank off those jerseys and leave that locker room. The Stanley Cup was theirs. All the goals, all the fights, all the penalties, all the practices, all of Freddie Shero's bizarre quotes were behind them now—at least for this season. They were savoring their accomplishment.

The celebration was going full blast when Joe Watson left the locker room for a few minutes and walked down the corridor. The crush on the ice had been so great that Joe had failed to shake hands with his old friend, Bobby Orr. Now they met privately in a room down the hall. "He was really dejected," Joe said, and by the tone of his voice you knew he felt genuinely sorry for Orr. "He shouldn't feel like that. He played his heart out. My goodness God, he played his heart out. . . . I tried to give him a swig of champagne. He said, 'I don't deserve it.' I said, 'Holy God, don't say you don't deserve it.' The way he kept their team together. . . . He must've played forty-five minutes."

Actually, Orr was on the ice thirty-five minutes and twenty-five seconds in the sixth and final game of the 1974 Stanley Cup playoffs. It wasn't enough. Bernie Parent played the full sixty.

*   *   *

Not everybody loves hockey. But everybody loves a winner. And everybody loves a parade. And the Philadelphia parade that saluted these winners boggled the mind.

They rode along Broad Street through that clutching, grabbing, laughing, cheering mob of people, and it was the Bullies who got bullied. "You should've seen the way I looked right after [the parade]," Bobby Taylor, the Flyers' backup goalie, said a day or so later. "My wrists were all swollen. My thumb—you should've seen it. And the Bird [Don Saleski] had the sleeve torn off his jacket."

"Right at the start somebody grabbed my glasses," Simon Nolet said. "Took them right off . . . And Moose [Dupont], they ripped his coat."

"Some jerk tried to pour wine down the back of my pants," chimed in Tom Bladon. "At least if they pour it over your head you might get a few drops."

"They were throwing full cans of beer in the car for us to drink," Bobby Clarke said. "*Throwing* them! We were riding in a red Cadillac, this guy's own personal car. Such a nice car, they asked if they could use it for the parade. There are big dents in it now. They ripped the lights off."

A city had gone temporarily insane over a group of Canadian hockey players. People who had never cared about ice hockey, who didn't know the rules and didn't want to know them, suddenly found themselves caught up in the excitement. A winner can do that for a town, even a big town. Granted, some of the celebrants got carried away in 1974, but there was no denying that the success of the Flyers had made a much-maligned city feel good about itself. Philadelphians had been kidded about their city and about their sports teams too long; now the shoe, or at least the skate, was on the other foot.

*   *   *

There's something about the first one that makes it the best, the most memorable. The Flyers won again in 1975, and it was a big event . . . but not quite as big as that first one.

As in '74, the biggest challenge came in the semis. The Flyers beat the up-and-coming New York Islanders three in a row and seemed to be breezing. But then the Islanders turned around and won three in a row. Tempers grew so short then that when a Philadelphia hockey writer, Bill Fleischman of *The Daily News,* suggested in print that a Flyer loss in the seventh game would be a foldup comparable to the Phillies blowing of the [1964] pennant, Ed Snider screamed at him in the locker room.

If nothing else, the '75 Stanley Cup finals proved that the hockey season runs too long. By late May, when the series between the Flyers and the Buffalo Sabres was finally nearing its conclusion, the temperature was so high inside the non-air-conditioned Buffalo Auditorium that fog developed above the ice. "It was so bloody hot out there, it was unbearable," Flyers' defenseman Ed Van Impe said after the third game.

To add to the bizarre atmosphere, a bat got loose and made several low passes over the ice surface. Between the bat and the fog, it was a setting better suited to Sherlock Holmes than Bobby Clarke. There were the two best teams in the National Hockey League skating around in a fog. Literally. But although the Sabres took games three and four at home, they couldn't stop the Flyers in game six—and the Stanley Cup remained in Philadelphia. "That little piece of tin," defenseman Ted Harris—the one man who bridged the huge gap between the Ramblers of the '50s and the Flyers of the '70s—called it as he, and his teammates, celebrated in the visiting locker room after the climactic, 2–0 victory.

Bob Kelly scored the first goal and Bill Clement the second as the Flyers qualified for another triumphant ride down Broad Street. "When so many people come out to cheer you," Bobby Clarke said, "you feel you're on top of the world. Maybe that's as close to heaven as we'll ever get."

For Freddie Shero, though, the search for newer, bigger hockey heavens went on. By the end of the 1977–78 season, his love affair with Philadelphia and the Flyers had ended. He had one year to go on a contract, but his heart was no longer in it, he said, as he sat in the office of his agent in downtown Philadelphia, a Stanley Cup championship ring glittering on each hand, and explained why he had decided to give up coaching. "Right now," he said, "I don't feel like coaching in any sport. Right now I just feel like I've lost something. I can't seem to generate any enthusiasm."

The feeling, he claimed that day, had hit him after the Boston Bruins had kayoed the Flyers in the Stanley Cup semifinals. "I didn't feel I did the job," this strange, almost mysterious man said. "I don't want to stay if I can't do the job."

He sounded very sincere that day. Already, there were rumors that the Rangers were after him, but Freddie made it seem as if coaching the Flyers or the Rangers or anybody was out of the question. "The way I feel," he said, "I can't conceive of coaching anywhere now. I've had enough success. I've come to the conclusion even if we won again I wouldn't be satisfied with myself. And if winning's not enough for me, it's obvious I need something else."

Apparently what he really needed—or wanted—was a chance to be general manager as well as coach. That wasn't to be in Philadelphia, where Keith Allen was solidly entrenched in the front-office job. So, after saying repeatedly that he wouldn't take another coaching job, Freddie Shero surfaced as GM-coach of the Rangers. Except for his first year, however, when he knocked the Flyers out of the playoffs and reached the Stanley Cup finals against Montreal, the old magic never reappeared.

Freddie remains one of those rare coaches who left Philadelphia because he wanted to, not because he had to. It's sheer folly to try to follow the workings of Freddie Shero's mind, but maybe he was simply afraid that if he stayed in Philadelphia too long the city's Hockey Writers' Association would get around to choosing him as the recipient of their coveted—and generally fatal—"Class Guy Award."

The first year it went to Bernie Parent, who promptly sustained an eye injury that cut short his career.

The next year it went to Gary Dornhoefer, who retired at the end of the season.

The year after that it went to Joe Watson, who was then traded to Colorado.

And the year after that it went to Andre Dupont, who accepted it with obvious misgivings and said, "I know this award is the kiss of death. I hope I'm here next year." His hopes were not realized; the Flyers shipped him off to Quebec.

The Philly writers are no dummies, though. Displaying

remarkable foresight, they made the first couple of "Class Guy" award presentations at the Airport Hilton. That way the recipient could accept his award, head straight for the plane, and leave town immediately.

Freddie Shero owes a vote of thanks to the Philadelphia hockey writers for never naming him their "Class Guy" of the year. I hope he appreciates what they didn't do for him.

9

Love Letters in the Sand

AT THE BEGINNING HE WAS RICHIE ALLEN. THEN HE WAS RICH *Allen*. Still later, he was *Dick Allen*. But Richie, Rich, or Dick, one thing remained the same. He was an enigma.

The man's talent was enormous. There's no telling what Richie Allen could have done if he had been determined to make the most of that talent. He might have been up there with the Aarons, the Mayses, the Mantles. He had Hall-of-Fame ability mixed with a curious urge to self-destruct. As a hitter, he was a thrill to watch, attacking the ball and frequently driving it tremendous distances. But as time went on, he got more headlines for his penchant to resist authority, to push his managers and push them some more until, inevitably, they broke, than he did for his ability to play the game of baseball. And that was a crying shame.

It's easy, when chronicling the Allen years in Philadelphia, to zero in on the squabbles, the controversies, the times he showed up late or didn't show up at all until he seems like the worst guy who ever swung a bat or ducked a sportswriter. And yet, there was another side to the man—a side that only rarely was put on display for the media or the fans. Richie. . . Rich . . . Dick . . . call him what you will . . . he could, and usually did, go out of his way to be cordial to the little guys—the groundskeepers, for example. To the umpires and some of his teammates he was a great guy, down to earth and helpful to the extreme.

One of the young players Allen went out of his way to help was Larry Hisle. Like Allen, Hisle arrived in the big leagues with great talent and matching expectations. Unlike Allen, Hisle would never rebel against authority, would never talk back to a manager, would never be unavailable to the press, would never refuse to sign an autograph. If there's such a thing as being too nice, that was Larry Hisle. And Philadelphia was a tough place for a super-nice kid to break in.

"I know when I was with the Phillies the toughest thing for me was to come to the ball park," Larry said years later, after making it—and making it big—in the American League. "As soon as I put on my uniform, something inside told me, it's not right."

The pressure was gigantic. The fans were impatient. The result was disastrous. After a good first year, Hisle wilted under that awful pressure, crumpled under the insistent booing by the fans. Maybe if Richie Allen had remained with the Phillies, Hisle would have handled it better.

"The first year, Richie helped me," Hisle recalled. "I'd strike out, Richie would make me laugh. I'd look up to Richie. I think it would've helped me quite a bit if he stayed. I'll never forget how much he helped me my rookie season. I started off slow. I was upset. After one game Richie said, 'Come with me . . .' We went to a place called the Cadillac Club. Hal Greer was there. They all knew Richie. It made me feel great. Usually a bad day [in baseball] stays with me a long, long time. That night I forgot it for a while."

That's the side of Richie Allen that Larry Hisle saw. That's the side of Richie Allen that Mike Schmidt would see several years later. It was even the side that Gene Mauch, the first manager to lose his job largely because of his inability to handle Allen, saw for a while during Richie's rookie season in that almost-wonderful year, 1964.

"I never enjoyed a player more than I enjoyed Richie Allen in 1964," Mauch said a year after leaving the Phillies. "We both had a lot of fun. It wasn't so much fun at the end."

But even knowing all the heartaches associated with the Allen years, even with his own firing fresh in his mind, Mauch remained enamored of that awesome talent. "I can't think of anybody I'd rather have walk up to a mirror, look at himself and say, 'I'm going to take the next five years and do everything I can [in baseball] so I can do what I want to do the next forty years of my life,' " Mauch said. "And he can do that. Five years of total dedication is not much of a price to pay for forty years of comfort. . . . I tried. I think my greatest feeling of inadequacy was my inability to convince him how reasonable this thinking is. That feeling of inadequacy finally disappeared when I realized no one on earth could make him feel that way—except himself. He wants independence. Not family. Not job. Not accomplishment. Not acceptance. Only independence. You just can't be that way.

"I think I know how he feels. He came from meager circumstances. So did I. He was happy as a poor kid. So was I. Now he probably figures, what do I need all this worry for? But you do have things to worry about."

And the men who attempted to manage the Phillies in the Allen years, starting with Gene Mauch, had plenty to worry about too.

The incidents came at a mile-a-minute clip, but the one that really began it all—the one that undoubtedly turned some of the fans against Allen—may have been the unfairest rap of all. It happened on the evening of July 3, 1965. The Phillies were taking pre-game batting practice at Connie Mack Stadium.

Needling is very much a part of professional baseball, and the needlers are generally at their sharpest during such relaxed periods as this. But a Phillie first baseman named Frank Thomas sometimes carried needling to the extreme. And on this evening, apparently, Thomas went too far. One word led to another, and finally the words led to fists.

It was a touchy situation. Allen was black. Thomas was white. Allen was still a kid, a rising, young star. Thomas was a veteran who had served time with the likes of the early Mets. If someone had to go, it didn't take a genius to figure out the one. Immediately after the game that night the Phillies gave Frank Thomas his walking papers, and the Thomas fans—there were quite a few—naturally blamed Allen for their man's departure. Richie's side of the story never really came out—until a few years later.

"I should've told you guys my side of it," Allen told a group of Philly writers in the spring of '69, "but Gene Mauch wouldn't let me. He said he was going to fine me if I said anything." So, rather than risk a sizeable fine—reportedly in the neighborhood of $2,000—Allen remained mum, and the fans grew increasingly hostile.

After the Thomas Affair, the Richie Allen saga took some

bizarre twists and turns. Historians might make note of some of the following chronological high (low?) lights. . . .

July 22, 1966—Allen benched by Mauch and fined for breaking curfew in San Francisco.

July 8, 1967—Arrived late for a home game and was benched and fined again by Mauch who, in a fit of cock-eyed optimism, said, "Let me tell you something; I anticipate Richie Allen showing up on time every day from now on."

July 19, 1967—Late again, Allen explained that his car had broken down. Mauch laughed it off this time, saying: "That son of a gun, the only thing he cares about is playing. But if that car of his starts to cost him, he'll care."

August 24, 1967—"That car of his" started to cost him. Allen seriously hurt his right hand and wrist when, the player said, his hand went through a headlight while pushing his 1950 jalopy.

March 8, 1968—Took off without permission from spring training, flying home from Clearwater and returning two days later to find a note in his mailbox from general manager John Quinn, informing him that he had been fined.

April 30, 1968—Oversleeping, he missed team bus to New York, then arrived late for game with Mets when he got stuck in traffic on the way to Shea Stadium. Mauch benched him and fined him.

May 29, 1968—Allen went horseback riding and pulled a muscle before twi-night doubleheader with the Cubs. He limped through the first game and part of the second game before Mauch yanked him.

June 9, 1968—Allen's highly publicized "sit-down strike" on West Coast trip hit its peak when he stretched out in a corner of the dugout during a game with the Giants while wearing sun glasses. "He was just lounging there," teammate Bill White said, "and after I came in [from the field] one inning I threw a ball at him. I figured he was sleeping . . . but he caught the ball. Just as it was about to hit him in the stomach, he caught it with one hand. . . . Maybe he's a little more alert than we think he is."

June 11, 1968—Allen returned to Phillies' lineup after his two-week layoff or vacation (take your pick) and indicated he was ready to play all along. "What do you want me to do, call him a liar?" Mauch snapped at the press. "You guys get in a hassle with him. I've had mine."

August 27, 1968—Allen appeared in court following a bar-room fight. The charges were dropped. "The man is his own worst enemy," said the chief magistrate.

March 8, 1968—While Phillies awaited his arrival in training camp, Allen's picture appeared in newspapers around the country. The "missing" player was in Miami, having dinner with Joe Namath.

May 2, 1969—Scheduled to leave Philadelphia with the team for an early-morning flight to St. Louis, Allen missed the plane, then missed the afternoon flight as well, and didn't get to St. Louis until the following day, missing one full game and part of another. New Phillies' manager Bob Skinner fined him $1,000.

June 24, 1969—Failed to show up for twi-night doubleheader with the Mets and was suspended.

And there was more. Much more . . .

Gene Mauch tried everything in his long-running campaign to win his war with Richie Allen. On opening day of the 1967 season, Mauch had his star carry the lineup card to home plate before the game in what amounted to a dress rehearsal for the team captaincy. Obviously, Mauch thought—or at least hoped—that the added responsibility would prompt Richie to turn over a new leaf.

"He [Mauch] just handed it to me," Allen said after the game. Asked if he'd like to be named team captain of the Phillies, he replied, "I'd consider it quite an honor. I'd be anything, do anything to help."

At times like that, it must have been easy for Mauch—or for anybody—to see the other side of Richie Allen, the side capable of leading a big-league baseball team to great heights. But his actions were often far different from his words, and he became the no. 1 target of that most knowledgeable, most outspoken, most ornery breed of American sports fan, the Philadelphia Boobird. "The boos don't bother me," Allen insisted early in the 1967 season. "They don't bother me at all. I was groomed for this. I was groomed for getting booed. In '64 they booed me because I couldn't catch the ball. In '65, they booed me because of Thomas. . . . The fans can do what they want. All I want to do is win."

But the only real chance he had to win in his first tour of duty with the Phillies was in his rookie season, and that chance eluded him. If Mauch really "enjoyed" managing Allen in '64, by '68—with the war between the two going full blast—things were so bad that Gene finally said, during what turned out to be his last West coast trip as a Phillie, "He'll never wear a Phillies uniform again as long as I'm the manager."

It was no coincidence that a few days later Mauch was no longer the Phillies manager.

The incident that occurred on April 30 of Mauch's final year typified the disintegrating relationship between the two strong-willed men. The Phillies were on a hot streak. They had won seven of their last nine games and had Chris Short ready to open a three-game series in New York against the Mets. Everything was peaches and cream—until the two team buses left Connie Mack Stadium at 9:30 in the morning with no Richie Allen in sight.

By the time he arrived at Shea, game-time was only twenty minutes away and Mauch had already filled out a lineup card with Johnny Briggs playing left field in Allen's place. Asked what had held him up, Richie told the press with a smile, "I stopped off at Aqueduct."

To compound things, the Phillies lost the game, 1–0, and Mauch, doing a not-so-slow burn, told the guard stationed outside the visiting clubhouse not to let the press in until he conducted a post-game team meeting.

Time passed. The press waited. The guard guarded. Then the door opened and a player walked out, sipping a cup of hot soup. Next a coach appeared, munching on a piece of pizza. Meeting? What meeting? The guard agreed to check with Mauch. He returned, shaking his head. "No meeting," he said. "He [Mauch] isn't saying a word. He's just sitting there in his office. He said to tell you he's still holding a meeting."

So it went as the Mauch-Allen war wound down. By mid-June of 1968, there was a new manager in charge, a generally soft-spoken, friendly fellow named Bob Skinner. If Mauch's intense approach to the game hadn't set well with Allen, maybe Skinner's comparatively low-key approach would.

"Richie Allen is a great player," Skinner said after taking the job. "He could be the outstanding player in the league. I know there were problems about showing up late and other things, but they happened before I came."

Ah, hope springs eternal in baseball . . . and it sprang especially high in the spring of '69. Allen arrived only a week after the official reporting date, showing up nattily attired in a white shirt with ruffled collar and cuffs and an Edwardian blue suit. He was wearing long, thick sideburns and a mustache—no big deal except in those days the Phillies frowned upon facial hair and made a production out of making their hired hands remove same.

After getting to Jack Russell Stadium, the Phillies' spring training field, Allen and his new manager spent nearly half an hour in animated conversation near the right-field bullpen, while reporters and several young players watched in fascination from a safe distance. "Gee," one writer commented, "I hope Richie isn't too hard on him." In truth, he wasn't. First thing Allen did following his meeting with Skinner was shave off his mustache. "As I've said before," the manager said, "There's been a lot of misunderstanding about this fella."

Stick around, Bob.

By early May of that season, Skinner was chirping a different tune. Surely, the Friday morning that Allen didn't show up at Philadelphia International Airport in time to catch the early, non-stop flight to St. Louis was largely responsible for the manager's revamped attitude toward his hard-to-handle superstar.

Allen had no reasonable excuse for showing up a day late in St. Louis. This was, after all, the jet age. A man could fly from one coast to the other in five hours. He could eat breakfast in New York and wolf down an early lunch in San Francisco. He could take off from Philadelphia International at 4 P.M.(EDT) and land in St. Louis at 5:05 P.M. (CDT), in plenty of time for that night's ball game.

Or, he could miss all the planes and not get to St. Louis that day, at all.

Richie Allen chose the latter course. Originally due to leave Philadelphia with the team at 8 A.M. Friday, he finally turned up in St. Louis at 8 P.M. Saturday. The U.S. mail travels faster than that. A train can make it in about twenty hours, a bus in less than twenty-two. Allen traveled by jet and made it in thirty. Such is progress.

Skinner, needless to relate, was furious. "John [Quinn] called me this morning and said he's on a flight that gets in at one," the manager told the press on Saturday. "I said, 'Dammit, we've got a 1:15 game.' He said, 'That's the flight he's on.' "

The Phillies were at bat in the top of the second inning when Allen wandered in.

"What took you so long?" a writer, who had been staked out next to the clubhouse door, asked him.

Allen put down his suitcase and grinned. "[Army] reserve meeting," he replied, giggling. "[Don] Money and [John] Briggs and those guys get weekends off."

It might have been a reasonable excuse—if Allen had been in the reserves. His little joke out of the way, Richie grew serious. "I didn't have no itinerary or nothing," he said. "Anyway, I don't feature going so early in the morning. They should've gone Thursday night. They don't have to be so cheap. . . . Those early flights are no good. The traffic's bad. Anyway, I wasn't going to bust my tail to get here because last year I got fined a day's pay for a barroom brawl they didn't even look into. . . . They had a chance to get rid of me last winter, and they didn't. It's their fault."

The Phillies were batting in the fifth when Allen walked ever so slowly out of the clubhouse, a batting helmet on his head, a bat in his hand. Later, he met with Skinner behind closed doors for nearly twenty minutes, after which the manager announced that Allen had been fined $1,000. "One of the worst things you can do in baseball," Skinner emphasized, "is miss a game."

If Allen was sorry for what he had done, he hid it beautifully. "I just bet another loser," the horse-loving Phillie said. "It was slow coming out of the gate."

Typically, when he returned to the lineup the next day Richie slammed a long, RBI double off the center-field wall, hit a 390-foot sacrifice fly, and added a line-drive single to left.

When the Sunday getaway game was over, Allen was on his way to the team bus when a little boy moved into his path. The kid was holding a bat in one hand, an autograph book in the other. "Hey Rich," he called out as Allen dodged past him, "you gonna catch the plane this time?" Richie grinned. "The kid oughtta be smart enough to know I don't miss anything going back," he said.

Things went from bad to worse after that. When Allen missed a late-June twi-nighter at Shea, Skinner had all he could take. Turned out, Richie had stopped off at the race track on his way to New York. He said he was driving to Shea when he heard on the radio that Skinner had suspended him. "The man didn't know whether I was dead on the highway or what," Allen said later. It seemed quite clear to everybody but the player that if, in fact, he had been involved in an accident or had any legitimate excuse, Skinner would have immediately lifted the suspension. Since Allen didn't show up, at all, the suspension stood.

A long wait ensued. Finally, on July 20, the day the United States landed on the moon, Allen returned. It was truly a historic day, as Phillies infielder Cookie Rojas, no great Allen booster at the time, was quick to observe. "This must be the greatest day in history," Cookie said. "The astronauts come down on the moon, and Richie Allen comes down to earth."

"Richie sure picked a helluva day," said his friend, John Briggs.

Allen picked it because the day before he had met with Phillies owner Bob Carpenter in a suburban restaurant. Richie's wife, Barbara, and his agent and confidant, Clem Capozzoli, attended the meeting. General manager Quinn and manager Skinner did not. Typically, after agreeing to meet with Skinner at 9 A.M. the next morning—a Sunday—Allen arrived at 11 A.M. leaving Skinner to cool his heels for two hours. "I must have gotten mixed up on the time," the manager said without making an effort to conceal his anger.

Richie's next move was a pip. Ten days after returning, he decided to move his uniform, his equipment, even the piece of adhesive tape with his name and number on it, out of the player's dressing area in the club-house. While Skinner and the rest of the players sat through a lengthy rain delay, Allen sought privacy in a storage room located between Skinner's office and the clubhouse proper.

"He just asked to dress there and I said all right," explained

Unk Russell, the Phillies' veteran clubhouse man. "I didn't think he was serious. I said, 'You mean it?' He said, 'Yeah, sure.' What was I going to say to him?"

So the rainy day turned into Richie's moving day. By the time the game was rained out, shortly before 8 P.M., Allen's old locker was absolutely bare.

His new quarters were rather strange, to put it mildly. Besides Richie, the room contained a variety of goodies ranging from sixteen cases of beer to a large supply of bubble gum. Also, there were fifteen cases of cola, two quart bottles of after-bath lotion, a jar of coffee, a coffee maker, a few dozen plastic cups, several rolls of toilet paper, some batting helmets, and a collection of old Phillies' jackets and uniforms still marked with the names of former wearers.

There seemed to be some irony in the fact that one of the pin-striped shirts hanging there was inscribed, "Mauch–'68," on the inside of the collar.

Poor Skinner didn't know what to say. "I couldn't care less where a player's locker is as long as it's in the clubhouse," he finally sputtered. "I've got so many things to worry about I'm not going to worry about where Allen dresses."

However, shortly after meeting with the press, Skinner talked to Kenny Bush, then the assistant clubhouse man, and minutes later Bush began moving Allen's things back to his old locker. Richie, who left the stadium shortly after the game was postponed, was not there to direct the latest move.

"What are you doing?" relief-pitcher Dick Farrell asked Kenny Bush.

"Following orders," Bush told him.

"Oh," said right fielder Johnny Callison. "I thought Skinner was moving in here [the storage room], and Rich was moving in there [the manager's office]."

It was just a matter of time now before Skinner surrendered. In early August, after Allen had skipped an exhibition game in Reading, Pennsylvania, Bob resigned. By then it was painfully clear to him that, without solid backing from the front office, there was no way he could handle the deteriorating situation.

Things hit a new comic low before the season ended as Allen did everything in his power to make it painfully clear that he had no interest in remaining in Philadelphia. One night he hit upon a new wrinkle while playing first base, scrawling words in the dirt with his spikes.

No, he didn't turn Connie Mack Stadium into an X-rated ball park. The words Richie scrawled were clean. *B-O-O*, he would write in very large, easy-to-read letters. And *M-O-M*. And in a particularly pungent commentary on his desire to get this long, miserable season over with, *O-C-T 2*, which just happened to be the day it was scheduled to end, and a week before he was traded to the St. Louis Cardinals.

It took a man with a sense of humor to appreciate Allen's doodlings, or at least to ignore them.

"It didn't bother me," remarked Bill Giles' father, Warren, who was then the president of the National League.

But one night his honor, the commissioner, took in a Phillies game at Connie Mack Stadium—and oh boy, did it bother him!

Bowie Kuhn, in case you haven't noticed, is somewhat on the pompous side. At any rate, he became quite upset as he sat in the decaying ruins of old Connie Mack Stadium in late September 1969, watching the worst Phillies team of the last decade on a night when the first baseman seemed much more interested in scrawling words in the dirt than playing baseball. Naturally, when Kuhn got upset, so did John Quinn. So there they were, the commissioner of baseball and the general manager of the Phillies, dedicated to one cause: stopping Richie Allen from writing any more words in the dirt near first base with his spikes. Clearly, it was a time for action, and these were men of action. In a flash, they hit upon a plan. They called Warren Giles and dumped the whole thing in his lap. And to think, there are people who claim Bowie Kuhn doesn't know how to handle things.

A year or so before he died Warren Giles, a warm, wonderful man, related the story of how he saved the game of baseball by stopping Richie Allen from scrawling words in the dirt.

"John Quinn got all excited about it," Warren Giles said. "He called me at home, and he said, 'Allen's at first base drawing pictures [sic] in the dirt with his toe and the commissioner's here, seeing this. He wanted me to call you and see if you want to do something about it.' I said to him, 'John, you [the Phillies] must be behind [to get worked up over something like that].' "

A very perceptive man, Mr. Giles. Also a very good guesser, although the odds were clearly on his side. In those days, the Phillies were almost always behind. But, Quinn kept insisting, it was the letters in the dirt, not the numbers on the scoreboard that were responsible for this emergency phone call.

Think of it. Here was Richie Allen scrawling words—perfectly clean words—in the presence of the commissioner of baseball and the home team's general manager, and their solution was to call the president of the league at home. Historians can only guess at the details of the high-level conference that led up to that long-distance phone call. Most likely, it went something like this:

Quinn: Look down there, Mr. Commissioner. He's writing words in the dirt. Let's see. What does that spell? *B-O-O* . . . My goodness, he must be trying to spell your name, sir. I'm so embarrassed. Let me call down to the dugout and get word to him that you spell it with a *W*.

Kuhn: Now don't get upset, John. I mean, it is a difficult name to spell.

Quinn: Well, I still think it's time we did something about this. Don't you agree, Mr. Commissioner?

Kuhn: Absolutely. Uh, what do you have in mind?

Quinn: Actually, I thought I would leave it up to you, sir. After all, you *are* the commissioner.

Kuhn: You're 100 percent right, John. This calls for firm action on my part. I hereby authorize you to call Warren immediately.

In any event, whatever deep thought went into that phone call, it was made—a fact that mystified Warren Giles no end.

"He [Quinn] said to me, the commissioner thinks this is terrible," Mr. Giles related with some relish. "I said, 'Is he drawing obscene pictures?' 'No, no,' John told me, 'but I'm telling you something's got to be done about this thing.' "

Warren Giles wasn't about to argue with that logic. What the president of the National League couldn't understand was why somebody at the scene of the, er, crime couldn't handle it.

" 'It seems to me it's a club matter,' I told him," Mr. Giles said. " 'Well,' he replied, 'the commissioner said he thought it was a league matter.' "

It took a while, but John Quinn finally convinced Warren

Giles that Richie Allen scrawling letters in the dirt was too much for the club or the commissioner to handle and that it was up to the league president to take a firm stand.

"I said, 'OK, OK,' " Warren Giles recalled, "and I called Richie the next day. I got him coming in the clubhouse after practice. I told him who it was and he said, 'What have I done now?' "

Mr. Giles informed him.

"He said, 'What's so bad about that?'

" 'It isn't earth-shaking,' I said, 'but it *is* bad in a way. It shows your mind is wandering when you stand at first base.'

" 'It relaxes me,' he said, 'I've done that all my life.'

"I said, 'Don't give me that crap. I wasn't born yesterday. You played the outfield. There's grass in the outfield. You don't draw pictures in the grass.'

He said, 'You guys—you big shots—you always have the answers. What are you going to do with me?'

"I said, 'If you continue, next time you do it I'm going to ask the umpires to get the groundskeepers to rake it out. And then, if you do it again, I'm going to ask them to put you out of the ball game. Then you're in a hassle with the umpires, and the umpires are in a hassle with the crowd.'

" 'Well, OK,' he said, 'but that's a helluva thing to make a telephone call about.' "

It was indeed. Warren Giles couldn't have agreed more. But Richie Allen was right about one thing. By the time he returned to Philadelphia, in the mid-'70s, the Phillies had come up with a foolproof way to prevent him from scrawling those "love letters in the sand." It was called AstroTurf.

As Allen said, those baseball big shots are smart. If only he had been as smart the folks in Cooperstown might be dusting off a new wing for him even now.

10

The Philly Follies

IF YOU THINK THE ESTABLISHED PHILADELPHIA SPORTS teams—the genuine big leaguers—had their share of problems over the years, you should have seen the outfits that tried to stake a claim in the city . . . and failed dismally, almost entirely through their own misdirected efforts.

In relatively recent times, Philadelphia sports fans have had a chance to watch such dubious enterprises as world team tennis and box lacrosse. If you don't know what box lacrosse is, don't ask. Just consider yourself lucky. Suffice it to say the box-lacrosse people who passed through Philly, trying to peddle tickets for a team called the Wings, used newspaper ads that promised, "Bumping, kicking, whacking, slashing, shoving." There have been cleaner gang wars in Philadelphia. Hell, there have been cleaner hockey games.

Perhaps the least noticed of all the pseudo-big-league teams that popped up, ever so briefly, in Philadelphia was a pro basketball team known as the Tuck Tapers, whose claim to major-league status was as transparent as the tape their name promoted. The Tapers (and the American Basketball League) came to town to fill the void left by the departure of the Philadelphia Warriors to San Francisco. It must have seemed like a good idea at the time, but the Tapers were in themselves a void. Arriving in mid-November 1962, they lasted until the first week in January 1963. There were pickup teams on the Philadelphia playgrounds that attracted more attention and created more excitement. Practically nobody paid to watch the Tapers play, strong evidence that Philadelphia sports fans were smarter than average. The only time the Tuck Tapers made headline news in the Philadelphia papers was when they did the only decent thing they could do: fold.

The Tapers were merely blah. But the Blazers—ah, that was a team in keeping with long-time Philadelphia tradition. They were so outrageously bad, so grossly mismanaged, so incredibly unlucky that they provided the city with some real bellylaughs in a period when Philly sports fans didn't have a lot to laugh about.

The Blazers, in case their meteoric dash to obscurity escaped your notice, were a professional ice-hockey team in an "outlaw" league called the World Hockey Association, which got its name players, and its notoriety, by raiding the established National Hockey League.

Opening night for the Blazers, at Civic Center Convention Hall, was a classic, even by Philadelphia standards. Shortly before the game was scheduled to begin, the Zamboni machine, which resurfaces the ice, rumbled into view—and the ice cracked under its weight. Naturally, the opener had to be postponed, a fact that didn't endear the Blazers to the people who had turned out for the gala occasion. Disgruntled fans, informed of the postponement, showered the cracked ice with the souvenir hockey pucks they had been given upon entering the building.

In retrospect, though, that wasn't the worst night in Blazer history. But what could you expect? The guy who wound up running the team knew so little about ice hockey he thought the game was played in quarters. Even worse, he knew so little about ice hockey that he thought Derek Sanderson, a center with the Boston Bruins, was worth what he paid to get him.

Would Derek Sanderson really leave the Boston Bruins to play for the Philadelphia Blazers? Doug Favell, a one-time Bruin who was then playing goal for the Philadelphia Flyers, chuckled when the idea was mentioned to him in the summer of 1972. "I don't think so," Favell said. "He's a good friend of mine. He hates Philly."

If Sanderson hated Philly, Philly wasn't exactly in love with Sanderson, who had engaged in a highly publicized brawl with Flyer fans at the Spectrum. So naturally the Blazers and their front-office corps of hockey masterminds went all out to get him.

"Their offer is utterly fantastic," said Bob Woolf, the Boston attorney who represented Sanderson in what had to be the greatest steal since the Brinks job. "Jim Cooper is the most persistent person I ever met."

Cooper was the driving force behind the Blazers in those formative months, the man who talked Bernie Brown, a trucking magnate, into joining him in this crazy venture. Cooper may not have been quite as astute an observer of the hockey scene as he thought, but he was a heckuva promoter. And he had it in his head that Derek Sanderson was the player who would put the Blazers on the map, make them sure-fire successes in the hotly competitive Philadelphia sports market.

"The Blazers," Bob Woolf was surprised to find out, "would make Derek the highest paid athlete in America. No, in the world. Jim Cooper and Bernie Brown," Woolf added, "are in love with what they're doing. They want to produce a winner. They want to be competitive with the Flyers."

And so they waved a $2,650,000 offer at Derek Sanderson and his attorney. Even if he hated Philadelphia, Sanderson did not hate the thought of becoming rich. So it was that on August 3, 1972, while the Phillies were playing out the string on another last-place season, while the Eagles were preparing for a 2–11–1 disaster, while the 76ers were gearing up for the worst season in NBA history, the Philadelphia Blazers captured the sports headlines in the nation's fourth largest city by calling a press conference in the Rose Garden of the old, elegant Bellevue Stratford Hotel.

While the media converged on the Bellevue, Keith Allen, general manager of the NHL Flyers, sat in his Spectrum office and shook his head at the folly of it all. "Placing any athlete in that type of wage level is ridiculous and impractical," Allen said. "Sanderson's a good hockey player. He's a Joe Namath-type guy. He's got long hair and a mustache. But a superstar? Let's face it. In all honesty I think he would be centering our second line [behind—way, way behind Bobby Clarke]."

On this day, however, Keith Allen's opinion, no matter how sound, didn't seem to matter. All eyes were on the Bellevue Rose Garden, where four uniformed security men stood at the door to make sure, presumably, that no spies from the National Hockey League got inside. They surely didn't keep anybody else out. The Rose Garden was packed with people who wanted to catch a glimpse of a twenty-six-year-old hockey player who scored twenty-five goals the previous season with the Bruins. (Clarke, incidentally, had scored thirty-five with the Flyers.) It didn't faze the mob that Sanderson hadn't received a single NHL All-Star vote or that he wasn't in Bobby Clarke's class as a hockey player or that he didn't like Philadelphia. He was a millionaire, courtesy of the Blazers. That's what mattered.

Jim Cooper, the president of the Blazers, stood up to address the gathering. "We have come here today to announce a momentous event to the hockey world and the entire sports world," he began modestly, and his partner, trucker Bernie Brown, nodded approvingly. Propped up behind the two men were a pair of nearly lifesize pictures of—guess who. No, no, not Jim Cooper and Bernie Brown; the hockey player they had just highjacked from the Bruins. "You will notice behind me two photos, which have been described to me as wallet-sized photos of Derek Sanderson," Cooper said with his best Bob Hope delivery.

Silence greeted that statement. The president of the Philadelphia Blazers paused, waiting for the laugh his gagwriter must have assured him would come at this moment. More silence, interrupted by an occasional clearing of the throat and maybe a nervous cough or two. "I think you must all be asleep this morning," said the president, unable to hide his injured feelings.

Well, somebody had been asleep. How else could Derek Sanderson have walked off with that big a contract? But Jim Cooper wasn't looking at it that way. His little wisecrack having gone over like a lead balloon, he pressed onward, ever onward. For three-quarters of an hour he stood there, telling stories, waiting for laughs that seldom came, introducing guests, taking shots at the "other team in town." The man who had bought Derek Sanderson was having a wonderful time, even if some of his Rose Garden guests weren't.

"Right now," Jim Cooper was babbling, "I'd rather be the Philadelphia Blazers than the Boston Bruins." Which should tell you something about how much Cooper knew about hockey.

"I asked my daughter, Cindy, 'How important is it to you that we get Derek?' " the president went on. There was an undercurrent of whispering in his audience. Cooper stiffened perceptibly. "This is a true story," he admonished. "C'mon up, Cindy, tell them what you said."

And, unbelievable as it sounds, Jim Cooper's daughter, a

pretty, sixteen-year-old, had to run up to the head table and tell the story of how she had promised to give her allowance to Derek Sanderson if he would only become a Philadelphia Blazer. With that, Cindy Cooper turned and handed a five-dollar bill to the world's highest-paid athlete, who quickly accepted it. The murmur in the audience grew louder. Finally, some hard news. Pens scribbled. Tape recorders whirred. At long last the truth was out; the exact amount of money required to lure Derek Sanderson to Philadelphia was now known. He had received precisely $2,650,005.

Still, Cooper kept yakking. It got so bad that a wire-service reporter saw fit to interrupt him by calling out, "Hey Jim, you want to open this up for a few questions?"

Silly boy. Of course, Jim Cooper didn't want to open this up for a few questions. Not yet, at any rate. There were more people to introduce. More stories to tell. Trapped in the Rose Garden, there was nothing for the assembled throng to do but listen. Maybe that was why those four uniformed security men were stationed at the door: to make sure that nobody got out.

A man named Jim Browitt, identified as the WHA's administrator, was introduced by Cooper and, predictably, chose to say a few words. "You're going to see a parity you're not accustomed to in the other league," he promised. At least, most of the reporters in the Rose Garden thought the word he used was *parity*. In light of later events, it's entirely possible he said *parody*.

Anyhow, the Jim Cooper Show finally creaked to a close with Derek Sanderson letting everybody know how delighted he was to be a part of this great, new undertaking, and the guests were herded aboard two chartered buses for a ride to Kennedy Plaza, a few blocks away. There, Jim Cooper found yet another unsuspecting audience—some 200 curiosity seekers who heard him say, "Just like they signed the Declaration of Independence in Philadelphia, we now have a declaration of independence for all hockey players. They're all free."

Free, hell. This one had cost $2,650,005. But why quibble? As the Kennedy Plaza crowd pressed forward, Derek Sanderson accepted a replica of the Liberty Bell, no doubt presented to remind skeptics that the management of the Blazers wasn't the only thing in Philadelphia that was slightly cracked. Then it was back on the buses, and back to the Bellevue Stratford, all of three blocks away, for what Jim Cooper hailed as "a reception and luncheon in honor of this historic event."

There were, of course, other historic events involving the Philadelphia Blazers. They didn't win an awful lot of games, but they held a lot of nutty press conferences.

The Sanderson one obviously rated top billing, but even before Derek put in his first appearance the Blazers' credibility had been somewhat eroded by a press conference called to introduce a general manager who had decided, hours before, *not* to take the job. No kidding. I mean, nobody could make this stuff up. It had to really happen.

The reluctant GM was Murray Williamson, a well-known hockey figure who had coached an American Olympic team along the way. Williamson had arrived in Philadelphia on a Saturday night in early June 1972 to meet with Jim Cooper and Bernie Brown, co-owners of a club that, up to then, had no place to play and practically no players. They wined and dined Murray at the Vesper Club one night, at the Bellevue Stratford the next night. By Monday, they had him sold. "It was a handshake agreement," Cooper explained.

There was so much work to be done and so little time to do it that Williamson began operating in his new capacity as general manager of the Blazers on Monday afternoon, the day before the press conference. "I worked four hours," Williamson said. "We added eight players to their list. I opened negotiation with three [World Hockey Association] general managers regarding the training camp and trades. I talked with three lawyers regarding the terms under which National Leaguers would be available [to sign WHA contracts]. I talked to two coaches regarding their interest in Philadelphia."

Murray Williamson accomplished a lot in those four hours. The man is a worker, a go-getter. And some time that night, he got up and went.

"He did not feel he was able, under the pressure of time, to do the job," Jim Cooper said. "I give him credit for telling me, but I wish he had told me ten hours before. It would have saved us a lot of aggravation and embarrassment."

Cooper, it turned out, didn't discover that his general

manager had decided to become his ex-general manager until 11:30 Monday night, too late to call off that Tuesday press conference. By the time the media gathered the man who was to have been introduced was safely at home in Endina, Minnesota. "Yeah," he confirmed over the telephone, "I agreed to terms. Let's say the terms were agreeable. They have a good organization. Cooper and Brown are good for that league. . . . They're honest. They're wealthy. They're dynamic."

They sounded absolutely terrific. So how come Murray Williamson had hightailed it back to Minnesota?

"They have three months to put a team together," he replied. "It's not enough time. You make a move like that, there are a lot of loose ends to be tied together. They're running against the clock. They're starting to panic a little bit."

If Murray Williamson wanted to see some real panic, he should have stayed around. But that wasn't for him. "I'm a winner," he said. "I go into something to command the no. 1 spot. I want to build a no. 1. . . . You can move mountains if you have enough dynamite, as long as you have enough time to plant the sticks and light the fuses."

In those four hours on the job, Murray Williamson found no dynamite, no fuses. All he found was the mountain. So he packed up and went home. Don't ever let anybody tell you that Philadelphia hasn't had some smart general managers.

In truth, then, the opening-night disaster was only one in a long series of Blazer blunders that assured this team of a place in the Philadelphia junkyard. By late November, Jim Cooper had moved on to other—presumably, more lucrative—ventures, and Bernie Brown was solely in charge. Until then, Brown had been the silent partner, the man in the dark suit who seemed so out of place amid the hubbub of those flashy, Jim Cooper-directed, midsummer press conferences. It was Cooper who made all the speeches, shook all the hands, got all the front-office publicity, told all the bad jokes. It was Cooper who had made the big push to sign Derek Sanderson and John McKenzie, another Boston Bruins veteran who was hired as the Blazers' player-coach. The players all knew Jim Cooper, not Bernie Brown. They only knew Bernie Brown's money. And now, with the club crashing down around him, Brown decided it was time to make himself known.

"I blame myself," he said two days after bidding a not-particularly-fond farewell to the man who talked him into making Derek Sanderson a millionaire. "I sat back when my instincts told me everything we're doing is wrong. But when you don't know, you listen. I thought, 'Maybe he's right. Maybe I'm crazy.' [But] I guess I wasn't so crazy."

Even a man who didn't know a hockey puck from a ping-pong ball was bound to get upset over the attitudes of some of those high-priced, so-called stars. They showed up in training camp out of shape. They laughed their way through the workouts. And the highest-priced player of them all—good, old Derek—went so far as to make disparaging remarks about Philadelphia, which did nothing to endear either Sanderson or the Blazers to the city's sports fans. "It's been a joyride, in my opinion," Bernie Brown said. He meant for the players, not the owners.

Sanderson engaged in a private war with the Philly press too, knocking the writers who had done such a thorough job of knocking him. "The Philadelphia press is brutal," he was quoted in a New York paper shortly before Brown took over control of the Blazers. "I'm writing a book with a whole chapter on the [Philadelphia] sportswriters that's really going to do a number on them. How sometimes they're so drunk they can't remember the arena, and where they are, and what they're doing."

Granted, the Blazers were enough to drive any writer assigned to cover them to drink, but it would appear that Derek Sanderson was getting a bit carried away in that interview. Or maybe he was confusing the writers with his teammates.

"Derek's a kind of guy who's got to get his name in the paper," player-coach McKenzie said. "He'll figure out a way. He says a lot of things without thinking."

Which seemed only fair. After all, the Blazers had given him that whopping contract without doing very much real thinking either.

When it became painfully evident that the multi-million-dollar "steal" wasn't worth two cents to the Philadelphia Blazers, the club bought up the contract. Let the record show that one day after the Philadelphia Phillies gave Steve Carlton, their great left-handed pitcher, $165,000 to play in 1973, the Philadelphia Blazers gave Derek Sanderson a million dollars *not* to play in 1973. Truly, in Philadelphia sports, truth is often stranger than fiction.

In May 1973, the Blazers finally left the Philadelphia sports scene, packing up their sticks, their pucks, their memories, and heading for Vancouver where, they undoubtedly hoped, nobody had ever heard of them. While in Philly, they had averaged about 2,200 paid fans per game, about half of what they had announced to the press. The losses, according to most educated guesses, ran as high as $2.5 million, maybe more. "When I first got here," said GM Phil Watson, "Cooper was spending money like there was no tomorrow. He had a guy come in who was forty years old, a defenseman. He gaved him a three-year, no-cut contract. Think he wasn't laughing at us?"

If so, he wasn't the only one.

*   *   *

One good thing about the Blazers. They did so many foolish things, wound up with egg on their faces so many times that nobody really took them very seriously. The Philadelphia Bell was another story, one that provided a perfect example of how the press—even in as sophisticated, as hard-hitting a journalistic town as Philadelphia—can be conned into promoting something that doesn't deserve more than the most fleeting of mentions.

The Bell was Philadelphia's entry in the woebegone World Football League, the brainchild of a promoter named Gary Davidson, the fast-talker who gave us the World Hockey Association, the American Basketball Association and—well, you get the idea. Davidson, it seemed, could make a league out of anything. The next one he should call World Team Bankruptcy, just to give the suckers a clue.

Talk to Davidson, though, and you always got the idea that things were booming. "We think right now our expansion next year will be Tokyo and Mexico City," he said during a trip to Philadelphia in February 1974 to promote his new football league and to take part in a press conference at the Cafe Erlanger. In keeping with WHA-WFL tradition, the press conference was called off at the last minute. "Some loose ends," Davidson explained without the slightest hint of embarrassment. The man did not embarrass easily.

"Think if you were a football player, a stud," he was gushing in his hotel room that day, "and I came to you and said, 'Frank, baby, do you want to play in Tokyo or Buffalo?' "

The president of the World Football League did not think in small terms. Let the National Football League dillydally in such frozen wastelands as Buffalo. His league would set up camp in Tokyo. Come to think of it, that would have been fine. It was the WFL's decision to put a team in Philadelphia that hurt.

The Philadelphia Bell was as phony as a three-dollar bill, but for a while it got publicity worthy of a National Football League team. The press, caught up by the pro football fever, provided some measure of credibility for the team by accepting the announced crowd figures as the real McCoy.

The early games were played in July 1974 at John F. Kennedy Stadium in South Philadelphia, for many years the 102,000-seat site of the Army-Navy game. On July 10, the Bell played before an announced crowd of 55,534. Two weeks later, banner headlines in the Philly papers heralded a turnout of 64,719. The Bell, it appeared, was ringing loud and clear. If you read the papers or listened to the radio and TV announcers or, better yet, listened to Barry Leib, executive vice-president of Philadelphia's new pro team, you'd have thought the Bell was one of the hottest tickets in town. That 64,000-plus crowd was mostly paid, the Bell would have the city believe. Oh, there was talk of some 10,000 "sponsorship giveaways" and an admission that 19,500 tickets were sold at group discount rates, but the implication was that the remaining 35,000 tickets were sold at face value, and that well over 50,000 fans paid something to get in.

The truth was another story. And it was reflected in the attendance figures turned in by the Bell to the city for tax purposes. Suddenly, the 55,534 crowd on July 10 dwindled to 13,855 paid. And the 64,719 turnout on July 25 shriveled to 6,200. The Bell had given away tickets by the truckload. In Philadelphia, nearly everybody got free tickets to the WFL. There hadn't been that much paper floating around town since the Flyers won the Stanley Cup.

"The image they're creating of being a success is the biggest phony thing I've ever seen," said Phillies' executive vice-president Bill Giles.

There's nothing wrong with giving away tickets, but there *is* something wrong with misleading the public, and the Bell was plainly guilty of doing that, with the nwitting cooperation of the media—at least for a while. When the truth came out, the Bell and the WFL were on the way out.

"I admit we lied to everyone. What can I say? I never thought those figures would come out?" Barry Leib said, and John B. Kelly, Jr., then the president of the Bell—a purely honorary position—was more than a little miffed over the use of his name in such a phony venture. "I feel I've been used," said Kelly, then a Philadelphia councilman. "I've been had."

He wasn't the only one taken in by the new league that Gary Davidson foisted on an unsuspecting public. We'll never know how many athletes and front-office types worked for nothing, or at least for considerably less than they had been promised in the WFL. One such victim was Hal Cowan, now the sports-information director at Oregon State. Cowan left a similar post at the University of Oregon to become public-relations director for the *Portland Storm.* "The credibility in the league went kaplooey after the Philadelphia story [about the phony Bell crowds] broke," he said. "Right away we get a Telex from Gary Davidson: 'Under no circumstances reveal official attendance figures to anyone from the media or you will be fined.' "

That was nearly as bad as the time Cowan called the league office to check on the WFL All-Star team. "We had voted on a team," he said, "so I asked them when they were going to release it and was told they weren't. Eleven of the players picked for the team had bonus clauses. If they made the All-Star team they got extra money. It would've cost us $40,000 [in bonus money] to announce the team."

So the team went unannounced. And the WFL faded out of sight, haunted by the embarrassment of "the Philadelphia story" that hastened its demise.

11

Ready, Aim, Fire—Or, the Axman Cometh

CHICAGO HAD THE GREAT FIRE. PHILADELPHIA, ON THE OTHER hand, had the great firings. The simple fact is this: When a guy comes to Philadelphia to take a job as a coach or a manager or a general manager, he should rent, not buy.

In the last two decades alone, the list of professional sports firings in Philly could fill a page in your average phone book. Let's see . . . there was Nick Skorich, Eagles, in 1963; followed by Dolph Schayes, 76ers, 1966; Gene Mauch, Phillies, 1968; Bud Poile, Flyers, 1969; Joe Kuharich, Eagles, 1969; Vic Stasiuk, Flyers, 1971; Jerry Williams, Eagles, 1971; John Quinn, Phillies, 1972; Frank Lucchesi, Phillies, 1972; Ed Khayat, Eagles, 1972; Pete Retzlaff, Eagles, 1972; Roy Rubin, 76ers, 1973; Don DeJardin, 76ers, 1973; Mike McCormack, Eagles, 1975; and Danny Ozark, Phillies, 1979. A rather imposing list of victims, you'll have to agree. They all came to Philadelphia with the dream of building a championship team . . . and paid for their failures by winding up in front of the proverbial firing squad. The way things were going in the late '60s and the '70s, Philadelphia should have changed its city seal to get in the spirit of things. A picture of a coach (or manager or general manager) standing blindfolded with his hands tied behind his back would have been perfect.

Don't get the idea that the firings grew monotonous after a while. Not *these* firings. They had a special Philadelphia flavor, each a soap opera in its own right. There were firings in which the victims broke down and cried and firings in which the "fire-ers" looked more upset than the "fire-ees." There were firings in which the victims attended their own funerals, so to speak, and

153

a firing in which the victim, Gene Mauch, was some 3,000 miles away at the bedside of his sick wife. There was the firing in which the victim, Dolph Schayes, had just been named coach of the year, and firings in which the only award the victims got came in the form of severance pay.

There were mid-summer firings and Christmas-week firings, bitter firings and sweet firings, cruel firings and humane firings. In short, if you spent the '60s and the '70s following professional sports in Philadelphia, you were bound to find one or more firings to suit your taste. What I'm trying to say is, if your favorite pastime was watching sports figures get the ax, Philadelphia was the place to be. Let's face it—if you wanted to lower the unemployment rate in the country in those years the best way might have been to ban professional sports in Philadelphia.

Now I don't want to make it sound as if firing coaches, managers, what-have-you was Philadelphia's no. 1 sport in the '60s and ''70, but I have always thought it was a pity that Richard Nixon's famous "farewell speech" of 1962 hadn't been saved for use by the men who passed through the Philly sports scene in the years that followed. Think about it. Nixon's historic words would have been near-perfect for any number of Philly sports victims. All they'd have to do was read the speech verbatim . . . and insert their own names in place of Nixon's.

In case you've forgotten, the speech went like this: "The last play. [Pause.] I leave you gentlemen now, and you will now write it. You will interpret it. That's your right. But as I leave you, I want you to know —just think how much you're going to be missing. You won't have [*fill in appropriate name*] to kick around any more."

Gee, if only Danny Ozark or Roy Rubin had said that.

*   *   *

There were so many Philly firings it would be foolhardy to try to jam all the details into one book, so let's just hit the highlights. Here then are the most memorable in those bloody years . . .

Let's start with Mauch. When in doubt, it's always a good idea to start with Mauch. He was so lively, so controversial, so sharp, and he lasted so long.

Inheriting a terrible ball club, Mauch managed more than

eight years in Philadelphia, and six of his Phillie teams—from 1962 through 1967— won more games than they lost. Mayo Smith, another Philadelphia firingsquad victim, circa 1958, may have done the best job of putting Gene Mauch's achievement into perspective when he remarked, while managing the Detroit Tigers in the World Series of 1968, "I saw Gene Mauch the other day, and I told him, 'Dammit, you set a record nobody will ever break—managing eight years in Philadelphia.' "

With that in mind it seems only fitting that we open this firing free-for-all, this orgy of axing with the man who managed 1,331 Phillie games, more than anybody in the history of the Philadelphia National League baseball franchise.

Some of Mauch's attributes have been mentioned earlier, although it's only fair to note that—Jim Bunning, Ruben Amaro, Bobby Wine and all the other Mauch-lovers to the contrary—not everybody who played for him shared their feelings. Catcher Clay Dalrymple, for example, managed to keep his adoration of "Number 4" within bounds. "People assumed Gene and I were very close," Dalrymple said. "It's not true. He was the boss. In this game you can't quit and go to work for somebody else. You make the best of a situation. I knew right from the start Gene was a good baseball man, but he never untied the apron string with me. He never even let me call pitchouts on my own. Talking to Gene was like having your brain picked apart. He'd call you in the office to talk over the hitters. He'd ask you what you thought. Then he'd do it his way."

Ask Ruben Gomez about that. Better yet, if you're a Gene Mauch fan *don't* ask Ruben Gomez about that.

Gomez, a native of Puerto Rico, spent ten years in the big leagues, long enough to win seventy-six games and build up a deep-seated dislike for Mauch. Ruben had all of Gene that he could stand in 1960, Mauch's first year as manager of the Phillies. Gomez, whose "out" pitch was a screwball—a' la Fernando Valenzuela—thought he knew quite a bit about pitching by the time Mauch tried to tell him how to do it. After all, Ruben had made it to the big leagues in 1953; four times he won ten or more games in a season.

"I left Philadelphia," Gomez explained recently, "because I couldn't stand Mauch."

He objected to the way Mauch ran a ball game, how he called

pitches from the dugout. Maybe that was all right with a kid on the mound, Gomez figured, but it wasn't all right when the pitcher was a big-league veteran in his thirties. Ruben was 0–and–3 for Mauch in 1960. He couldn't wait to leave.

Several years passed—and then a strange thing happened. Gomez was in Puerto Rico, pitching winter ball, when his old buddy, Gene Mauch, arrived in town. "He comes to see me," Ruben said. "He says, 'I'm looking for a relief pitcher.' I name four guys. He doesn't want them. He says, 'I want you.' I said, 'I left because I couldn't stand you.' He said, 'If you come back, I'll let you pitch your own game.' "

With that understanding, Gomez said, he agreed to a second tour of duty with Mauch's Phillies.

An incident in spring training should have given Ruben a hint of what was to come. "He says to me, 'Do you mind throwing only screwballs [in today's game]?' " Gomez said. "I told him, 'Sure, I don't mind.' "

The scene shifts to Pittsburgh. It's the regular season now, the real thing, and the intense Mr. Mauch is staring at a situation that makes a manager's blood run cold: the bases loaded with Pirates and Roberto Clemente coming up. Gene waved to the bullpen for Ruben Gomez.

"The catcher [Clay Dalrymple] signals for a screwball," Gomez said. "I shake him off. Again he signals for a screwball. Again I shake him off. Again a screwball. Again I shake him off."

Ruben knew Clemente like the back of his hand. And he knew that Clemente knew him. Surely, Gomez thought, Clemente would be looking for a screwball. For that reason, the pitcher did not want to throw it on the first pitch.

"I call the catcher out," Ruben said. " 'I say to him, 'Don't you know anything else but screwball?' He says, 'He's calling all the pitches.' "

"He," of course, was Gene Mauch. Gomez saw red, or whatever color it is that angry, veteran, Puerto Rican screwball specialists see when they feel they've been betrayed.

"I say to the catcher, 'I'm throwing sinkers.' "

Clemente dug in, looking for a nice, juicy screwball to bat. "I throw him two sinkers for strikes," Gomez said. "Then I throw him two high, inside fastballs. I deck him twice. Then a little screwball to strike him out."

And Gene Mauch was ecstatic, right? He was waiting in front of the dugout with outstretched arms and a huge smile on his kisser, right? Hey, you don't know Gene Mauch. *He* was the boss. When he signaled for a screwball, he wanted a screwball. The manager was livid when Gomez strode into the dugout.

"He says, 'If you don't pitch what I tell you, you can go back.' " Ruben said. "I tell him, 'Sir, I go back.' "

And back he went, a two-time loser in the Gene Mauch sweepstakes. "He lied to me," complained Gomez. "He said I could pitch on my own, and then he tries to call the pitches for me."

Ruben suspected that his troubles with Mauch stemmed from an incident in Puerto Rico during Gene's playing days. "Mauch slid into second," Gomez said. "He went out of his way to get [Junior] Gilliam, and he cut him on the leg. So I hit him. I hit him in the head. Later, when he comes to manage the Phillies, he says, 'You remember me?' I say, 'Sure, I remember you. I hit you with a ball in the head.' He says, 'Don't you forget it.' I think, 'Now I know how I stand.' "

But even if Ruben Gomez was not a charter member of the Gene Mauch Fan Club, he was quick to admit that Mauch knew baseball. "I'm telling you, he's smart," Gomez said. "There are few managers that know as much as he knows about this game. He works his ass off. He's great with younger players. The only thing, in those years he couldn't deal with older players."

At least not with an older player named Ruben Gomez.

OK, so that's the way Mauch was, particularly in those early Phillie years. But he was bright, and he was fascinating. There may have been people who didn't like Gene Mauch, but nobody ever accused him of being dull. In a game filled with clones, he was an original.

You can ask Lowell Palmer about that. Palmer, in case his fleeting Phillies career escaped your notice, was a highly regarded, hard-throwing, young righthanded pitcher in the late '60s. While trying to earn a spot on the big-league staff one spring, Palmer—a good-looking devil—made a rather serious tactical error. He dated Gene Mauch's daughter. The very next day Mr. Palmer was reassigned to the Phillies' minor-league complex. Of course, the timing was pure coincidence . . . but Gene Mauch did have a way of getting a point across.

Anyhow, Mauch's days with the Phillies were clearly

numbered in June of 1968. By then it was painfully obvious that Gene and Richie Allen could no longer coexist, and that the Phillies, if forced to choose between them, would reluctantly opt for the young slugger.

On Friday night, June 14, the Phillies were shut out by Los Angeles Dodger righthander Bill Singer in the first game of a Connie Mack Stadium doubleheader, 6–0. Immediately after the game, it was announced that Mauch had left the club to fly to California to be with his sick wife. The very next afternoon, just prior to the game, the club announced that Mauch had been fired. It seemed like a terribly heartless way to do it at the time, but looking back on it now there seems little doubt that Mauch knew, before leaving Philadelphia between games of that Friday night doubleheader, that his long run as manager of the Phillies had come to an end.

On Sunday afternoon, June 16, PA man Eddie Ferenz greeted the Connie Mack Stadium crowd with these words: "Good afternoon, ladies and gentlemen. Turn to the center of your Phillies' scorecard for the following addition to the Phillies' roster: no. 19, Bob Skinner, manager."

There was, of course, also a deletion, but Ferenz—now the club's traveling secretary, didn't have to say, "Scratch no. 4, Gene Mauch, ex-manager." There were more than 29,000 fans in the stadium that day, and not one of them showed up with a "Mauch Must Go" sign. Obviously, they all knew that he went. And you got the feeling that even many of those who had been calling for his scalp as the club struggled along were actually sorry to see him go.

A strange thing happened that afternoon. Common sense tells you that it had to be planned, but nobody has ever owned up to it. At any rate, whatever sparks Gene Mauch left behind apparently ignited the auxiliary scoreboard in left field because one number—the number "4"—glowed brightly in the space allotted for the number of the man at bat. That number, of course, was Mauch's number, and even the most casual fan was aware of it. Over the years it had become commonplace to refer to Gene as "Number 4."

Well, the "4" kept glowing on that left-field board and, try as hard as they could, they couldn't turn the darn thing off. Denny Gavaghan, who operated the board from the press box, kept pushing a button, but nothing happened. "It's stuck," Denny finally said, staring at the ghostly "4" in left field. "I can't get it off."

That "4" haunted the Phillies the rest of the afternoon. To add to their misery, the club's new manager started Rick Wise, whose record was 4–4, and he lost the game on a run scored in the fourth inning. An hour after the final Phillie had been retired and the people had left Connie Mack Stadium, that "4" still glowed on the scoreboard in left field. Gene Mauch was gone, but the memory lingered on.

Three days later, Gene returned to Philadelphia to collect his things and to say goodbye. Nina Lee, his wife, was home from the hospital, and Mauch seemed more relaxed than he'd been in weeks. They held a press conference in the Elephant Room behind first base, where Mauch's successor had been introduced the previous Sunday morning, and there wasn't the slightest trace of bitterness in the ex-manager's behavior. Gene Mauch may have come in like a lion in 1960, but he went out like a lamb in 1968.

"This ain't gonna be anything big," he began. "It's just that I didn't want to run in, run out. I didn't want to make a big deal out of it either. If I had a luncheon, a cocktail party, you'd say, 'Gee whiz, that's not Mauch. What's he trying to do?' "

He paused, letting the words sink in. Those who had traveled with the club during the Mauch years smiled to themselves. Gene had never been known for his lavish spending habits. Throwing parties for the press wasn't high on his list of things to do.

"There's no graceful way to say goodbye," Mauch went on, his voice a dab huskier than usual, "just like there was no graceful way for Bob [Carpenter] and John [Quinn] to handle it. I don't want to make a big thing about this. It was very uncomfortable for Bob and John and, dammit, nine years is a long time. If anybody had said to me, 'You'll be here [nearly] nine years,' I'd have said, 'You're nuts.' "

He leaned forward, ground out the cigarette he'd been smoking, and said, "Something had to be done. . . . They couldn't foresee Nina Lee getting sick. It was a terribly tough situation for them. And suppose they waited to tell me. Suppose I found out some other way. It would have been ten times worse."

He struck a match, put the flame to another cigarette, and went on. "It just made me ill that the organization got rapped around the way it did. Put the shoe on the other foot. Suppose they don't fire me. Suppose they say, 'We're going to take care of our little manager. Gene Mauch's going to be our manager forever.' And they trade Richie Allen. . . ." He took a long, thoughtful drag. "What kind of life do you think I'd be leading around this town after that?"

It was a remarkably subdued performance by a man who had never been known for subdued performances before, and it lent credence to the speculation that the decision had actually been made before Mauch flew to California.

A short time after the firing a friend of Gene Mauch's, a Philadelphia trucker named Leonard Tose, hosted the former Phillies manager and his wife on a week-and-a-half-long cruise. "We went to Nantucket, Newport, up through there," Gene said the following spring when he returned to Florida as manager of the expansion Montreal Expos. "You think he'll get the Eagles? He'd make a helluva great addition to American sports. Print that, will you? I'd like him to read it. There are only three adult people I've been able to confide in—John Quinn, Bob Carpenter, and Leonard."

Mauch, of course, got his wish about Leonard Tose getting the Eagles. Gene also had a Philadelphia "homecoming" that exceeded his wildest expectations.

"Baseball's not dead in Philadelphia," he said that mid-April day when his Expos came to Connie Mack Stadium. "It's just asleep, waiting for something to happen." Six hours before the game was supposed to begin, Mauch drove to the old place, winding his car through Fairmount Park, then down 33d Street, and finally taking a right on Lehigh Avenue. "I've gone down this street about 700 times—hell, 1,500 times if you want to count both ways," he said. "The first couple of years I was just full of doubt and uncertainty all the time. The next six were beautiful. Just beautiful. The first two years I wondered if we'd ever win a game. The next six I expected to win every game."

The game got rained out that night, but the following evening Gene Mauch faced the Phillies for the first time. His pitcher was a young righthander named Bill Stoneman, who had pitched only one complete game in his big-league life. All Stoneman did was pitch a no-hitter. "As clever as you guys are," Mauch told the

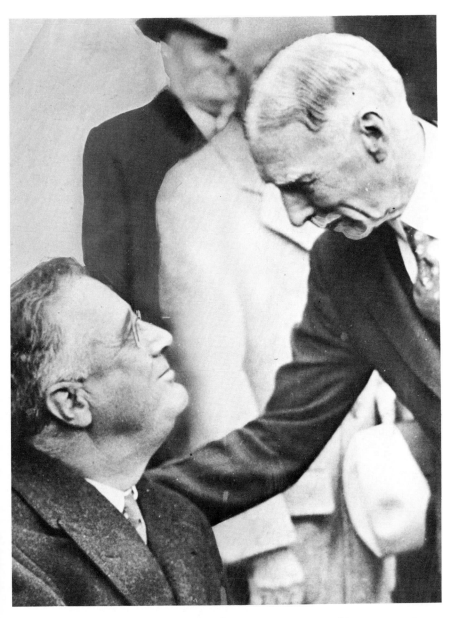

Here's one for the historians to savor: Franklin Delano Roosevelt is greeted by Connie Mack on a long-ago opening day. (Courtesy of The Sporting News)

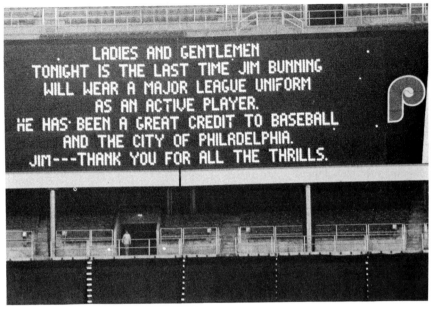

A sentimental moment at Vet Field. Bunning pitched a perfect game in 1964 at Shea Stadium. (Phillies photo)

The magnificent Phillies pitcher Robin Roberts. The Hall of Famer won 286 games while pitching for second-division teams and was a 20-game or more winner six consecutive years. (Phillies photo)

Left fielder Greg Luzinski shows the style that makes him one of the most formidable sluggers in the major leagues. (Phillies photo)

Pete Rose bowls over Astros catcher Bruce Bochy (13) to break up a tenth-inning deadlock in the 1980 NL playoffs. Rose scored from first base with a daring run home. Note loose ball at Bochy's right foot. (AP photo)

Richie Allen, author, gives Phillies fans the word. (Photo courtesy of the Philadelphia Inquirer)

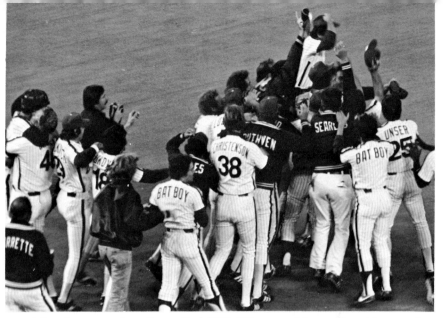

Tug McGraw has just struck out Kansas City's Willie Wilson to end the 1980 World Series, and it's time to celebrate. Out of the dugout rush the members of the first world championship Phillies team in history. (Phillies photo)

Danny Ozark, the long-lasting Phillies manager who led the team to contender position. (Phillies photo)

Pitcher Jim Bunning throws the first major league pitch in new Veterans Stadium. (Courtesy of Jim Bunning)

Paul Owens (left) and Dallas Green, the architects who built a championship baseball team for Philadelphia, let the cheering adoring throng know that they're no. 1. (Phillies photo)

Pete Rose shares a fizzy moment with Phillies manager Dallas Green immediately after winning the 1980 World Series. (UPI photo)

Phillies pitcher Tug McGraw celebrating the World Series triumph. The Phillies team trophy is at the right. (Phillies photo)

Champagne-soaked owner Ed Snider, left, singer Kate Smith, and Flyers star Bobby Clarke exult after winning the first Stanley Cup. (Flyers photo)

The Flyers' mystical coach Fred Shero with some of his blackboard wisdom. (Flyers photo)

A friendly disagreement at the Spectrum. (Flyers photo)

Bobby Clarke always attracts a crowd—even off the ice. Here, the man who has been called the heart, the soul, the guts of the Flyers, tells it the way it is to the media, including the author, following a game. (Flyers photo)

There was a time when it seemed as if they only occasionally interrupted the fights to play hockey at the Spectrum. The man in the white jersey against the boards (right) working over a member of the loyal opposition is—who else?—Dave Schultz. (Flyers photo)

Victory-hungry Philadelphia went wild when the Flyers copped their first Stanley Cup in 1974. (Flyers photo)

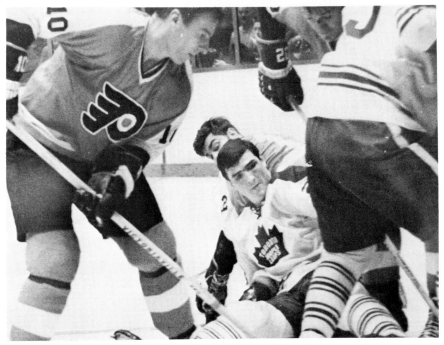

The Flyers' Bill Sutherland scores during the 1967-68 season. Pat Quinn, now Flyers coach but then with the Maple Leafs, is on ice. (Flyers photo)

It's a tense moment on the bench of the old Philadelphia Warriors as Coach Eddie Gottlieb, his shirt open, his tie askew, observes the action at the Arena. That's Matt Guokas, Sr., sitting two seats from Gotty. (Photo courtesy of the late Eddie Gottlieb)

Basketball wizard Julius Erving pops one in for the 76ers. Erving was the heart and soul of the fine 1980-81 club. (76ers photo)

Coack Dick Vermeil, who built the Eagles into a championship team. (Eagles photo)

Dick Vermeil, left, with former Eagles ironman Chuck Bednarik, now an assistant coach. (Eagles photo)

Bill Bergey, 66, in action. (Eagles photo)

Wide receiver Harold Carmichael looking for the ball. (Eagles photo)

Philly press when the game was over, "there isn't one of you here who could have written that script."

It was indeed a memorable night for the manager who had come so close to leading the Phillies into a World Series five years before. As Stoneman closed in on his no-hitter in the bottom of the ninth, the Philly fans—many of whom had booed him the year before—cheered, even chanted, "We want Mauch . . . We want Mauch," and a sign fluttered from the upper deck, "Please forgive Gene and bring him back."

Still, Mauch had been in Philadelphia long enough to know how fragile the love-hate relationship between a Phillies manager and the Phillie fans could be. When the visiting clubhouse attendant answered a knock on the door after the game he found a fan with a "gift" for the former manager. It was a big sheet with the words, "Welcome home Gene," scrawled on it.

"Some of your fans sent this over," the attendant said.

Gene Mauch looked at him. "If it's ticking," he said, "throw it out."

*   *   *

If the Mauch firing was among the friendliest in Philadelphia sports history, the Eagles' axing of Jerry Williams had to be one of the messiest.

No Eagles coach ever worked much harder or longer than Jerry Williams—no, not even Dick Vermeil. Williams was also a "workaholic" who spent long hours in the office and sometimes spent all night. He got the job after Mauch's buddy, Leonard Tose, bought the team from the financially troubled Jerry Wolman for $16,155,000. First thing Tose did was pick former Eagle hero Pete Retzlaff as his general manager, and Pete named Williams, an ex-Eagles player and assistant coach, as the new head coach.

The departure of Joe Kuharich as general manager-coach must have come as a terrible blow to all the novelty manufacturers in the city who found a bonanza in "Joe Must Go" items. There were "Joe Must Go" buttons, "Joe Must Go" bumper stickers, "Joe Must Go" T-shirts, "Joe Must Go" license plates. The least Leonard Tose could have done for the sake of the businessmen in town was to hire a coach whose first name was also Joe. But no, the next victim turned out to be a Jerry instead. And even though Jerry Williams' record as coach of the Eagles was seven wins, twenty-two defeats, and two ties in the two years and three games he lasted, the "Jerry Must Go" bumper sticker never really replaced the old, "Joe Must Go" model in the hearts or on the bumpers of Philadelphians.

The Eagles were 2-7-1 in Williams' second year when things got really bad. They lost to the Cardinals by nine at St. Louis, by nineteen to the Colts at Baltimore, and by eighteen to the Redskins at Washington. Leonard Tose was finding out that owning a National Football League club wasn't all it was cracked up to be, especially when the team you owned cracked up. He didn't take it well.

On the Monday after the Redskin game, Jerry Williams looked like hell. His face seemed unusually pale, his blue eyes deeply troubled. "I second-guess myself more than anybody else does," he said. "I took three pills [to get to sleep Sunday night]. I woke up at three o'clock anyway. I think I'm building up an immunity to pills. I lay there for a while. I couldn't get back to sleep, so I came to work."

On film, Williams discovered, the Eagles didn't look a heckuva lot better than they did in person. It must have been gruesome staring at the films of that '70 Eagles team, running and rerunning botched-up plays, but at no time did Jerry Williams offer alibis. That wasn't his style. An honest man, he seemed only too willing to accept the blame. And the owner seemed only too willing to give it to him.

"When you're 2-10 there's no excuse," Leonard Tose told the press that day. "There's nothing to say except you're 2-10."

Maybe Leonard wouldn't have thought 2-10-1 was so bad if he had known that two years down the road, with another coach, he'd be 2-11-1. But he had no way of knowing that, and the Eagles' record gnawed at him.

"I'm not a guy who interferes," he said, "but there comes a time for soul searching. The season is almost over, and we've won two games. Two games! It's hard to believe."

Eagle watchers in those days knew exactly what he meant. Two victories were hard to believe, but then you couldn't expect them to lose every game.

Tose didn't exactly give Jerry Williams a vote of confidence that Monday afternoon. What he gave him could best be described as a rousing vote of no-confidence. "I feel a greater consideration for the fans than any of you fellas have ever given me credit for," he told the press. "Philadelphia has the best fans. They're entitled to a championship team. At least to a winning season. . . . I would think if we don't do it next year it's only reasonable to expect that there'll be a helluva lot of changes."

Later, sitting in his private office, the owner was asked point-blank if there would be changes if the Eagles did not come up with a winning record in 1971. "Drastic changes," Tose replied quickly. "Completely drastic changes. . . . What we really need," he added, "is a convincing victory. That's what I've been hoping for all season. That's what we need."

Here they were, 2–11–1, and he wanted a *convincing* victory. A plain, ordinary, simple victory wouldn't do. Including the last four games of the '69 season, the Eagles had won twice and tied once in their last seventeen games, and Leonard Tose was looking for a *convincing* victory. I suspect most Eagles fans at that point in time would have considered a victory by forfeit rather nice.

Well, by golly, the Eagles won their final game of the '70 season, whipping the Pittsburgh Steelers, 30–20, at Franklin Field. The fans were not satisfied. Neither was the owner.

The next day, at the Eagles' weekly press luncheon, Leonard Tose gave his coach the strangest endorsement in the history of pro football. Jerry Williams was still coach of the Philadelphia Eagles, Leonard indicated, and he would be the coach of the Philadelphia Eagles in 1971—unless, of course, he was able to find somebody decent to take his place. "I'm in favor of a crash program tempered with judgment," was the rather interesting way Tose put it.

Poor Jerry. He had barely left the room when the talk about his possible successor started. The mention of George Allen's name seemed to bring a special sparkle to Leonard Tose's eyes. When a reporter said that he might phone Allen to see if he had any interest in the job, Tose poured gasoline on the already flaming rumor by replying, "If you talk to him, call my secretary. She'll know where I can be reached."

Basically, the owner said, he was looking for "a professional coach with a winning background."

"And if nobody fitting that description could be found, what then?" a writer asked.

"If we don't come up with anybody, it'll make sense to announce as soon as possible that Jerry will be back," Leonard Tose replied.

So it was that the Eagles staggered into the holiday season in 1970, beset by losses, by rumors, by questions. "You slowly find yourself answering questions you didn't anticipate, and you don't know what the hell the answer is," the owner said. Which summed it up rather neatly. I think.

Under the circumstances Jerry Williams' chances of succeeding as coach of the Eagles the following year were so small you needed a high-powered microscope to see them. Gamely, he carried on, hoping against hope for a miracle. Instead of a miracle, Jerry got a 37–14, opening-game pasting at Cincinnati, followed by a miserable home debut at the Vet, in which the Dallas Cowboys slaughtered the Eagles, 42–7, proving conclusively that Tose's Terrors could be just as bad in South Philadelphia as they had been in West Philadelphia. The biggest cheer of the day came early in the third period when the public address man said, "Ladies and gentlemen, the scoreboard clock is now functioning." Unfortunately, the Eagles never did function that afternoon.

The best thing you could say about the Eagles' offense in their first regular-season game at the Vet was that it seemed likely to solve the post-game traffic problem at the new stadium by getting the fans so disgusted that they began walking out at halftime. The danger was the ever-present possibility that some day the pre-game traffic would be so bad outside the stadium and the Eagles would be so bad inside the stadium that the people walking out early would bump into the people walking in late.

Those fans who stayed to the bitter end amused themselves by booing. The main targets were Pete Liske and Leroy Keyes. You had to feel sorry for Leroy, the no. 1 draft choice whose Eagles career never lived up to expectations. Midway in the fourth quarter he was belted in the mouth so hard that two of his teeth were loosened. There he was, stretched out on the Vet's green rug, while the Veterans Stadium faithful serenaded him with a rousing chorus of, "Goodbye Leroy, goodbye Leroy, goodbye Leroy, we hate to see you go." For those unfamiliar with the melody, it should be pointed out that the tune was the same as "Goodbye Jerry," which attained hit-parade status earlier in that long afternoon.

The week after that, the Eagles had the misfortune to play another home game. This time the opposition was provided by the San Francisco 49ers, who romped, 31–3. Jerry Williams didn't know it at the time, but his Eagles coaching career had ended.

The press conference called to announce the firing was a circus. "This was a joint decision between Retzlaff and myself," Leonard Tose said, but obviously it was nothing of the kind.

The longer the press conference went on, the more apparent it became that this was a hasty decision, an emotional decision, and, above all, a unilateral decision. Pete Retzlaff didn't order Jerry Williams' firing. Leonard Tose ordered it.

"I think Pete was coming to that decision," the owner said under stiff cross-examination. "I really do. But you'd better ask Pete."

The suggest was followed, and Pete Retzlaff did nothing to back up his boss' suggestion that the firing had been "a joint decision."

The first thing Pete said was, "I have no comment." Finally, he broke his silence by saying, "I think the world of Jerry. I think he's a fine football man. I feel . . ." At that point his voice broke. Recovering his composure, he added, "On the whole there's certainly no rejoicing on my part."

Retzlaff looked terrible. It had been his job to inform his friend that the axc had fallen. Early that morning Pete phoned Jerry's office and "asked him to step in."

The confrontation between the general manager and the coach he had been instructed to fire must have been terribly emotional. "I'm not very good at disguising my feelings," Retzlaff said.

Neither is Jerry Williams. He reminded Retzlaff that Tose had stated repeatedly that he would not, under any circumstances, fire a coach in mid-season. And he asked for a chance to save his job by being permitted to coach the Eagles against the Minnesota Vikings the following Sunday.

Retzlaff called Tose and told him that Williams wanted to talk to him. Another emotional confrontation, this one between the owner and the fired coach, ensued.

"I told him he was the first guy I ever fired," Tose said. "I told him, 'I'm sorry. I just think I owe it to the fans.' I think he asked for one more game. I told him, 'Jerry, if you won it, it wouldn't change my mind.' I didn't want to draw it out any more. I hope we do beat Minnesota, of course," Tose added. "You know how I feel about winning. It's blood with me."

Maybe so, but that was Jerry's blood he was spilling, and the ex-coach reacted bitterly, preparing a statement that said, in part, "Unfortunately, I was working for a man who is without courage and character."

Retzlaff had attempted to talk Williams out of taking that parting shot, but failed. "I didn't think it would serve anybody's purpose," Pete said. "He told me he felt this way. It was the way he felt it should be. . . . After all the time, the energy he directed [toward his job], to be canceled out, in effect, has to be a pretty severe emotional blow."

Tose, of course, was appalled. "Jerry says I have no courage and character," he responded. "I think it took a lot of courage and character to make this move. I'm disappointed [at Williams' reaction). No, that's a weak word. I'm shocked at what he said. This man has had complete cooperation. He was a party to every trade that's been made. Pete's been taking the rap on trades, but there was not a trade Jerry Williams couldn't have vetoed. . . . All we did was say to him, 'What do you want?' and try to do it for him. What we were, were fucking idiots."

To the best of my recollection, nobody in the Philadelphia press disputed the final evaluation.

Jerry Williams' bitterness didn't vanish quickly. The next morning *The Inquirer's* pro football writer, Gordon Forbes, and I met with him at the Penrose Diner, not far from Veterans Stadium, and the anger, the frustration, the bitterness were still there. "If I put into a business the hours I put into this football club, I wouldn't have to worry about my financial future," he said.

Leonard Tose had given him the opportunity to "resign," in return for which, Williams said, he would have received a year's salary. Jerry called it "a bribe."

"He wanted to come out smelling like a rose," the ex-coach said. "It was just an out-and-out bribe to get me to resign. . . . I wasn't invited to that press conference, but Pete said I had every right to be there if I wanted to be there. I went down at four, kind of in hopes that Tose would be there. He wasn't there yet, so I made my statement and went out. Out of respect for Ed [Khayat, Williams' successor as head coach], Pete and I left."

Jerry went home and watched film clips of Tose's press conference on television. That merely served to raise his anger another notch. "I feel justified in being to an extent vindictive because I don't feel people like Tose should be in football," Williams said. "If in some way I can contribute to the elimination of such ilk, I will feel that I have helped professional football. . . . It's a toy with him. Just a toy. Money has bought him everything. It bought him pseudo friends; it bought him a football franchise, which he is not capable of operating, and I was determined it was not going to buy me."

So Jerry Williams, a bright man, a hard-working man, a man with a law degree, refused to "resign" quietly. He went out screaming and kicking and attacking the owner who had axed him. The Williams-Tose affair shall always remain a Philadelphia standard by which nasty firings are measured.

                    *   *   *

If sad firings are your cup of tea, the tearful farewells of Flyers' coach Vic Stasiuk and Phillies' manager Frank Lucchesi rank high on the list. Both were immensely likeable men who loved their jobs. When the end came, it hit them like a ton of bricks.

Stasiuk was a totally honest, singularly dedicated man. He kept no secrets. What he thought was what he said. He was a throwback to an age when athletes got paid much less and, he felt, put out much more.

"Vic," Flyers' general manager Keith Allen said, "is a big, rough, honest guy. He's an idealist. He thinks the game has got to be played one way."

But his way didn't work in Philadelphia, nor in California afterwards. When Allen broke the bad news to him at the Spectrum, Stasiuk took it hard.

"I'm sure he was somewhat stunned," Keith said, and the tone of the general manager's voice indicated that he too had found the firing a most unpleasant experience. "Look," he said, "I don't want to knock this guy. He's the most dedicated individual I've ever run into in sports."

As tough as he was, Vic Stasiuk wasn't afraid to show his emotions, not even afraid to shed a few tears and talk about it later. "I cried [when Allen told him he was fired]," Vic said. "I sat in Keith's office, and I cried. I tried not to show it, but . . ."

But if Stasiuk's firing tugged at the heartstrings, Lucchesi's was worse.

He was a charismatic guy, this bouncy, little Italian with the heart of gold, who had spent a lifetime in the minor leagues helping kids, making friends, dreaming of the day when the big leagues would beckon. The Phillies may have had managers who won more games than Lucchesi, but never in the city's history had there been a manager who won over the fans as quickly as he did. The people seemed instantly to identify with this long-time minor leaguer who had fought his way to the top. Some would have considered managing the Phillies in the early '70s a thankless, virtually hopeless job; Frank Lucchesi considered it the greatest job in the world, a fantasy come to life. His enthusiasm and his joy were catching. Lucchesi had a way of communicating with people. He liked the press, and the press liked him; and as a result even before he arrived in town from his first spring training, the Philadelphia public felt they knew the man, and they liked what they knew. As long as he lives, Lucchesi will remember the opening of the 1970 baseball season at Connie Mack Stadium. They introduced him to the big crowd, and he popped out of the dugout in that jaunty way of his, a stranger in a big, supposedly tough city, and the people showered him with affection.

Lucchesi doffed his cap, and the applause grew louder; many of the people stood to welcome the new manager. Frank, a highly emotional man, was nonplussed. Here he was, in a place where the natives supposedly devoured Phillie managers for lunch, and they were cheering him before he'd managed a single game. His eyes filled with tears. It was a welcome he would never forget . . . a welcome that would make it extra difficult for him to accept his forced departure in July of 1972.

Before he left, Lucchesi must have signed a million autographs, made a zillion friends. If somebody wanted him to make a speech or visit a hospital or make a phone call to a sick kid, he did it . . . and seemed to love doing it. From a public-relations standpoint, the Phillies never had a manager who was more effective than Frank Lucchesi. At a time when the Phillies were in the early stages of a long, hard rebuilding program, he was a perfect man for the job. He was patient with the kids—most of whom he had managed in the minors—and he was great with the press and the fans.

At least one player who went on to become a National League All-Star owes his big-league career to Lucchesi and isn't reluctant to say so. Larry Bowa played for Lucchesi in the Double A Eastern League and gain in the Triple A Pacific Coast League. Frank loved the fiery, little shortstop. He understood him. And he was determined to stick with him.

There's every reason to believe that another manager, one who didn't know Bowa the way Lucchesi did, would have given up on the kid when his batting average seemed stuck somewhere below .200 in the early stages of his rookie year. Lucchesi kept playing him, kept building him up. And it paid off.

"I've worked for everything I have in baseball," Bowa said one day during 1981 spring training, "and I'll work when I get out of baseball, and I'll work when I'm getting ready to die. That's the way I am. I don't want anybody to do any favors for me. As far as my salary is concerned, every penny I've earned. Just one guy gave me a break, that's how I look at it. Frank Lucchesi gave me the biggest break of my life, and if I owe anything to anybody, I owe everything to Frank Lucchesi. If not for him, I wouldn't have had the opportunity to play in the big leagues. He gave me that opportunity. We were in last place, and he died with me, and I owe it to him. I've written him letters [to tell him]. And I sent him my World Series glove at the end of the [1980] season for his son. I'm breaking in a glove now because I gave him my 'gamer' that I used for three years. That's what the man means to me."

As much as Lucchesi meant to Bowa, the Phillies' job meant even more to Lucchesi. Under any circumstances, his firing would have been sad. The way the Phillies did it, it was brutal. Funny, you'd have thought with all the practice they'd had at getting rid of managers by 1972 they would know how to conduct a decent firing.

Naturally, Lucchesi had heard the rumors that began circulating as the long, losing summer of '72 commenced. One of those rumors seemed based on hard, cold fact. A most reliable source—it was, of all people, Dallas Green—told Allen Lewis of *The Inquirer* that a managerial change appeared to be in the offing. Lewis, who was no longer covering baseball, gave the information to his office, and his office notified the man who was covering the Phillies at the time.

That man was Bruce Keidan, and he wasted no time seeking out the truth. In the course of the investigation, a phone call was placed to the home of Dave Bristol, believed to be one of the leading candidates for the Phillies' job. Dave wasn't there, but a member of the family passed along the information that the Phillies had, indeed, been trying to get in touch with Bristol. The evidence seemed overwhelming: Lucchesi was out, and Bristol was in.

The Phillies were playing a Saturday-night home game, and Keidan informed Lucchesi that his paper had learned from an "unimpeachable source" that Frank was about to be fired and that Bristol was about to be hired. Lucchesi was jolted. Despite the rumors, he had forced himself to think that his old friend and new Phillies' general manager, Paul Owens, would never do such a thing to him. That night I spoke to Lucchesi long-distance from Eugene, Oregon, where I was covering the Olympic Trials. Frank was terribly upset; he didn't know what to do next.

"I told him [Keidan], 'I don't believe it,' " Lucchesi told me over the phone. "I don't think they'd do a thing like this. The last week or ten days they indicated I'd be all right, at least through the end of this season. I've been with the organization eighteen, nineteen years. I don't have to go in and ask them, 'Am I all right? Are you getting ready to fire me?' I don't have red blood in me. I have Phillie blood in me."

But Keidan's words haunted him. Lucchesi went through a sleepless Saturday night, and something that happened early Sunday morning didn't soothe his nerves.

The Phillies had been planning a Sunday-night cookout in Delaware. All members of the official family and their families were invited. For days Frank Powell, assistant to the Phillies' president, had made it a point to remind Frank of the gala event every time he saw him. "Don't forget Sunday night, Frank," Powell kept saying.

Then, as luck would have it, Lucchesi ran into Powell at the ball park on Sunday morning, following that sleepless Saturday night. This time, instead of reminding him for the umpteenth time about the cookout, Powell told Lucchesi that the affair had been called off. "Bob [Carpenter] can't make it," Powell explained. "And Paul's tied up."

Maybe it was Lucchesi's imagination, but Powell seemed a little nervous when he relayed that information. Now the manager was really worried. Perhaps it was all a coincidence that the Phillies had phoned Dave Bristol's home and that the cookout was canceled. On the other hand, there seemed to be a distinct possibility that the Phillies had decided to move their cookout to Monday with Frank Lucchesi as the main course.

The manager sought advice; I told him there was only one thing to do, only one way to put his mind at ease. Confront Owens with the latest batch of rumors and speculations and ask him, point-blank, if the decision had been made to fire the manager the following day. The worst that could happen was confirmation from Owens. At least then Frank would know; he wouldn't have to go through another night of twisting and turning and wondering. Lucchesi agreed. That was the thing to do.

Paul Owens and Dallas Green, then farm director of the Phillies, were in Paul's office that Sunday morning when Lucchesi walked in to find out if he was about to be replaced by Dave Bristol.

"I said, 'Look, I've known you fifteen, sixteen years, and you've never conned me,' " Frank told me a few minutes later, relating the conversation. " 'I'd like to know the story.' "

So Owens told him the "story." He told him Bristol had been contacted for information on an American League player the Phillies were trying to get in a waiver deal.

"Paul told me there's nothing going on," Lucchesi said over the phone shortly before the Sunday game began. "If something does happen now, it would be unbelievable. If it isn't true, you'll have a heartbroken man here."

For the first time in quite a while some of the spark had returned to Lucchesi's voice, some of the bounce was back in his walk. He was convinced that the rumors were all false, that there was, in fact, "nothing going on."

And so the next day, when the ax fell, Frank Lucchesi broke down and cried as he faced the press. His friend had fibbed to him, misled him. It was a rotten thing to do.

The Phillies, of course, said they had done nothing of the kind and played a little semantics game to prove it. "If I thought for a minute I'd lied to Frank Lucchesi, I'd feel worse than you do," Paul Owens told me. "I have to live with Paul Owens. I have to look at myself in the mirror in the morning."

Then why wasn't Frank told the truth Sunday morning when he sought it?

"He asked specifically about the Bristol thing," Dallas Green explained. "I said, 'Frank, we tried to contact Dave Bristol to find out about an American League player. That's the only reason. He's the only guy I know who would give us the information with no ax to grind. . . .' Frank said, 'Fine, that's all I want to know.'

"If Frank had come right out and asked, 'Am I going to be fired tomorrow or next week?' we'd probably have broken down."

"I could not have looked him in the eye [and lied]," Owens said.

"These two guys," Ruly Carpenter added, "there's no way they would have lied to Frank Lucchesi if he had asked them, 'Am I a goner?' "

Beautiful, right? All Frank Lucchesi had to do was ask the right question in the right way, and he would have been spared the agony of being built up Sunday for a brutal letdown on Monday. The Phillies' official version of the deception was ludicrous. Why did they think he was asking them about Bristol? Did they really think that Frank gave a damn whether the name of his successor was Bristol or Stengel or Durocher—or, as it turned out, Owens? Lucchesi was there to find out one thing: Did he still have his job? In the most literal sense, they may have given him an honest answer when he asked, "Am I going to be replaced by Dave Bristol tomorrow?" and they assured him there was nothing to it. But the truth was they intentionally deceived him into thinking the job was still his. Frank Lucchesi deserved something better than that.

*   *   *

If the Lucchesi firing had soap-opera overtones, how about the Eddie Khayat rehiring in 1971 that set the stage for the Eddie Khayat firing of 1972?

Khayat had taken over the 0-3 Eagles following Jerry Williams' stormy departure, and he proceeded to turn things around. After losses to the Minnesota Vikings and Oakland Raiders dropped the Eagles to 0-and-5, Khayat's team put together back-to-back victories over the New York Giants and the Denver Broncos, and the drive back to respectability had begun. When the '71 Eagles closed the season with a rush, winning four of their last five games, Leonard Tose was elated. The final victory—a 41-28 romp over the Giants at Yankee Stadium—was especially heartwarming to the owner. It seemed to him that he had been vindicated in his decision to change coaches, and as the score mounted against the Giants, the owner's disposition became brighter and brighter. By the third quarter, he was smiling. By the fourth quarter, his mind was made up. He was going to rehire his general manager and his coach for 1972, and he was going to do it immediately after the game.

"I thought we completely dominated the game," Tose beamed. "I said, 'Why not [make an immediate announcement]?' "

"Complete domination" was the key. That's what the owner wanted. Not just a victory. Not merely a 6-7-1 season. He wanted "complete domination" of the Giants, and he got it. So Pete Retzlaff and Eddie Khayat received an early Christmas present on that December 19 in the visiting locker room at Yankee Stadium.

"Pete did not know it and Eddie Khayat did not know it until I walked into the dressing room," Tose said. "I didn't tell them. . . . I didn't say a word. I just said to Pete, 'I want you down in the dressing room.' "

"If that's the way he wants to do it, fine," Retzlaff told the press, "but he told me on the way down."

OK, so maybe the owner let it slip out, but at least the news came as a surprise to Khayat and the players, whose cheers could be heard through the closed locker-room door. Before the door was opened, the players tossed Khayat into the shower and gave Retzlaff a game ball.

It was such a beautiful Christmas story, such a marvelously happy ending. What a shame 1971 had to be followed by 1972.

What happened to the '72 Eagles shouldn't happen to a dog. The '71 Eagles may have won six of eleven under Khayat, but the '72 Eagles won two of fourteen—and one of their losses was a 62–10 disaster at—yep, you guessed it—Yankee Stadium against the Giants. Talk about complete domination . . .

"The thing that ticks me off about this game," quipped Charlie Swift, the Eagles' radio play-by-play man at the time, "I had the Eagles and fifty."

"All but a handful quit," Khayat said. "That's a crying shame."

It didn't take a particularly astute observer to figure out that the jobs Khayat and Retzlaff had won at Yankee Stadium in '71 they had lost at the same site in '72. The fans were enraged over the poor performance of the '72 team. So was the owner. Retzlaff, a hero as a player, became a villain as a general manager. "This is the guy who had his uniform retired, who had a day at Franklin Field," said Jim Murray, Retzlaff's assistant who would go on to become a latter-day Eagles' GM. "He came in as a shining knight on a white horse."

And the horse had thrown him.

And some of his old fans had turned on him.

"Most of the hate calls I take are so way out, so vulgar, so sick," Murray said. "He doesn't know about half of them."

Retzlaff handled it all with great strength. He wasn't the type of man who went to pieces even when all around him were going to pieces.

"I thought I could help this organization, and I wanted to help this organization," he said as the dismal season neared its conclusion. "The Eagles and this whole town have done so much for me. It would have been a nice way to say thank you, to give them what they were looking for ever since 1961. I'm just sorry it hasn't worked out better in the past four seasons."

The Eagles' final loss—a one-pointer to the Cardinals at St. Louis in the last game of the season—was the first game that Leonard Tose failed to attend since he bought the club. Pete Retzlaff couldn't help but note the difference that a year had made. "Eddie was in the shower this time last year," the soon-to-be ex-general manager said.

This time they were both in hot water.

The twin firings, when it came on the Monday before Christmas, was virtually painless. Both victims were thoroughly prepared. There was no shouting, no name-calling. Eddie Khayat even went out of his way to reaffirm his love for Philadelphia shortly after the official announcement that he was no longer gainfully employed there. "I get the same feeling flying into Philadelphia," he said, "that a fella gets seeing an old girl friend he hasn't seen in a long time. I loved this town as soon as I hit it. People have been so good to me."

Leonard Tose echoed the friendly sentiments that were so much in evidence on this day. "They're fine young men," the owner said. "They're going to use their offices while they're looking for jobs. Same for Pete. Pete's not cleaning out his desk, anything like that."

It was all so pleasant, so friendly, so civil, so different from the previous Eagles' firing.

"Well," Leonard Tose asked when it was over, "did we do it professionally?"

*   *   *

If the Retzlaff-Khayat firing was among the friendliest in the city's history, the 76ers' firing of general manager Don DeJardin was surely the most reluctant.

DeJardin, a West Point graduate, was honest and trustworthy and as straight-arrow as a person could be. In short, he wasn't at all cut out to be a general manager in the crazy, mixed-up world of professional basketball.

DeJardin's boss, 76ers' owner Irv Kosloff, was honest and trustworthy and patient—just about the nicest guy who ever owned a pro team. Kos simply hated to hurt anybody. If you were trying to find somebody who was the extreme opposite of George Steinbrenner, you wouldn't have to look past Irv Kosloff. In short, he wasn't at all cut out to own a professional basketball team.

The screwy thing about DeJardin's firing in September of 1973, months after that awful 9-and-73 season had ended, was that Don almost surely could have stayed on as GM for an indefinite period if he had been willing to work without a contract. But

Don forced the issue and wound up forcing himself out of the NBA, which was a pretty good idea at that. DeJardin currently resides in Pasadena, where he is a highly successful business executive. Typically, he harbors not the slightest bitterness over his Philadelphia experience, as unbelievable as it was.

"I learned to consider Philadelphia a great sports town," he said. "I think the fans are terrific. I don't think you could get a better sports climate anywhere than you get in Philadelphia. I think any sports franchise given a modicum of success would be a successful franchise in this city."

DeJardin's last 76er team didn't enjoy that "modicum of success," largely as a result of those terrible draft decisions made before he arrived.

It's only fair to note that Don was in part responsible for the rapid improvement of the 76ers in the years immediately following his departure. For instance, the final no. 1 draft pick of the DeJardin regime was Doug Collins, who developed into an NBA All-Star until injuries cut him down. And it was DeJardin who had the foresight to grab NBA draft rights to George McGinnis, when the latter was still playing for Indiana in the ABA. Although McGinnis didn't remain for long as a 76er star, his signing helped to give the team credibility in its fight back to the top.

Don DeJardin was that rare individual who had the ability to place things—even such a highly personal, unpleasant thing as his own unexpected firing—into perspective. He possessed a delightful sense of humor, made all the more delightful by the fact that he could laugh at himself as well as at others.

A few hours after his firing DeJardin entered the lobby of a City Line Avenue Motel to keep an appointment with a writer. He was calm and smiling and . . . well, he was the Don DeJardin his friends had come to know so well. Those who never really got to know him in Philadelphia missed a treat.

It wasn't until that day that DeJardin had learned, for the first time, that Kosloff was thinking of firing him. For days the general manager had tried to finalize things with the owner, and for days Kos put him off. Finally, they met face-to-face, and DeJardin laid it on the line. "I said to him, 'Look, if you're not satisfied with the job I've done, all you have to say is, you're finished. I'm not going to punch you in the nose. I'll just shake hands and leave.' "

Still the owner had delayed making a decision. Furthermore, he avoided seeing DeJardin for the next few days . . . or even talking to him on the phone. Then, on a Sunday morning, Don reached his boss at home, and Kos told him he'd decided to make a change. Clearly, the decision pained Kosloff more than it pained DeJardin.

The press conference called by the 76ers to announce Don De-Jardin's firing was truly a classic. The man who had been fired looked so calm, so cool, so poised. The man who had done the firing looked so miserable, so uncertain.

Kos *was* uncertain. The more he talked at that press conference, the more it became obvious that he hadn't wanted to fire DeJardin. In fact, the owner readily conceded that he wouldn't have fired Don if the general manager had been willing to go on without a contract.

"Do you mean if Don hadn't forced the issue, he might have gone on being your general manager for the entire season and perhaps for seasons to come?" a writer asked.

"That's right," Irv Kosloff replied.

"Do you have any regrets about firing him?"

"I do."

"Do you think you might have made a mistake?"

"I might have."

"Then it's possible after you spend the next month or so looking for a general manager you might come to the conclusion that Don DeJardin was a pretty good man, after all, and that you could do worse?"

Kos nodded. "A lot worse," he said.

Don DeJardin found it all highly amusing. He knew Irv Kosloff to be a genuinely nice man, so nice that he had resisted De-Jardin's attempts to fire Roy Rubin for a remarkably long time, considering the record.

No fired general manager ever left with more class, or with a more genuine smile on his face, or with a better sense of humor.

"Maybe what they'll do is have a 'General Manager of the Week' contest," Don suggested laughingly when the press conference was over.

It seemed like a great idea, one that fit in perfectly with all those other Philadelphia jokes. Let's see, first prize would be one week as a general manager of the 76ers. Second prize would be two weeks.

12

The Ozark Years

BASEBALL MANAGERS HAVE IT TOUGH. THEY MAKE A MOVE—ANY move and a guy sitting in the top row of the upper deck knows about it and, if it doesn't pan out, complains about it. "What's that dummy doin', putting up Whoozis to hit for Whatsis? Who told him he could manage?"

Football is different. There's a mystique, a mystery about the game that the average Joe can't quite fathom. Why should he? Even the coaches don't know what went wrong on the critical play until they've studied the films. A man succeeds as a football coach, and he almost automatically qualifies as a near genius. Merely to understand football lingo a person has to take a four-year graduate course or, failing in that, spend a minimum of three Monday nights listening to Howard Cosell.

Even hockey has a certain aura about it. To the uneducated eye, it may look like a bunch of hooligans running into each other on a skating rink in pursuit of a small chunk of vulcanized rubber, but a team starts winning and immediately we hear about "the system" that made it all possible. Freddie Shero became famous as the brain behind "a system" that mere ticket-buying mortals couldn't be expected to understand. It wasn't until years later that people began to suspect that Freddie didn't really understand it either.

Ah, but baseball is different. Anybody who knows first base from left field is convinced that he (or she) can make moves at least as well as the poor guy who's paid to do it. That's one of the great charms of the sport. It's all out in the open for the world to see . . . and second-guess.

Occasionally a manager comes along who builds a reputation

for having a higher-than-average mentality. Gene Mauch comes readily to mind. Ask baseball people to name the brainiest managers of the last couple of decades, and surely Mauch's name would appear high on the list, if not at the very top. And yet the fact remains that Gene Mauch has never finished no. 1, never so much as won a division title. All of which lends support to the theory that baseball managers don't need brains to win, merely talent.

If Philadelphians—and the Philadelphia press—marveled at Mauch's brainpower, they had very little difficulty keeping their admiration for the IQ's of latter-day Phillies managers under control. One problem was, two of the men who led the team through the rags-to-near-riches '70s led the league in malaprops.

Now I'm going to be honest with you, as Frank Lucchesi would say. There's nothing terrible about malaprops. Amos 'n' Andy made a fortune out of them. Besides, who ever said that a man had to major in English to be a successful baseball manager? Sparky Anderson, who did a lot of winning with the Reds and is still recognized as one of the game's foremost managers, piles up more double negatives than Pete Rose does doubles.

Nobody really minded that Lucchesi, a most devoted and likeable man, occasionally used the wrong word. In fact, there was something genuinely amusing about listening to a big-league manager say, in all sincerity, "Nobody's going to make a scrapgoat out of me." Frank was wrong, of course. The Phillies did make a scrapgoat out of him, but we've covered that already.

Looking back on it now, the Lucchesi years performed a great service: They prepared Philadelphians for the Ozark years. Frank was a jolting contrast to the still-sharp Mauch image that lingered on long after Mauch was fired in '68. Gene was highly quotable . . . when he wanted to be. If he didn't want to be, if somebody in the press aroused his anger, Mauch was entirely capable of refusing to talk to the guy for days, even weeks. Lucchesi, on the other hand, was cooperative almost to a fault. When he said his door was always open, he meant it. Few managers ever did a better job of communicating with the press, and through the press the fans, than Frank Lucchesi. He even had his own pre-game radio show in 1971. What's that you say? Lots of managers have radio shows. True enough. But Lucchesi had a one-man show. There was no announcer asking him questions, merely a producer, Gene Kirby, to keep him posted on the time and perhaps slip a piece of paper in front of him with a word or a key phrase designed to remind the star of the show of the next topic.

"The Skipper Lucchesi Show" was one of its kind because the star was one of a kind—warm and friendly, a good talker who genuinely liked people and absolutely loved his job.

"He would say, 'This is Skipper Lucchesi. . . .'," recalled Gene Kirby, now an administrative assistant with the Montreal Expos, "and off he'd go. He could talk, no question about it. We'd do it in his office, or maybe we'd go down the right-field line in Wrigley Field or in the corner of the dugout. 'What'll I do if I have to kill time?' he said one day. I said, 'Frank, you never kill time on radio, you *use* time. If you kill it, what about the people listening?' He always remembered that."

The warmth, the sincerity of the man came through on "The Skipper Lucchesi Show." And if an occasional malaprop came through as well, it merely added to the human quality of the Phillies manager. But if Frank rated high in the malaprop league, Danny Ozark made a determined bid to wrest away the title in the seven years that followed, coming up with such classics as, "This thing is beyond my apprehension," and, on an occasion when team morale was being questioned, "Morality is not an issue at this time."

Gosh, Danny was fun, in his way.

There will never be anything to match the Ozark years. The Phillies were the joke of the National League East when he arrived. Before he left, they were three-time champions of the National League East . . . and yet when something went wrong, as it invariably did, the joke was always on Danny.

There may never have been a big-league baseball manager who accomplished more, in terms of wins and losses, than Danny Ozark did in his years with the Phillies . . . and received less credit for the accomplishment. Maybe it was the way he looked—the sad, hound-dog expression he usually wore—that hurt his image. Or the way he talked and the things he said; sooner or later, it seemed, Danny would always put his foot in his mouth. Whatever the reasons, almost from the day he arrived in

Philadelphia after a lengthy career in the Dodgers organization, Ozark was generally perceived as a man who wasn't smart enough to manage a big-league ball club. That perception, of course, was ridiculous because it was based on the fallacious assumption that a big-league manager had to be smart. What nonsense. The only truly smart manager in the history of major-league baseball was Connie Mack, who had the foresight to own the team he managed. The rest of the managers come and go, come and go in a never-ending game of musical chairs. Danny Ozark's greatest claim to fame is that he came and stayed as long as he did.

It wasn't easy. From day one, Ozark was on the defensive. For weeks—months even—speculation on the identity of the new Phillies manager had centered on Dave Bristol and Jim Bunning and Richie Ashburn, all names that meant something to Philadelphia baseball fans. The name *Ozark* meant nothing except to those who traveled to Arkansas a lot by air.

If Danny's arrival produced more dismay than acclaim, the Phillies front office had to accept some of the blame. It was Paul Owens, after all, who had led other candidates—and the Philly press—to believe that someone with a bigger name than *Ozark* would be managing the 1973 Phillies.

One possibility was Bunning, who had just completed his first season of managing in the Phillies farm system. Jim's year at Double A Reading had been somewhat rocky, but his timing seemed perfect. The Phillies were searching for a manager. There had been a mid-season shakeup; first Owens had moved up to replace John Quinn as general manager, then Owens had fired Lucchesi and taken over himself as interim field manager.

You could make a strong argument that Bunning wasn't ready for the job, that one season in a Double A league wasn't enough. Maybe it wasn't—and yet look at some of the inexperienced managers who were handed big-league jobs. Joe Torre's first managing job at any level was with the New York Mets. Jeff Torborg got his start with the Cleveland Indians. And for a few days in late 1972, Jim Bunning thought lightning was going to strike him.

The Carpenters—Bob and Ruly—Paul Owens, and Dallas Green met with Bunning at the end of the Phillies' dismal '72 season. It was Jim's first formal interview for a big-league managing job.

"They asked me what I would do with the ball club," Bunning said. "They asked me who I would trade, what players I would retain, who I thought were the guts of our ball club in Philadelphia."

The session seemed to go well. When it was over, Dallas Green, then the Phillies farm director, called his old friend into the office and told him that Owens had remarked, "Bunning gave all the right answers." Owens even wondered aloud, Green told Bunning, if Dallas had helped him bone for the "exam."

"He accused Dallas of prepping me," Bunning said. "Hell, Dallas didn't even know the questions. Paul had prepared them himself. 'Would you trade [twenty-seven-game winner] Steve Carlton?' I said, 'Of course. If I can strengthen my ball club by trading Steve Carlton, I'll trade him.' "

The hottest rumor at the time, however, was that Dave Bristol, former manager of the Cincinnati Reds and Milwaukee Brewers, was the leading candidate for the Phillies job. Bristol, in fact, was interviewed in Philadelphia and, like Bunning, came away thinking he had given all the right answers.

The days passsed; the 1972 World Series between Oakland and Cincinnati began. Bunning lived across the river from Cincinnati, in Fort Thomas, Kentucky. It seemed to him like a good time to find out where he stood. Once again, he contacted Dallas Green. "I want to talk to Paul Owens, one on one," Jim told him.

The meeting was arranged. They met in Owens' suite at the Netherland-Hilton Hotel in downtown Cincinnati. Typically, Bunning wasted little time getting to the point. "I asked him flat out, 'Well, what's it look like?' " Jim recalled.

Owens, an outgoing, friendly man, looked him in the eye. "You're *that* close," he said, and he held his thumb and forefinger a fraction of an inch apart.

"That's good enough for me," Bunning replied. "I'm not going to worry about it any more. It's up to you now."

Jim Bunning left the general manager's suite thinking that he really was "that close" to becoming manager of the Philadelphia Phillies. What he didn't know was that Dave Bristol came away from his meeting with Paul Owens thinking that he too was "that close."

"Everybody," Bunning said years later, "was 'that close.' How close is close unless you actually get it? I found out later I had no chance. They did their homework well. They deceived everybody." Jim discovered the extent of that deception when the World Series returned to Cincinnati for the sixth and seventh games. Ray Kelly, a writer for *The Philadelphia Bulletin*, had talked to Owens in Oakland, and Owens—"in an unsober mood," Bunning said—"told him there was no way Jim Bunning was ever going to manage for him."

Owens had also talked to Ralph Bernstein of the Associated Press in the World Series' hospitality room bar in the basement of the Oakland Coliseum, triggering an AP story that claimed Dave Bristol had the job. "Owens' exact words were, 'In my mind Dave Bristol is my manager,' " Bernstein said. "Later, just to be sure, I double-checked with him [Owens], and he repeated it."

Bernstein phoned Bunning to tell him the news and to get his reaction. "You know more than I do," Jim told him. "I don't think you're right, but you go ahead and write whatever you want." Bernstein, confident that he had his information from the best possible source, the general manager of the Phillies, wrote the story. He too had been deceived.

When word finally leaked out that the new Phillies manager was Danny Ozark, a long-time minor-league manager and big-league coach, the overwhelming reaction was, "Who's he?" Ozark's name had never been seriously mentioned in the press speculation, even though Phillies executive vice-president Bill Giles had told at least one writer, weeks before, that he had "a candidate for the job you'll love—Danny Ozark." Apparently, Giles did his bit to help sell Ozark to the rest of the Phillies front office.

Ruly Carpenter, who had just taken over control of the club from his dad, probably wasn't that hard to sell. He was impressed by organization men, especially when they came from the Dodgers organization. A Bristol or a Bunning might rock the boat. A Danny Ozark, from all indications, would be a company man through and through.

The two men who believed they were "that close" to the job, Bunning and Bristol, found out that Ozark had it the evening before the official announcement. I phoned Bristol at his North Carolina home to tell him. "That can't be right," Dave replied. "I've got the job." Bus Saidt, a sportswriter from Trenton, called Bunning to inform him that an announcement was imminent and that Paul Owens had indicated to the press that the new Phillies manager had already been informed. "Have you been notified?" Saidt asked. "No," answered Bunning.

Bristol promptly called Owens to ask him if what he had been told by a Philadelphia writer was true. Paul acknowledged that it was. The following morning Owens phoned Bunning from the airport in Tampa to let him know that Danny Ozark was the man. "I wished him well," Jim said.

Ozark needed all the good wishes he could get. He was taking over a club that had lost ninety-seven games the year before, a club that hadn't finished higher than fifth in six years. And he could hardly be called the people's choice for the job. Still, it wasn't his fault that he had been chosen over Dave Bristol, Jim Bunning, and the rest. It wasn't his fault that Paul Owens, with his penchant for telling people what they want to hear, had led two others to believe that the job was theirs. Danny Ozark had the job now. And he would keep it longer than anybody thought possible.

Gene Mauch had charisma. When he entered a room, you could feel the electricity. Frank Lucchesi had charisma too; another kind, to be sure, but charisma just the same. To meet Frank was to like him, to want to see him succeed. That ovation he received *before* his first game as Phillies manager was a tribute to the Lucchesi brand of charisma.

Danny Ozark had no charisma. He was just a big, slow-moving man who looked and acted pretty much the same, win or lose. Eventually, there were some moments when his emotions spilled over; no man can manage a Phillies team for nearly seven years—and deal with the Philadelphia press and the Philadelphia fans that long—without snapping occasionally. But when you first met Danny Ozark, it was hard to tell how he felt. Lucchesi wore his emotions on his sleeve. Ozark kept his deep inside. He was forty-eight when he got the Phillies job; he had waited years for the opportunity to manage a big-league team, and yet when the good news came Danny took it in stride. "When they called me," he said the day after the press conference at which he was introduced, "I wasn't overly excited. I didn't jump up and say, 'Whoopee!' "

Danny Ozark was simply not the jump-up-and-say-whoopee type. But if he kept his emotions inside, his true feelings were seldom a secret. If you talked to Danny long enough, you usually found out how he really felt. The man was open—sometimes too open for his own good. As the years went by, it was difficult not to like the man—unless you were a member of his pitching staff. One of the major criticisms leveled at Ozark was that he didn't know how to handle pitchers. What made the criticism serious was that it was mostly his own pitchers who leveled it.

For a while it appeared that Ozark's first season might also be his last. To nobody's great surprise the '73 Phillies finished exactly where the '72 and '71 Phillies finished: dead last. But if the standings were no great surprise, the way the club was playing in early September came as a severe disappointment. After back-to-back 11–5 and 12–0 losses to Montreal, criticism grew . . . and some of that criticism came from the general manager of the Phillies.

The team was in New York when Paul Owens let his feelings be known late one night in the hotel bar. He asked me what I thought of Ozark's managing, and I told him I had serious doubts. He answered that he had them too. The conversation went on and on; Owens made some strong, anti-Ozark remarks, but under the circumstances I assumed they were off the record. The next day I went to his room, reminded him of the conversation, and asked him if any of it was for publication. Paul said it was, and he reiterated most of what he had said the previous night, and then asked me when it was going to be printed. I told him I planned to write the story before the game that night and, because some of the quotes seemed so strong, I offered to let him read them before I sent them in to make sure they were totally accurate and expressed the thoughts he was trying to convey. We agreed to meet outside the press room at Shea Stadium at a designated time, early in the ball game. Paul read the story, and reread the story, and nodded and said, "Yes, that's fine."

So the column got in the paper. In it Owens called Ozark "a sound fundamentalist, a good baseball man," but suggested that he had failed to establish a rapport, a line of communication with his players. "If I decide a change would help, I think it would be my responsibility to make a change," Paul said. "That's why I get paid—to make decisions. It's got to be my baby. I'm not afraid of the responsibility or the criticism. I'm not going to pass the buck. I want to win not for Paul Owens, but for these kids [the players, many of whom had come up through the farm system under

Owens' guiding hand] and for the people we've surrounded ourselves with. I want to get the best out of these kids. . . .

"There's a lot of pressure in managing today," Owens went on. "Kids are more intelligent today. We, as management, have to change with the times. It's instinct. Some people have it; some people don't. We have to evaluate if every ounce, so to speak, was gotten out of this ball club —physically, emotionally, psychologically. We've got to be objective about it. . . . In the position we're in I can't be concerned with personalities. I had to fire Frank Lucchesi, who I loved like my own brother. Maybe better than my own brother. Sometimes you have to do things to help the organization."

Owens said he and Ruly Carpenter had met with Ozark and discussed some of the problems. "I think I'm like a guy waiting for a miracle," the general manager said. "Like a guy when it hasn't rained for thirty-eight days, waiting for a downpour. He's got three weeks [to the end of the season]. You have to be fair. When you lead, you *have* to be fair. I would rather be fair with him and get my own head cut off."

The more he talked, the more plain it became that he was less than thrilled over his manager's first-year performance in dealing with his players. "I told Danny," he said, " 'I've talked to you about little things during the season. If you don't know I'm talking about communicating [with players], if you don't understand that, then *we're* not communicating."

The Phillies were last, sixteen games under .500 when Owens spoke those strong words to, and about, his manager. They finished last, twenty games under .500. Yet a week before the season ended, the general manager announced that Danny would be back. "I didn't lie to you," he told me. "I tried to be honest. There was a problem, and I was investigating. If I feel my car's not running right, I've got to find out if I've got a loose plug. All I know is, I kept my eye on everything, and after two weeks I was satisfied."

Yeah, Paul, but how about the communications problem? "I honestly felt in my mind that he had made a complete turnaround in that area," Owens said. "I had three, four players come to me and say, 'He's changed. He changed completely.' If a man shows me he's got the gumption to take the bull by the horns to make a 100 percent turnabout —well, in my opinion he answered his own situation. This is what I was waiting for, what I was hoping for."

The feeling persisted that Ruly Carpenter had jumped to Ozark's defense in those difficult, early months and that the owner may not have been too pleased with Owens' critical comments in the press. If so, nobody would admit it.

One of the strangest things about the episode was this: On the day my column appeared filled with all those quotes that Paul Owens had read, and reread, and approved, a writer from another Philadelphia paper told me that the general manager had accused me of misquoting him. Such are the games that the Phillies brass and the Philly press play.

For all the negative things that have been written and said about Ozark, the man grew on you after a while. He worked hard. He was sincere. He was honest. And he frequently left you with a smile on your face. Nothing wrong with that.

There was no pretense about Danny. If you met him, and you didn't know what he did for a living, you'd never guess that he was a big-league manager. One spring he and his wife stayed at a motel on heavily traveled Route 19 in Clearwater, Florida—the same motel where some of the minor leaguers stayed. There was nothing wrong with the place, but it wasn't where you'd expect to find the manager of the Phillies staying. Also, many big-league managers go to fancy, high-priced restaurants. Danny's idea of a night out during spring training was to take his wife, Ginny, to The Toast of the Town, a moderately priced chain operation on Route 19. Nothing wrong with that either. Danny simply didn't feel comfortable with the big-money types. He'd spent a lot of years living on a minor-league salary. He came to the Phillies as a down-to-earth, forty-eight-year-old man. He left as a down-to-earth, fifty-five-year-old man, unspoiled by his time in the big-league spotlight.

It seemed incredible at the time, but Danny Ozark began the 1979 season—his last in Philadelphia—as the dean of National League managers. "You know," he said that spring, "I never came to realize it until Shenk [Phillies publicist Larry Shenk] said something about it. I told him, 'I don't know if that's good or that's bad,' But after being fired [by the press] for seven years, I guess it's not too damn bad."

No. In fact, it was pretty damn good.

It should be pointed out that Danny and Ginny Ozark worked very well as a team. Surely, one of the fondest—and most amusing—memories of the Ozark years is that of Danny's better half stuffing the All-Star ballot boxes with Phillie votes . . . and getting Danny to help her.

The 1978 "election" for All-Star starters was Ginny's big push. Who can ever forget that trip to Chicago in early July when she arrived with a giant box of ballots? For years we had been hearing about rigged elections in Cook County. Ginny Ozark, with Danny's ever-loving help, gave us a rare opportunity to catch a glimpse of it first hand. If only Mayor Daley had still been alive, how proud he would have been. There, inside a green-carpeted hotel room, those two master ballot-stuffers, Ginny and Danny Ozark, were hard at work, punching out holes next to such names as Larry Bowa and Greg Luzinski and Garry Maddox and Bake McBride and Bob Boone and Mike Schmidt.

"My wife's up there punching cards in the hotel right now," Danny said that late morning in July as he sat in the visiting manager's office at Wrigley Field. "You oughtta see my room. She's been punching out so many All-Star ballots on that green rug it looks like I've got dandruff."

Danny, I suspect, had come to the ball park extra early that day just to get a reprieve from ballot-punching. You might say he was punched out. Let it be recorded, though, that his form was excellent. "What you do," explained Danny, "you take a ballpoint pen and you start punching. I'm getting pretty good at it. I can do about fifteen at a time."

When a clubhouse visitor wondered why the manager of a big-league club would spend his free hours on the road sticking a ballpoint pen through All-Star ballots, Danny was quick to explain. "My wife makes me do it," he said. "She gives me a stack, and I'll finish it."

Never in the course of history had Chicago seen a political machine to rival Ginny and Danny Ozark. Richard Nixon thought he had it tough there in 1960, but even a Republican had a better chance to get a vote in Chicago in November of '60 than a non-Phillie had of getting one from Ginny and Danny in that Chicago hotel room in July of '78.

Don't get the idea that Danny Ozark spent all his waking hours punching holes with ballpoint pens. The man was always on the lookout for ways to win baseball games too. Just because

Danny didn't have the image of a Rhodes scholar is no reason to think that he couldn't dream up some clever trick plays with which to befuddle the opposition.

Larry Bowa will always remember one of Danny's 1978 brainstorms. "A goofy play," the manager termed it, and he was right because it put his All-Star shortstop in the unenviable position of running top speed toward a man swinging a bat.

The Phillies had a 4–3 lead over the Mets in New York when Ozark tried to steal a run with runners on first and third and two out in the top of the seventh. Although Jose Cardenal, the batter, had a two-strike count —and therefore would have to swing if the next pitch was over the plate —Danny put on his unique version of the double steal. Bowa, the runner on third, and Jerry Martin, the runner on first, were supposed to break. Pinpoint timing was of the essence. The idea was to startle the pitcher—a lefty named Paul Siebert—who would see Martin out of the corner of his eye and throw to first, thereby giving Bowa a clear shot to swipe home. "We worked it in spring training," Danny explained. On this day, however, it didn't work. Martin broke too late; instead of throwing to first base, Siebert threw to the plate. Or, as Ozark put it so eloquently after the game, "We flubbed the dub a little bit."

As flubbed dubs go, this one was a classic. Poor Bowa. There he was, running full speed ahead, all the while knowing he had a reasonable chance of having his head dented by a line drive. "I could hurt Bowa," Cardenal was quick to point out. "It is very dangerous. Very, very dangerous. When I swung, I turned around and Bowa is ten feet from me. I [would] hate to be that guy at third base."

"It was scary," confirmed Bowa.

Ozark was frightened too when he saw the Mets' pitcher come to the plate, instead of throw to first the way he was supposed to do. (That was the trouble with the play; Danny had only worked on it with the Phillies in spring training. The Mets didn't know anything about it.)

"A lot of negative thoughts were going through my mind when that thing was going on," Ozark said. "I may see it tonight when I go to sleep. I think I shut my eyes when I saw what was happening."

By then, it was in the hands of fate. "The ball was right there," Cardenal said. "I had to swing."

Are you wondering how Larry Bowa could keep running at a time like that? Ozark was nice enough to explain.

"Something like that comes up, when you're trying to execute a play," he said, "and I think all fear goes out of a runner's mind. He wants to win so badly at that moment that the guy's life isn't that important."

No kidding, that's what the man said.

Oh yeah, let the record show that Jose Cardenal fouled the pitch into the first-base stands; Larry Bowa was saved. It can be assumed that the next time Danny Ozark tries that play he'll make sure there's a less valuable player on third base.

If poking fun at Ozark became a popular pastime, Danny was partly responsible. Some of the things he said, some of the statements he made, left him wide open for attack. Take, for example, Ozark's announced decision to switch his All-Star third-baseman Mike Schmidt to second base in 1979.

"I think," Danny said, "Mike Schmidt is going to turn the double play as well as anyone in baseball. Give him two weeks [at second base] in spring training, and you won't be able to tell the difference between Mike Schmidt and Joe Morgan."

That statement was so patently absurd that you had to assume Ozark dreamt it up in late January of '79, just before the Phillies' annual press caravan, to create some controversy and some headlines. Common sense told you that a team with the best left side of the infield in all of baseball wasn't about to break it up, particularly when that meant putting its no. 1 home run hitter on second base, where his oft-injured knees would be fair game for anybody trying to break up a double play.

Ah, but Danny stuck to his story as the press caravan rolled into Princeton, New Jersey. Mike Schmidt, he assured the sellout throng, was going to be a helluva second baseman.

In the audience that noon happened to be Jack Martin, who played some shortstop for the Phillies in 1914. He had listented to Ozark's profound comments, and now this ninety-one-year-old man was asked to say a few words. Presumably, the Phillies brass expected him to tell everybody how happy he was to be there—or anywhere at that age—perhaps say a few kind words about the

Phillies and sit down. Uh-uh. Jack Martin, it turned out, was a pretty sharp, if well aged, cookie.

Turning to stare the surprised Ozark squarely in the snout, Martin referred to the move the manager had so eloquently described and said, "The hell with that. You ain't gonna make that change, are you?"

Danny was momentarily speechless. As accustomed as he was to dealing with critics, he wasn't about to talk back to one who'd been around for over nine decades. Still, when the luncheon was over, Ozark insisted that he wasn't kidding about moving Schmidt to second base.

"All right, Danny," a writer said, "what do you think the odds are that you'll open the season with Mike Schmidt at second base?"

Ozark pondered the question for a moment or so. "About 50-50," he finally said with a straight face. "But," he added, "If you ask me if we have a chance to make a trade for a second baseman [before the season], I'd say we have a 60-40 chance."

Figure that one out, sports fans. A 50-50 chance that Schmidt would open the season at second, and a 60-40 chance that the Phillies would trade for a new second baseman before the season began. How comforting it was to know that two months before opening day Danny Ozark's computer-like brain was already in mid-season form. P.S.: The 60-40 shot came in. Three weeks later, the Phillies acquired Manny Trillo from the Cubs.

Some of Ozark's moves seemed to make as little sense as some of his words. But just when you thought he didn't know what he was doing, just when you were ready to lower the boom on some outrageous piece of Ozarkian strategy, Danny would come out smelling like a rose.

For example, there was the time in 1977 when a Chicago Cubs lefthander named Willie Hernandez was pitching in relief, trying to protect a three-run lead against the Phillies with two out in the top of the eighth. The Phillies had a runner on third and Jay Johnstone scheduled to bat. In the visitors' dugout Dave Johnson, his batting helmet already in place, stood with a bat in his hands, waiting for Danny Ozark to tell him to pinch-hit.

Everybody in Wrigley Field that day knew Ozark was going to send up a righthanded pinch hitter for the lefthanded-swinging Johnstone. It was an obvious move. Johnstone practically never was permitted to hit against lefthanders; no way Ozark would let him hit now.

Except he did. And Johnstone confounded the percentage-players by hitting a two-run homer. By allowing Jay to bat, Ozark had Dave Johnson available for ninth-inning pinch-hit duty, and Johnson hit the homer that tied the game, setting the stage for an eleventh-inning Phillie victory. Of such moves and non-moves are geniuses made.

And why, pray tell, did Danny Ozark permit Jay Johnstone to hit against the lefthanded Hernandez with the Phillies three runs behind in the eighth? Because, the manager explained later with a straight face, Jay had not glanced back toward the dugout but rather had walked straight up to the plate from the on-deck circle. "I don't like a hitter to look back to see if somebody else is coming up," Danny said. "If he'd done that—if there'd been doubt in his mind—I might've taken him out."

That logic seemed so unassailable that the writers switched their attention to Johnstone in an effort to find out why, in fact, he hadn't glanced back toward the Phillies dugout to see if a pinch hitter was on his way to the plate. "Didn't you think you were coming out?" Jay was asked. "On this club," he replied, "I learned to give up that [thinking] a long time ago. There are so many surprises here you learn to roll with the punches."

If Danny Ozark, performing solo, provided a few smiles, then the comedy team of Ozark and Johnstone was good for some good, old-fashioned belly laughs. They were baseball's answer to the Odd Couple, always needling each other, always breaking up the audience. Next to Crosby and Hope, or maybe Martin and Lewis, Ozark and Johnstone might have been the funniest comedy team ever to hit the big time. Excuse me. Better make that billing Johnstone and Ozark. Jay would never forgive me.

As luck would have it—I'll leave it up to you to decide if the luck was good or bad—Ozark and Johnstone were reunited on the Los Angeles Dodgers following Danny's Philly firing. "Danny and I probably talked more the last two weeks than the five years I was in Philly," Jay said in the spring of '80. "We've had some good conversations."

Sadly, those conversations are not available on eight-track or cassette. They'd be worth a fortune.

"Aah," said Jay, "we always got along. He just used me for whatever purpose he did. I knew that. He knew it. We were kidding the other day. He said, 'You know, all those people still think we never got along.' I said, 'Yeah, Danny, I know.' He said, 'Yeah, and they're right.' "

Funny stuff. I can hardly wait till they make their first movie.

As low key as Danny Ozark was, there were times during his Philly years when he blew his top. On one memorable Sunday afternoon in 1976, Danny actually threatened to punch a Philadelphia writer. Some managers will do anything to get the players on their side.

Seriously, though, Ozark's blowup was so uncharacteristic that it deserves a closer look. After all, that very spring he had said, "I'm not going to punch a guy in the nose or throw him out of my clubhouse because I dislike him because of what he wrote about me. Certainly I don't like a lot of things that are said about me, but the next day I come out to the ball park and forget it."

On this day, though, Danny exploded. Not surprisingly, Richie Allen was at the bottom of the eruption. Ozark had never really wanted Allen on his Phillies ball club; when it appeared the Phillies might get him back in the winter of 1974–75, Danny made no effort to hide his feelings.

"I want to win badly," Ozark said at the winter meetings in New Orleans. "I want to win as badly as all Philadelphia wants to win. But there would have to be a lot of sacrifices made by me and by the players on this club if we got Richie Allen. We'd have to shut our eyes to a lot of things."

Danny was merely echoing the sentiments of Sparky Anderson, among others, who said when asked if he wanted Allen on his club: "If my head's going to roll, I want to be the one who rolls it."

When the Phillies announced during spring training of '75 that they had given up on acquiring Allen, Ozark was visibly elated. When a Philadelphia writer told him that it might be the biggest break of his Phillie career, Danny broke out laughing and threw a bear hug around the guy. "I'm not going to say I'm happy," he said, but he didn't have to say it. His actions said it for him.

Then, lo and behold, the Phillies wound up acquiring Allen, anyway. Danny had to pretend he liked the idea, when in fact he hated it. He had to stand there and listen to Paul Owens tell the press that Richie Allen had never really caused any problems when he—and everybody else—knew that Allen had caused all sorts of problems.

So it was that Danny Ozark lost his temper when Allen showed up in no condition to play on that Sunday afternoon in April of 1976. The lineup had already been sent up to the press box, mimeographed, and distributed to the writers. Allen's name was on it. When a last-minute change was announced, scratching Allen, everybody clucked knowingly and looked forward to the post-game inquisition.

One of the writers at the game that day was Bob Fachet, of *The Washington Post*, in town to cover that night's Stanley Cup hockey game at the Spectrum. Bob wasn't covering the Phillies game, merely watching it. But he had time to kill between the end of the baseball game and the start of the hockey game, so he decided to hear what Ozark had to say.

"I didn't go down in the first [press] elevator," Fachet said. "The press conference was already under way in Ozark's office when I got down there."

Before he arrived, Bus Saidt of the *Trenton Times* had popped the big question: "Why not Allen at first base?" Ozark's answer raised a few eyebrows. "You didn't see him go up there, did you?" he snapped. And then he added, "Allen was unable to play. If I had a reason other than that I think you should know of, then I would tell you."

Along about then, Fachet arrived. It was perfect timing: The hockey writer was there in the nick of time to cover a fight.

"Danny," Bob said, "maybe you've answered this already . . . but Allen was in the starting lineup and taken out. Can you tell us why?"

The question was reasonable. It was Ozark's answer that struck Fachet as more than a little strange. "He said something like, 'It has nothing to do with you and nothing to do with me,' " Bob recalled.

That cryptic comment prompted Bus Saidt to turn to another writer and ask, in a stage whisper, "What's going on around here?"

It was then, Fachet said, that Ozark "went crazy."

"If you've got a controversial question, ask it," he shouted, jumping up as the words and the venom poured out. "That's the end of it. He didn't play because I didn't think he was right to play. Stupid questions."

With that, he went storming out of his office, through the adjacent coaches' room and into the clubhouse proper, slamming the door as he went and kicking the wall and a wastepaper basket. "*Out!*" he bellowed. "The whole fucking bunch of you."

The startled writers, more than twenty of them, began to leave. But the AP's Ralph Bernstein, who happened to be chairman of the local Baseball Writers Assocation at the time, stood up for his journalistic rights. "You can't do that," he informed Ozark.

Danny was in no mood to listen to reason, least of all reason as seen through the eyes of a sportswriter. He made a move to get at Bernstein, threatening to punch him.

"Go ahead, hit me," Bernstein told him.

Ozark charged but was restrained by clubhouse manager Kenny Bush. "It was like he [Ozark] snapped," Fachet said.

That ugly scene led to yet another as several writers marched up to the lobby of the Phillies executive offices and asked to see Ruly Carpenter. The president of the club was just heading out when he encountered the press. The conversation began on a friendly level, then heated up. If there was ever a doubt about Ruly's attitude toward the press, it vanished that day.

When Bernstein began to tell him the details of what had happened downstairs, Carpenter interrupted him. "Ralph, look," he began angrily, "Danny Ozark is sick and tired of this bullshit. Every game he loses you go down and second-guess him. I'm getting sick and tired of it too."

Just then, the elevator arrived. Carpenter entered it and, as the doors were closing behind him, he muttered an unflattering reference to the "sons of bitches" of the Fourth Estate.

That episode had to rank as the most unpleasant, by far, of the Ozark years, although Danny would get upset on other occasions before his seven-year stay ran its course. In August of 1979, not long before the ax fell, Ozark got so fed up with the second-guessing that he chose not to speak to the sportswriters. He closed his office door to the press and even removed his nameplate from the door, perhaps in the hope that the writers would forget him. The silent treatment lasted five days. But it was typical of Danny that during that period he learned that one of the writers who had been especially critical of him was in the hospital, and he phoned the man to see how he was. Even when he was on the verge of losing his job, even when he was at his angriest, Danny Ozark remained a decent human being.

Later he was asked why he had taken his nameplate off the door. "If they [the writers] are going to speculate," he answered, "I wanted them to really speculate. Kenny Bush [the clubhouse man] was mad at me. I took the sign [nameplate] off the door and put it in my drawer, and he found it and he put it back up. So next time I took it and I really hid it, and he couldn't find it."

Think of that for a while. Here's a manager of a big-league baseball team spending his valuable time hiding the nameplate on his door from the clubhouse man. That's what seven years as manager of a Philadelphia team can do to a guy.

The fact of the matter is, Danny probably owed his longevity to the very sportswriters who tried so diligently to get him fired in his early years. Knowing Ruly Carpenter and his feelings about the press, you had to believe that the harder the writers pressed to get Ozark fired, the more intent Ruly became on keeping him. And, in the end, Ruly's support of Ozark was justified in light of those three consecutive division titles. But the big prize—the National League pennant and a place in the World Series —kept eluding Danny's Phillies, even though at least two of those Eastern Division championship teams appeared to be good enough to win.

*   *   *

Best in the East was good enough for the '76 Phillies. The '75 team had made a run at a division title and fallen short, getting mathematically eliminated in Pittsburgh . . . although Danny refused to admit it at the time, insisting there was still a chance despite the disheartening fact that his club had dropped seven games behind the Pirates with six to play. Had he been pressed further on the subject that night Danny probably would have explained that the Phillies' chances of winning were no better than 50-50, while the Pirates were 60-40. Whatever your feelings about Ozark's managerial skills, you have to admit the man was a mathematical wizard.

The Phillies have never been known to do anything the easy

way, but what happened to the '76 club on its way to that first divisional championship was ridiculous. In late August, they led the Pirates by a whopping fifteen-and-a-half games. Two weeks later, their lead was down to five-and-one-half games. A week and a half after that it was down to three games. The Ghost of 1964 haunted Philadelphia streets. But just when it appeared as if the '76 Phillies were going to choose America's bicentennial year to stage the greatest foldup in baseball history, they pulled themselves together. Give Danny Ozark some of the credit for that. He didn't panic. He didn't rave and rant. Through that long, long slump that turned a runaway into a pennant race, he acted like a manager who expected to win. Perhaps in the final analysis that's why his shaken team did win.

Baseball is very much a mental game. Hot hitters expect to hit, so they hit. Hot teams expect to win, so they keep winning. Then suddenly, inexplicably, it all turns around. Hot hitters become cold hitters. Winning teams become losing teams. For the '76 Phillies of Danny Ozark, the greatest challenge they faced was to start thinking, acting, playing like winners again after their seemingly insurmountable lead all but disappeared. "I can imagine what's going through their minds," Pittsburgh's Al Oliver said the first week of September after the Pirates had closed to within five-and-a-half games. "All of a sudden certain guys can be trying too hard, trying to do things they don't normally do. They can be thinking of 1964."

They had no choice but to think of 1964, and that fabled Phillies collapse. Day after day, that's all they heard. "Nineteen-sixty-four is a thing of the past," second baseman Dave Cash said. "You bury the past." But for a while—an alarmingly long while—it appeared as if the past might bury them.

"God knows we're not trying to make out," Larry Bowa said in Pittsburgh. "It's very important for us to get some support when we get home. People think we're faking it. They think we've been living it up [on the road]. I'll tell you, I haven't eaten in a week. It's killing me."

That's how these things happen. Slumps—hitting slumps, losing slumps, all types of slumps—become a state of mind. There was no escaping the pressure of that suddenly tough pennant race, no forgetting the realities of a September slump. Always there were phone calls to remind them, newspapers to remind them, interviewers to remind them. Mike Schmidt bought a New York paper at the newsstand in the Phillies' Pittsburgh Hotel because he didn't want to read about the Pirates and the Phillies. He turned to the sports page, expecting to read about the Yankees or the Mets, the Giants or the Jets, and the headline hit him between the eyes. "There's a Big Apple Tree Growing in Philadelphia," it said.

Bob Boone got a 1 A.M. phone call in New York from a guy who gave the name of a nationally known sportswriter and began asking questions. "Is the pressure starting to get to you guys?" he inquired for openers.

Mike Schmidt got a call at two in the morning. "The guy was calling me names," he said, "telling me I was choking. Bowa got a letter that said, 'It's gonna be tar-and-feather time when you get back home.' "

It was a new experience for them, a devastating experience. A couple of weeks earlier they were thinking about getting ready to play the Cincinnati Reds in the National League championship series. Now they were thinking about what it would be like to blow this thing, to be remembered as the team that let a fifteen-and-a-half-game lead get away. "Before [with the Mets] I had everything to gain, nothing to lose," reliever Tug McGraw said. "This is the first time I've got everything to gain and *everything* to lose." His meaning was clear. Those pennant-winning Mets teams of '69 and '73 weren't supposed to win. The Phillies of '76 not only were supposed to win but *had it won.* Let this one get away, and these players, this franchise might never recover. "I worry more about what would happen to them mentally in the winter than anything else," Paul Owens said after the lead shrank to four-and-a-half. "They would have to live with it. I mean, if we *do* lose, it would be the biggest comeback of all time." Also the biggest comedown.

"Maybe we ought to do something—even if it's wrong," Owens suggested that night. "I mean get in a fight with the other team. Do *something.*" Oddly enough, Gene Mauch had said the same thing to another Phillies team, twelve years before.

Crazy things kept happening to Ozark's careening ball club. Rick Bosetti, a fleet-footed, free-spirited, young outfield prospect developed in the farm system, came up in September, just as the slump was growing serious. Bosetti was one of those daring baserunners, who kept opposing pitchers—and his own manager—in a constant state of worry. "I hope," he had kidded upon arrival in Philadelphia, "I don't get picked off." He didn't. At least not the first time that Danny Ozark sent him in as a pinch runner. But the second time—representing the tying run in the bottom of the ninth with nobody out—Rick Reuschel of the Cubs caught him flat-footed. Philly fans don't forget quickly. A few nights later Bosetti, sent in to pinch run at third, loosened up by sprinting toward left field and back. "Hey Bosetti," a guy called out from the third base box seats, "home plate is the *other* way." Happily, Bosetti had a sense of humor.

The low point came in Chicago in mid-September. Before the game, Larry Bowa got on Lou Boudreau's radio show and told the Cubs announcer, "We're going through a lot of adversity now. I think the Man upstairs is testing us. When we do win this thing, it'll be like taking a 2,000-pound brick off our backs."

Before the afternoon had ended, the brick got heavier. Trailing a patchwork Cubs team until the late innings, the Phillies put together a last-ditch rally. Bob Boone's two-out single got them close, Larry Bowa's triple into the right-field corner got them even. They were going to win it now; you could sense it. But they didn't.

In the twelfth inning a twisting, wind-blown pop fly started them on their way to another excruciating defeat. Bowa, baseball's finest defensive shortstop—and the most consistent of all time—called for the pop fly . . . and missed it. It didn't matter how hard the wind was blowing. It didn't matter how bright the sun. Larry Bowa never missed pop flies. But he missed this one. And another game went down the drain. Back to the clubhouse they trooped, trailed by a flock of reporters. Over and over again, they asked Bowa what happened on that wind-blown pop fly near second base, and over and over again the shortstop replied, "I dropped the ball. It's as simple as that. I just dropped the ball."

The Ghost of '64 kept haunting them. Something had to be done to drive it away. Bobby Wine, a member of the '64 Phillies, was a coach for the '76 team. "I went to Danny in Chicago," he said, "and I asked him if I could talk to the team about it. Danny said, 'Fine.' He said, 'Whatever you think will help the club, go ahead and do it.'

"I felt that people in general—not so much the players, but

the media, radio, TV, everybody—were always bringing up '64. 'Do you think this club will be like '64? Do you think you're going to blow it?' Stuff like that. I just wanted to tell the guys that I thought this club was no comparison to '64. This club has a lot more talent than we had then. We had two guys playing regularly in '64—Allen and Callison. The rest of us were platoon players, part-time players.

"I said, 'This club is a major-league club. We've got nine guys out there who are going to play every day. You can't compare the two clubs. You guys weren't around when that happened. So all the extra pressure being put on you by friends, people, fans, everywhere you go has nothing to do with the guys. You're the Phillies of this year, not '64.'

"That's all I said. No big deal, except I know some of them were thinking about it. I know some of them came to me and asked, 'How did you guys feel in '64? How'd the fans react?' "

Maybe Bobby Wine's first-hand account of the '64 disaster did some good. Surely, there was no sense in trying to pretend that 1964 wasn't on everybody's mind.

The day after the twelfth-inning defeat in Chicago a radio man cornered Danny Ozark in the dugout and asked, "Does the team feel it's '64 all over again?" Displaying remarkable patience, Danny explained, for the umpteenth time, that his team didn't feel that way, that it was 1976, not 1964. Greg Luzinski stood nearby, listening to the interview. "I'd like to win just to shut them up," he said. "Win this thing, and we'll never hear that again. The way it is now, that's always the first thing they ask. They don't say, 'Hi, how are you?' They say, 'What's the difference between this and '64?' You get sick of it. Hell, I was fourteen years old in '64."

The Phillies beat the Cubs the next day behind Steve Carlton . . . and in a few days, almost as suddenly as the awful slump had started, it was over. The Phillies came home and started winning. The Pirates started losing. No more panic. No more looking at the scoreboard to see how the Pirates made out.

The sound of laughter could be heard in the Phillies clubhouse again. Larry Bowa was eating again. It was almost as if that terrifying skid had never happened.

It was September 26, 1976. The Phillies were in Montreal, getting ready to play the Expos in little Jarry Park. "I'm starting to shake now," said Paul Owens. "Lucky I got this warm coat on."

The agony of the early-September slump was behind them now; the joy of the official division-clinching awaited them. "It was probably the biggest test in the history of this ball club," Dave Cash said. "I think the future [of the Phillies] was riding on it. If we hadn't come back I think this club, confidence-wise, would have been destroyed forever."

But they did come back, and now the day that Larry Bowa, Mike Schmidt, Greg Luzinski, Bob Boone—all of them—had dreamed about through their years in the organization was at hand. Sunday, September 26, 1976: the day the Phillies would win the National League East.

"Hey, Larry," Bobby Tolan called out, "if Pittsburgh's seven out with six to go, think they'll have a chance?"

Bowa jumped on the line, chortling as he recalled Ozark's refusal to surrender when the '75 Phillies were seven down with six to go. "Hey Danny," the shortstop had yelled after the previous day's victory. "Come out here, Danny. The magic number is one. Any combination of one and we win. . . . Hey, Boonie, we're having a meeting tomorrow morning to tell Danny the magic number is one."

And there was Danny—sweet, lovably Danny—lured out of the shower room by his fun-loving players, standing in the middle of the clubhouse, the water dripping off him, listening to Greg Luzinski say: "The number's one, Danny. We want you to know it's one."

Even Ruly Carpenter got a charge out of it. "You guys got the magic number straightened out?" he inquired. "Yeah," Luzinski assured him. "We told him what it is so he doesn't mess it up with the press."

Through it all, Ozark stood there, good-naturedly. The long-awaited moment was at hand. The Phillies, a franchise that had spent the better part of a century losing, were about to win something. "Some of us have been together a long time," Luzinski said. "We were here when it was rought going. We've seen it build up. And now we're so close."

"I don't want to overreact yet," Bowa said. "But when it happens, I'll show you some emotion then."

And then it happened. As rain clouds moved in over Jarry Park, the magic moment arrived. Jim Lonborg did the pitching.

Greg Luzinski supplied the power, hitting a game-winning, three-run homer in the sixth inning. Final score: Phillies 4, Expos 1.

Paul Owens, a highly emotional man, was sitting in a box seat behind home late as Lonborg faced the Expos in the home ninth. This was Owens' club. He had nursed these guys through the minors. He had suffered with them through the last-place years in the majors. And now they were about to clinch first place in the National League East. He could feel the excitement racing through that long, still-lean body.

Larry Bowa, standing out there at shortstop, could feel something too. "It was like a trance came over me," he said. "I started shaking. I didn't think about it the whole game. Then we got the second out and suddenly I thought, 'This is it.' "

He had been a part of some bad Phillies teams . . . and now he was about to be a part of Philadelphia's first baseball winner in twenty-six years. Jim Lonborg threw the final, title-clinching strike, and Bowa went wild—shouting, laughing, leaping. The initial celebration over, the players rushed to the clubhouse in deep right field; their general manager was waiting for them. As luck would have it, Paul Owens and the shortstop he signed for a $2,000 bonus eleven years before came together just outside the clubhouse door. Their eyes met, and Bowa reacted instantly. "He jumped right in my arms," Owens said. The two men embraced, like a father and a son who hadn't seen each other for years.

"Guys were telling me, 'Don't overreact' " Bowa said, and he shook his head because, dammit, he wasn't going to hide his feelings on a day like this. "It's sweet, *sweet*," he was screaming in the clubhouse. "Damn, it's sweet." And to emphasize the point he dumped half a bottle of champagne over Ruly Carpenter's head.

"I feel like crying," Paul Owens said as he observed the scene, and a few minutes later he *was* crying. "I guess in my mind that's what it's all about," Greg Luzinski said. "Just to see Paul get up on that stand and to see those tears come out of his eyes."

Finally, the hilarity abated, the champagne disappeared, the clubhouse grew comparatively quiet. Bob Boone looked at Larry Bowa, smiled, and said, "Well, another pennant, huh Bo?" And they both laughed.

*   *   *

"This is going to be the greatest series they've ever seen," Danny Ozark said before the Phillies met the Reds in the best-of-five showdown for the National League pennant.

But it wasn't. The Reds won two in a row at Veterans Stadium, then rallied in the ninth to win the third game in Cincinnati. Twenty-six years the Phillies had waited to play in a post-season series, and this was it: a three-game blowout. Despite Ozark's high expectations, it really wasn't all that surprising. The Reds, after all, were at their peak. They had Pete Rose, Joe Morgan, Johnny Bench, George Foster, Tony Perez, a powerhouse of a baseball team. After sweeping the Phillies in the playoffs, they swept the Yankees in the World Series. It would be another year before the Phillies could be reasonably expected to win the National League pennant.

*   *   *

The '77 Phillies were good. Make no mistake about that. Greg Luzinski was at the peak of his game, slugging 39 home runs, driving in 130 runs, batting .309; if George Foster hadn't gone completely wild in Cincinnati, Greg would have been the National League's Most Valuable Player. Paired with Luzinski was Mike Schmidt, who hit 38 homers and knocked in 101 runs. Steve Carlton went 13–10 with a 2.64 earned run average and won the Cy Young Award. It was the year the Phillies should have won the pennant.

It was the year Danny Ozark would get blamed for *not* winning the pennant.

The clinching of the National League East wasn't quite as meaningful this time; the Phillies were after bigger things. In '76 they had celebrated in Montreal with champagne imported from France. In '77 they celebrated in Chicago with a California brand known (not too well) as Chateau Deer Path. Nobody complained, though. It was great for pouring over people's heads.

As clinchers go, this one was crazy. At one point in the game Danny Ozark wanted to send up a pinch hitter for pitcher Larry Christenson with the bases loaded. Christenson talked him out of it and hit a grand-slam home run. The score was Phillies 12, Cubs 4, when Tug McGraw arrived on the scene for mopup duty. The lefthander struck out the first two batters he faced in the eighth inning on six pitches, then gave up five hits in a row and suddenly the score was Phillies 12, Cubs 9.

"Tug comes in the dugout [after the inning], and he's laughing," Tim McCarver said. "Bowa looked at him and started screaming. 'What's so funny?' he was yelling. 'We haven't got the thing clinched yet. We got to get more runs.' I mean he's *screaming.*"

He yelled so loud that the Phillies heard him, scoring three more runs to win going away. But if the game was crazy, the celebration that followed was even crazier. First baseman Tommy Hutton gloved Bowa's throw for the final out, McGraw set a Wrigley Field high jump record, finally landing on all fours near first base, and Luzinski charged over to a box seat near the Phillies first-base dugout, plucked Ginny Ozark's hat off her head, and ran triumphantly to the clubhouse.

"They had a bet," Danny Ozark explained. "Greg said, 'When we win it, I'm getting your hat. You better wear a good one.' "

Ginny, a team player, came through under pressure. "A $30 hat," her husband said later as Luzinski paraded around the clubhouse wearing Ginny's bonnet, by now soaked through and through with Chateau Deer Path.

Danny's concern over the fate of his wife's hat disappeared as the celebration went on, growing nosier and nuttier by the minute. Good, old, quiet, unemotional Danny suddenly appeared wearing a crumpled Disney World rain hat and a wild look in his eyes. (That Chateau Deer Path must be strong stuff.) Armed with a can of shaving cream, the practically peerless leader romped through the clubhouse looking for victims.

Not far away—in the visiting clubhouse in Wrigley Field nobody is ever far away—Luzinski, still wearing Ginny's hat, was doing a Philadelphia Mummer's strut and singing, "Oh, Them Golden Slippers." Danny was so impressed he put down the shaving cream and went in search of more champagne.

"Hey Bull," he hollered, "look at this turkey over here." The manager nodded in the direction of outfielder Ollie Brown, who had just showered and was in the process of putting on clean clothes.

"No, no," Brown screamed as Ozark approached, waving a bottle of Chateau Deer Path menacingly in front of him.

"Yes, yes," retorted Danny, and he proceeded to give Brown's clean clothes a champagne rinse.

So it went until finally the jubilant, drunken champions of the National League East, dressed in undershirts and baseball pants, carrying their street clothes over their backs, trooped down the old, iron stairway that leads from the clubhouse. Ginny Ozark, hatless, was waiting for them at the bottom with a bottle of Chateau Deer Path, the contents of which she dumped over their heads. Observers tried to imagine what the next celebration—the one following the Phillies clinching of the pennant—would be like. But imagination was all it was. Although they didn't know it at the time, that crazy celebration in Chicago was to be the Phillies' last victory party of the year.

*   *   *

The Phillies expected to beat Ozark's old team, the Los Angeles Dodgers. This was their year. Ozark felt it. Owens felt it. Ruly Carpenter felt it. The ball players felt it. "I've got a feeling this thing could be three in a row," Greg Luzinski bubbled before the series opener. "I don't know why, but I feel it."

And then, to add substance to his words, Luzinski smashed a long home run on his first at-bat in game one at Dodger Stadium. The Phillies roared off to a four-run lead, lost it on one swing of Ron Cey's bat, then came back to win in the ninth. "Momentum's a big thing in a series like this," said Schmikdt, whose clutch ninth-inning hit broke the tie. "The momentum took a drastic swing on Cey's home run. For us to rise to the occasion and turn the momentum back around—that's a tough thing to do."

Their confidence knew no bounds. They were good, and they knew it. All the Dodgers had going for them at this point, it seemed, was Don Rickles, one of manager Tommy Lasorda's show-biz friends. Lasorda invited him in to the Dodgers clubhouse before game two, presumably to loosen up his players. Rickles responded with what amounted to a full-scale night club act. "Lose tonight," the insult comic informed his captive audience, "and I got day jobs for all of you."

"We have to go through this all the time," Dodger pitcher Tommy John explained to a visitor as Rickles went from locker to locker, from victim to victim.

"How ya doin', Goodson?" he said to Ed Goodson, a utility-man with a .167 regular-season average. "There's some talk you're getting on the field tonight. Not in the game, on the field . . . He's the only guy who's going to end the season owing points . . .

"Hey, Davey, good to see you," he told second baseman Davey Lopes, who happens to be black. "I spoke to my neighborhood. You can move in Friday . . . Hey Vic [to Vic Davalillo, the 5-8 outfielder from Venezuela], I spoke to the people at the Immigration Bureau. They say you're too short."

On and on he went, his victims—most of them, at least—roaring with laughter. Imagine Danny Ozark permitting such a scene in his clubhouse.

"Danny's in his dressing room now," Rickles told the Dodgers. "He's trying to find his shoes."

Little did anyone think at the time that the Dodgers would still be laughing at the end of the series.

Los Angeles' second-game win—the main event after Rickles' opening act—hardly diminished the Phillies' confidence. After all, they had won one out of two in LA; now they were going home. Two more victories, and they'd be in the World Series.

The first of those two victories was one out away on that unforgettable night, October 7, 1977. The Phillies had rallied to take a 5-3 lead. Gene Garber was pitching brilliantly in relief, forcing the Dodgers to beat the ball into the AstroTurf. The crowd of 63,719 was roaring. One more out. That's all it took. One more lousy out.

They would have gotten it too if Danny Ozark had made the obvious defense move in the top of the ninth and put Jerry Martin in left field in place of Luzinski. He'd done it before on many occasions. Unaccountably, he didn't do it now.

If Luzinski had caught Manny Mota's long fly ball for the final out, nobody would have asked Danny why Martin was still in the dugout. But Greg took a step in on what appeared to be a routine fly ball, then had to retreat when "it got up in that wind tunnel and just carried." Luzinski got his glove on it at the fence, but couldn't hold it. Instead of a game-ending out, it was a Dodger double. And then all hell broke loose. The Phillies still came within a hair of winning the game when Lopes hit a sharp grounder to third. The ball hit Schmidt's glove and caromed toward short. Bowa made a brilliant play, grabbing the ball and firing to first. It was a bang-bang call, and it went against the Phillies. Lopes was ruled safe, and the inning was still alive. It didn't end until the Dodgers had scored three times, turning a 5–3 deficit into a 6–5 win.

Danny Ozark never really lived that one down. He would always be remembered for the defensive move he didn't make and for the game—and probably the pennant—that got away as a result. Asked to explain why Luzinski had not been removed following the Phillies' two-run rally in the eighth, Ozark answered, "In this kind of a series, you don't know what's going to happen. If they [the Dodgers] tie it [or go ahead], Bull's coming up third [in the bottom of the ninth]."

His reasoning was astounding. Instead of managing to protect a two-run lead in the top of the ninth, he was concerned with having his top RBI man available to bat in the bottom of the ninth in the event the Dodgers scored two or three runs. It was negative thinking carried to the extreme.

"He broke in on the ball a little bit," the stunned manager said as he sat in his office, replaying the ninth inning in his mind. "If he got back right away, he'd have caught it very easily, I thought. If I knew the same ball was going to be hit, I'd have put the other guy in there. But Mota's a guy that doesn't pull."

The confidence was gone now. The home-field advantage didn't mean a thing. The team that had expected to win now knew it was destined to lose. That one game . . . that one inning . . . that one play . . . that one non-move by Ozark turned the series around. What happened the next night in the rain was merely a grim anticlimax, a miserable ending to what had been a super Phillies season. With National League president Chub Fenney sitting in a first-base box seat, the rain pelting down on him, Tommy John beat Steve Carlton, 4–1. But the pennant had really been lost the night before, when Danny Ozark was thinking offense at a time he should have been thinking defense.

I remember having dinner with Greg Luzinski and Paul Owens several weeks later. The general manager was still upset over the move Danny Ozark had failed to make, and the longer the night wore on the more upset he became. Ozark, however, refused to acknowledge—at least publicly—that he might have cost the Phillies the pennant. In late November of that year the manager was asked in a phone interview, "What would you do if you could do one thing differently in the playoffs?" Danny replied, "Nothing."

"I can't believe he said that," Larry Bowa said on the day the Phillies previewed their 1977 highlights film. "I hope he was misquoted. It would be like me, if I went 0–for–20 in the playoffs, saying that I wouldn't do anything different. We lost three out of four in the playoffs; we'd *better* do something different."

The loss of the '77 playoffs stayed with the Bowas, the Schmidts, the Luzinskis, the Boones for a long time. Especially, it stayed with Paul Owens, who felt in his heart that he had the best team in baseball that year. Even now, when asked to pinpoint his toughest moment in baseball, Owens recalls the ninth inning of the third game of the 1977 championship series—"when we had a two-run lead and blew it."

"I thought in '77 we were mature enough [as a club] to handle the playoffs," he said. "I think that was my most disappointing time. It bothered me for a couple of weeks after that. It's like you want to be a recluse or something."

The move that wasn't made, the fly ball that wasn't caught, the pennant that wasn't won gnawed at him for a lot longer than a couple of weeks. "The thing that bothered me most," Owens said in 1981, "was when you play that way all year, when every time you get to the eighth or the ninth with a lead you put Jerry Martin out there, why didn't he do it that night? If ever there was a time to do it, that was it. I think Danny realized it himself. I think if he had it all to do over, he would've made the move."

*   *   *

Danny Ozark had one more shot at leading the Phillies into a World Series. His 1978 team struggled mightily all season, winning only 90 games (compared to 101 in '76 and again in '77). The Pirates once again had come out of nowhere with a late-season spurt that nearly caught the Phillies on the final weekend of the season. There was an incredible, double defeat to the Pirates in a Friday twi-nighter—on a high, routine fly ball that wasn't caught in game one and a ninth-inning balk in game two—that touched off a horn-honking celebration in Pittsburgh, so sure were Pirate fans that the Phillies would never recover. And then, the very next day, there was a first-inning grand slam that Willie Stargell sent soaring over the center-field fence against Randy Lerch. But Lerch hung in there, socked a pair of homers of his own, and the Phillies came clawing back. Finally, Greg Luzinski unloaded the home run that put the Phillies ahead to stay.

There was the customary ninth-inning scare. The Pirates scored four quick runs, and Stargell, swinging a hot bat, came up representing the tying run. But Ron Reed poured three pitches past him, and the Phillies survived, 10–8. A third straight Eastern Division title was theirs. Again, the Dodgers blocked the path to the World Series.

After what had happened in '77, you'd have thought Danny Ozark would have been cautious in his pre-playoff pronouncements. Uh-uh, not our Danny. Not only did he predict that the Phillies would beat the Dodgers, but he said they'd do it in three straight.

His brave prediction looked good—until the first game, which the Dodgers won at the Vet, 9–5. That should have been enough to make Danny regret having stuck himself out on a limb with his three-in-a-row prediction. Again, uh-uh. "I predicted three in a row, sure," he said brightly, "but I didn't predict what order. . . . I still feel we're going to win three in a row."

So saying, Ozark returned to the dugout and watched closely as Tommy John shut out the Phillies on four hits in game two, 4–0. Ah, no big deal. The Phillies still had a chance to win three in a row.

And for a while it looked as if they might actually do it.

Steve Carlton won the third game, 9–4, in Los Angeles, and game four went into extra innings. Tug McGraw retired two Dodgers in the tenth, then Dusty Baker lined one to center. Garry Maddox, one of the game's premier defensive center fielders, came gliding in. He reached down, got his glove on the ball . . . and then dropped it.

Had the next Dodger batter, Bill Russell, gone out, Maddox' error would have been a footnote instead of a headline. But Russell didn't go out; he lashed a base hit to center, and the Dodgers had themselves another National League pennant. The Phillies? They faced another cold winter.

One picture remains from that afternoon at Dodger Stadium, that of Garry Maddox walking slowly . . . very slowly . . . off the field following Russell's game-winning hit as the fans raced out on the field and Dodger players cavorted on the infield and papers came floating out of the upper deck. God, what a long walk that must have been for Garry Maddox.

He is a very thoughtful, a very special human being, and on that day, in that most uncomfortable of moments, he showed just how special he is. Rather than hide from the press, he made himself available, answered all the questions, took all the blame. "The ball was right in my glove," he said. "I missed the ball. I cost us a heckuva chance to be world champions. I'll never forget it the rest of my life. . . . You face a number of different crises in your life. This is one of them."

"I guess," said Danny Ozark, "all the bad things happen to the good guys." He was referring to Maddox, but he might as well have been talking about himself.

*   *   *

Danny Ozark deserved a better ending to his Phillies career than the 1979 season. The team got hit by a succession of injuries . . . and defeats, tumbling to fourth place. The boos grew louder by the night.

Poor Danny. All he had to do was stick his face out of the dugout, and the people let him have it. The Phillies were struggling to get above .500, and Danny Ozark was going through hell.

"It used to be fun to come out here and look at the guys," he said in the wee hours one morning after the Cincinnati Reds had won a game at the Vet. "This has been the worst week of my life. We're playing Class D baseball. My first team here didn't have the talent, but we played better baseball than this."

Danny was willing to try practically anything to keep his listing ship from sinking. "I don't have a lot of answers," he readily admitted one day in Montreal. "I have a lot of questions, but I don't have any answers." Poor, *poor* Danny. Things were getting so bad he was starting to sound like a sportswriter.

Life with the '79 Phillies became a never-ending bag of surprises. One Friday night in Cincinnati, Ozark batted his pitcher,

Steve Carlton, in the no. 8 spot. Nope. That wasn't the answer. Carlton hit into a rally-killing double play his first time up, struck out with the go-ahead run on base his last time up. Next day, with the game on national TV, he put his catcher on third base, his third baseman at short, and Carlton's personal catcher, Tim McCarver, behind the plate even though Randy Lerch was pitching. "Run that by me again," Greg Luzinski said to coach Bobby Wine after hearing the starting lineup. So Wine repeated it—and by God, it came out the same way the second time: McCarver catching, Mike Schmidt at short, Bob Boone at third, Bud Harrelson at second. "That's what's fun about coming to the ball park," Luzinski finally said. "Every day something different."

"I don't mind breaking out my old high school position in front of a small crowd," Schmidt said, "but the whole nation is watching."

To everybody's surprise that odd-ball lineup was leading, 1–0, after five. Then George Foster stepped up in the sixth with a man on base and sent the ball sailing high above the fence in straightaway center field. Considering the fact that it came off a changeup, it was an unbelievable wallop. In fact, Ozark *didn't* believe it. As Foster trotted around the bases, the beleaguered Phillies manager screamed at McCarver from the dugout. Turned out he wanted the catcher to grab the bat Foster had used to propel his mammoth shot. "I thought there was a strong possibility George might've been using one of those loaded bats," Danny explained. "I'm screaming at Timmy to go out and pick it up, but first thing you know the batboy's got it, and he hustled it into the [Cincinnati] dugout."

"Loaded" bats, real or imagined, were only a small part of the problem as the Phillies plunged deeper and deeper in the National League East, so deep that "We Want Sparky" signs began popping up at the Vet with great regularity—until the Detroit Tigers made them obsolete by signing Sparky Anderson to a five-year contract in mid-June.

Still the rumors persisted. In late June, the Phillies lost a game in Montreal and the headline in *The Montreal Gazette* the next day said, "Ozark Still Phils' Manager Despite Another Expos Win." Danny had just about recovered from that when he picked up *The Montreal Star* and read, "Will Ozark Be Next Expo Victim?"

Danny handled himself remarkably well during that trying period. Some managers, faced with a diet of defeats and media "firings" would have become surly. Ozark went in the opposite direction. Instead of blowing up at the writers who poured into his office after a tough defeat, he sat behind the desk and delivered self-deprecating one-liners. Most any time you could find him there, talking about how his wife was getting their place in Florida ready for his imminent return. And, he said one day with that wonderful, deadpan delivery, "Well, I guess I can get a job—picking grapefruits." It was funny, and it was also sad. After listening to him for a while you couldn't help but think, "Here, the Phillies need a Gene Mauch to straighten them out, and they've come up with a Rodney Dangerfield." Or, as a writer for *The Montreal Star* put it after the Expos had handed the Phillies yet another one-run defeat: "A curious thing happened. The guest of honor turned into the life of his own wake."

"The stuff he says, he probably doesn't even think about how it's going to look [in the papers]," Larry Bowa said. "Then the next day he probably reads it and says, 'Did I say that?' He's h is own worst enemy."

By late August, Danny's "enemies list" had grown. The way the Phillies were playing you'd have thought the entire twenty-five-man roster was out to get him that job as a grapefruit picker in Vero Beach. The club went through a stretch of forty-one victories in ninety-seven games. Ozark's days were numbered. The headliners were finally going to come true.

A dreadful home stand was coming to a close; the Phillies were bound for Atlanta. Rather than fire him in Philadelphia, the Phillies let him go south with the team. Danny was in the hotel when traveling-secretary Eddie Ferenz told him that Paul Owens wanted to see him in his room.

"I thought it was probably to go over the waiver list, something like that," Danny said. "I went upstairs thinking about—well, when are we bringing the [minor-league] guys up from Oklahoma City? But Paul just told me, 'We're going to make a change.' I was stunned a little bit."

To the very end, no matter how the losses piled up, no matter how loud the boos became, no matter how often he sat behind the desk in his office telling those self-deprecating jokes, Danny Ozark had felt confident that the people who hired him would not fire him. And certainly Ruly Carpenter didn't want to fire him, putting it off as long as he possibly could despite all the pressures—some from within the organization. Eventually, though, Ruly had to give in.

Danny Ozark, who had accomplished one of the great upsets in major-league-baseball history by lasting long enough in Philadelphia to become the dean of National League managers, was finally an ex-manager.

The toughest part, he said, had been when he spoke to the players. There may have been some strong critics of Ozark on the ball club—especially on the pitching staff—but there were also a number of men who felt very close to him. "I felt worse when I talked to them and shook hands with them than at any other part of the day," Danny said. "When you see grown men with tears in their eyes putting their arms around you and stuff like that, it kind of makes you feel like, you know, like I meant something to them. I felt like, 'Gee, I hope they don't miss me *that* much. Life has to go on.'"

Later that night, after the ball game, Ozark met with several of the players in the hotel bar. "Bowa, Bull, a lot of guys stopped in," he said. "We just talked about the first year here, and we talked about the second year, and the third year, and the kind of fun we had together. That kind of set up my emotions. You listen to that stuff, and you think back to all the nice things that happened. You think about all the guys you came up with that same year, and you see them now at the pinnacle of their careers—All-Star players, superstars. It was nice that I was part of it, and I do feel that I did contribute something to their futures."

He did indeed. The big, lumbering guy with the hound-dog look may have been the target for a lot of jokes in his seven years as manager of the Phillies, but it's hard to laugh off the fact that he inherited a last-place club and, after one year in the cellar, finished in the first division five straight years before falling back.

If Danny Ozark deserves the blame for blowing the 1977 playoffs, he also deserves some credit for the 594 games his Phillies teams won (against 510 defeats). "I think he was as instrumental as we were in building the whole thing up," Paul Owens said recently. "Danny was a strong teacher. He had patience. I don't think we can give Danny enough credit for the job he did in seven years."

The guy who didn't holler "Whoopee" when he got the Phillies job didn't raise a rumpus when he lost it. "The criticism I've taken, I can't understand it," he told me during spring training, a few years before. "Sometimes people say, 'You're too honest,' but I'm not going to lie to anybody. That's not my way. . . . They say, 'Don't talk to them [the critics], and if I felt like I was wrong maybe I wouldn't talk to them. If I did a lousy job, I would go hide in the corner. But I'm going to talk to you. It doesn't bother me. I can sleep at night. If you can sleep with *yourself*, great. I'm not going to belt you or anything. You have a job to do. I think I'm better at my job than you are, and I think I'm better at my job than two million people who come to the ball park. I'm not going to leave the city and say, 'Those so-and-sos, they're the ones that got me fired.' I don't believe in that."

Danny Ozark lived up to that promise. He left quietly, with his head high. He left like a man. Who else but Danny Ozark would, on the very day he was fired, agree to sit in the Phillies' TV booth and do color commentary on that night's game?

Danny did a fine job on TV too, although some of us were a mite disappointed that he didn't utter at least one choice malaprop to remember him by. Oh well, suffice it to say that he made good on one of his early promises: to establish a better rapport with his players. Let me check back in my notes and see just how Danny worded it. Oh yes, here it is: "My repertoire," he said, "will be better." Why more Philadelphia sportswriters didn't take him seriously at the time is, quite frankly, beyond my apprehension.

13

Great Teams Don't Always Finish First

IN 1972–73 THE PHILADELPHIA 76ERS HAD BEEN A JOKE. NINE wins and seventy-three losses. Yessir, just one big laugh after another.

But the 76ers didn't remain a joke. They signed a superstar from the American Basketball Association named George McGinnis, and later they signed an even brighter ABA alum named Julius Erving, who could do things on the basketball court that boggled the mind. In addition, they tried a new approach to the NBA draft: They picked players who could play. I mean, really play—the way Doug Collins played, for instance. In the mid–'70s the laughs stopped; the great expectations began.

Maybe that was the trouble. People began expecting too much from the 76ers.

You could see it on their faces the night of October 27, 1975. The NBA was starting a new season—and there was traffic on South Broad Street. Cars were actually lined up, fifteen or twenty deep, waiting to get into the Spectrum parking lot. No, the Flyers weren't playing. Sinatra wasn't singing. The Philadelphia 76ers were playing . . . and the people were going to see them, lured by the likes of George McGinnis and Billy Cunningham and Doug Collins, buoyed by the distinct possibility that the home team might actually win the game.

The demand for tickets was so great that Collins, the first-round draft choice who became an All-Star, needed three extras and wound up having to buy them. What a difference a team makes.

The people stood and cheered for forty seconds when McGinnis was introduced. He stood there, the spotlight shining down on him, the applause caressing his ears. It was a beautiful moment for him. "These people," he said, "are just unbelievable. I never saw a crowd anywhere so hungry for victory."

And the sellout crowd got a victory that night. McGinnis and his new playmates beat Kareem Abdul-Jabbar and the Los Angeles Lakers. The cheers echoed through the building, rolled out into Broad Street. "I know what the Flyers feel like now," said Collins. "I'm just happy for Mr. Kosloff [owner Irv Kosloff]. He weathered the storm. He's a super person."

A new era, it seemed, had been born. Or, at least, an old era had been reborn. Philadelphians, after all, had watched good basketball teams before. The 1946–47 Warriors, coached by Eddie Gottlieb and led by Joe Fulks, won the post-season playoffs in the first year of the Basketball Association of America—forerunner of the NBA—by whipping the Chicago Stags in five games. And the 1955–56 team, powered by Paul Arizin (24.2 points per game) and Neil Johnston (22.1) and coached by George Senesky, became NBA champs by beating the Fort Wayne Pistons in five.

Then came the greatest Philadelphia pro basketball team of them all— so great that it was named the best team in the history of the NBA. The 1966–67 Philadelphia 76ers had it all. Wilt Chamberlain averaged 24.1 points that year, two more than Hal Greer. Chet Walker scored at a 19.3 clip, and Billy Cunningham, a terror of a sixth man, averaged 18.5. Then there was Wally Jones, the Villanova kid known as Wally Wonder, who threw in those rainbow jumpers (they'd have been worth three points today), and massive Luke Jackson. Jones averaged 13.2 in the regular season, Jackson 12.0. No wonder the Sixers went 68–13 that season. No wonder they crushed Boston, four games to one, in the Eastern finals, and beat the San Francisco Warriors—the transplanted Philly franchise—in six. No wonder they were honored in 1980 as the NBA's all-time best.

But if pro basketball in Philadelphia had scaled the heights with the '67 Sixers, it crash-landed with a terrible thud in '68. That was the year Philly had the Boston Celtics set up for another five-game kill, leading them three games to one and coming home for game five. Somehow, Red Auerbach walked out of that mess puffing contentedly on a victory cigar. The Celts won the fifth game at the Spectrum, the sixth game at Boston Garden, and the seventh in

Philly when Chamberlain, unaccountably, stopped shooting in the second half. Wilt wound up taking only nine shots in the entire game—just two, including a tap, in the second half. That was hard to believe for a man who once *averaged* 50.4 points per game over a full pro season. Asked why, Wilt said that Alex Hannum didn't tell him to shoot. To this day nobody, including Hannum, has been able to figure out why it would be necessary to *tell* Wilt *to shoot*. That would be like Miller Huggins having to tell Babe Ruth to swing.

Pro basketball had always been a struggle in Philadelphia—a few giddy highs, a lot of sickening lows. It took all of Eddie Gottlieb's ingenuity, all of his dedication to keep it going for all those years, and after Gotty temporarily went west—selling his Warriors to San Francisco in the spring of 1962—the struggle grew even more difficult.

Want to know how bad things can get? Try this on for size. When major-league pro basketball returned to Philadelphia with the coming of the 76ers, the new team in town found itself facing an incredible, morning-newspaper news blackout. *The Philadelphia Inquirer*, then owned by Walter Annenberg, never—but never—put a 76ers story on the first sports page during this rather bizarre period. What's more, its sports columnists—I was one of them—were instructed not to write about the team. The topper came in the form of an intra-office memo that established hard-and-fast guidelines for covering 76ers games. The memo didn't beat around the bush. Seventy-Sixers game stories, it advised, were to be limited to two paragraphs unless the team lost, in which case a third paragraph would be permitted. I remember thinking that if the 76ers lost by a really bad score some night—you know, by seventy or eighty points—that Mr. Annenberg might soften his stand and permit the paper's pro basketball writer to sneak in a fourth graph. That never happened, however. Two paragraphs for wins, three for losses—no matter how lopsided—was the rule. In fairness, however, it should be pointed out that some of those paragraphs got to be rather long.

The reason for *The Inquirer's* novel approach to covering the 76ers remained a mystery for some time. Eventually, it was determined that a sportscaster named Les Keiter was the innocent cause of the whole thing. Keiter, a colorful announcer who would describe long jump shots that found their marks as "ring-tailed howitzers," achieved considerable popularity as the radio voice of Philadelphia's Big Five college basketball games. He came to the city to work for the radio and TV stations then owned by *Inquirer* publisher Annenberg, and built such a following that the 76ers tried to hire him away as their general manager. The result of that unsuccessful attempt, apparently, was that *Inquirer* memo, surely a classic of its kind. Keiter, now a successful sportscaster in Hawaii, still laughs about it. The 76ers, however, weren't doing too much laughing at the time.

So it was that despite the achievements of the 1967 team, the 76ers knew more than their fair share of hard times in Philadelphia, ranging from 9–and–73 to two-graphs-if-they-win, three-graphs-if-they-lose. All of which made opening night of the McGinnis Era in 1975 a very special occasion, perhaps too special. The people expected a championship team, and they didn't get it.

The 1976–77 team—the George McGinnis–Julius Erving team—had a chance to deliver, gaining a place in the NBA finals against the Jack Ramsay–coached Portland Trail Blazers. But at a time when they needed him at his best, George McGinnis was at his worst . . . so bad in the opening game that Coach Gene Shue benched him with just over two minutes to go, and a one-time solid 76ers' lead whittled down to two. Philly went on to win that first game, and the second too, but the sight of "superstar McGinnis" spending the vital, closing minutes sitting on the bench, wrapped in a warmup jacket, was hard to forget. He shot 3–for–12 in that opening championship-series game and pulled down just two rebounds in twenty-two minutes. Clearly, he would have to do a lot better than that if the Sixers were to hold off the Bill Walton-led Trail Blazers.

"It's tough [being benched with the game on the line]," McGinnis said in the locker room after the first game. "I'm not going to hide it. I'm not going to say it's groovy. Through my whole career in situations like that I've been in there. I've been in slumps before, but never in a playoff situation. It's tough. It's tough while I'm playing. It's even tougher when I go home because I'm very hard on myself. You know what you can do. You know when you get a little fifteen-footer it's nothing but candy."

Not then, it wasn't. On that night he had passed up one of

those simple fifteen-footers at a time when the 76ers desperately needed two points; he had hesitated when he should have been sticking the ball in the hole, and the result had been a traveling violation that prompted Shue to sit him down. "He's a great player," the coach said. "I just expect him to come on and win this series for us. I just feel he's going to explode."

But he didn't explode. And, despite winning the first two games, the Sixers lost the series in six. Those great expectations had been dashed. Not even two superstars on one team—not even the dream combination of George McGinnis and Julius Erving—could carry this franchise back to the heights it had reached, however briefly, a decade before. That failure labeled the Philadelphia 76ers as "underachievers" in the eyes of many of the city's sports followers, and that image remains to this day. It's not an easy image to live down.

When McGinnis departed in August of '78, it was as a somewhat bitter, disillusioned man, which was a shame. Few athletes had ever been accepted so generously in Philadelphia by fans and media alike. George had come to town as the Three Million Dollar Man whose job it was to restore pro basketball to major-league status in the city. And he succeeded. Don't underestimate the importance of McGinnis' arrival. As general manager Pat Williams said, "I think that was the point that pro basketball turned around in Philadelphia."

But if McGinnis put the 76ers on the map, if he provided them with almost instant respectability, he did not carry them to the top of the mountain. The 76ers' front court, it turned out, was not big enough for two offensive-minded, crowd-pleasing superstars. "George and Julius tried so hard to complement each other," Billy Cunningham said. "I just don't think they were able to do it."

So it became evident by the end of the 1978 playoffs that one of them had to go, and that one was obviously McGinnis. Sadly, he left kicking and screaming, not the way you would have expected George McGinnis to do anything. At almost all times during his three years in the city—even during those very rough times in the playoffs—he had handled himself with dignity and class. And he was treated with dignity and class. When other Philly stars flopped, they were treated roughly by the fans; even Greg Luzinski, one of the most popular Phillies of all time, became the target of the boobirds when his production fell off. Not George McGinnis. "You think of all the athletes in this town who went through bad times and were ridden out of town on a rail," Pat Williams said at the press conference called to announce McGinnis' departure. "It never happened with George, which I think is remarkable."

What did happen, though, must have been just as hard for George McGinnis to take. He had outlived his usefulness in Philadelphia. The team that had to have him a few years before no longer needed him, and no longer wanted him. That had to be a terrible blow. Throughout his career, teams had begged for his services. Colleges ran after him. Pro teams ran after him. And now this. The pain, the injured pride, call it what you will, was most evident when McGinnis, his agent, Williams, and the customary sprinkling of attorneys met on the twentieth floor of the United Engineers Building in downtown Philadelphia.

For five hours they met and talked and waited for George McGinnis to sign the piece of paper that would permit the 76ers to trade him to Denver. "I saw a George McGinnis I never saw before," Pat Williams said the next day. "[I saw] a hostile George McGinnis. Hostile to me as a symbol of the 76ers, I guess. He was glaring. His teeth were grinding. He was an angry young man. I think the bottom line is that he didn't want to go. If the deal collapsed, it would've been all right."

All right with George. Not with the 76ers. "He knew we didn't want him anymore," Williams said. "I think he's very upset, very distraught. He's embarrassed. His pride is hurt. This is the first time in his life he was told somebody didn't want him. When he was in high school, 300 colleges were after him. The Knicks wanted him so much they signed him illegally. We chased after him. Now, at age twenty-eight, he's been rejected. I guess it stung him. It wounded him."

For the man who restored pro basketball to major-league status in Philadelphia, it was a tough way to go. But then, nothing has ever been easy where the 76ers are involved.

"From October of '76 when we signed Doctor J, only excellence would suffice in this town," Pat Williams said, and he was right. From the day Julius Erving arrived to join McGinnis, anything short of a champinship would be regarded as a failure by the fans. "When you have an Erving, a McGinnis, people feel you have to be a championship team," Williams said.

But the McGinnis-Erving Sixers couldn't win the championship in '77, and the Erving Sixers, despite a strong supporting cast, couldn't do it in '81. That was the cruelest blow of all.

*   *   *

Occasionally there are pro teams that deserve to be called great. Each year there are pro teams that earn the right to be called champions. Not all the great teams become championship teams.

There are some who will disagree with that statement. They'll say that a truly great team must be a championship team as well. I disagree. In sports, the better team—even if it was markedly better over the long season —doesn't always win a short series. Maybe a key player gets hurt. Maybe a star falls into a terrible slump, the way McGinnis did in '77. Maybe the other team simply plays so well in the short series that nobody—not even a team that demonstrated its greatness over a sixteen-game season, or an eighty-two-game season, or a one-hundred-sixty-two-game season —can stave off defeat. Casey Stengel's last Yankee team, in 1960, had Mickey Mantle, Roger Maris, and Yogi Berra in the heart of the batting order, an awesome trio. Those Yankees crushed the Pittsburgh Pirates by outrageous scores—16–3 in the second game, 10–0 in the third game, 12–0 in the sixth game. They batted .338 as a team in the World Series, got ten homers, twenty-seven extra-base hits, outscored the Pirates, 55–27 . . . and lost the Series, four games to three.

Then there were the 76ers of 1968. They won sixty games in the regular season, coasting home eight ahead of the Celtics. Wilt, apparently trying to prove his versatility, won the rebounding title *and* the assists title. The Celtics were supposed to be overmatched in the playoffs, but Billy Cunningham broke his wrist early in the series, then had to sit there watching the 76ers blow their three-games-to-one lead.

And how about the Baltimore Colts, the team that got rave notices as it wrapped up the NFL title in '68? Those Colts were "great"—until Joe Namath and the Jets, two-and-a-half touchdown underdogs—took them apart in Super Bowl III.

Great teams usually win championships, but not always. Two recent Philadelphia teams are living proof of that.

The 1979–80 Flyers didn't win the Stanley Cup, that battered, silver relic that men fight for, slash for, hook for, trip for, and generally go out of their ever-loving minds for; but they did go thirty-five consecutive games without a defeat. Let's face it: Less-than-great teams have won the Stanley Cup. Only a great team, in any professional sport, could play thirty-five straight league games—from mid-October of one year to early January of the next —without losing.

Surely, the Flyers must have been tired on some of those nights; but if they were, they hid it beautifully. Eight times in the course of their streak they trailed by as many as two goals, and in one of those eight games they began their comeback from three goals behind. Nothing fazed them. Inspired by the non-stop hustling of an aging Bobby Clarke, they kept skating, kept digging, kept refusing to lose. In game 14 of the streak they trailed, 2–0, at St. Louis . . . and gained a 3–3 tie on a shorthanded goal by Bill Barber at 6:53 of the third period. In game 23, they trailed the Los Angeles Kings, 3–0, at the Spectrum . . . and dethroned them, 9–4. In game 24, they went into the final minute trailing the Chicago Black Hawks . . . and managed to pull out a 4–4 tie.

On and on, they skated, until it became evident that the all-time National Hockey League record—twenty-eight straight games without a loss, set by the Montreal Canadiens—was in danger of tumbling. The games kept getting tougher. In no. 25, the Flyers had to overcome a 3–1 deficit before beating Quebec, 6–4, at the Spectrum. In no. 26, the Buffalo Sabres had them, 2–1, in the third before the Flyers pulled it out, 3–2. No. 27 was a 1–1 tie with the New York Rangers at Madison Square Garden.

The opponent for the record-tying 28th game in the streak was Pittsburgh. The Penguins were no big deal, but on the night of December 20, 1979, at the Spectrum, they were all the Flyers could handle. Greg Millen, the Pittsburgh goalie, was brilliant, stopping thirty-four Philly shots. The one he didn't stop came with 4:08 to go and the Penguins leading, 1–0. Young Behn Wilson, the target of Spectrum boobirds, brought the crowd to its feet by beating Millen on a power play. It didn't matter that the goal was disputed by the visitors, who claimed Wilson had illegally kicked the puck in the net. The Flyers had salvaged a 1–1 tie; the streak was still alive.

Into Boston they went in quest of a new record. "It'll be a real feather in their cap if they break the record in Boston," said Scotty Bowman, who coached the Montreal team that went twenty-eight in a row without losing two seasons before.

Boston Garden, that old barn next to North Station, was a difficult place for a visiting team to win a game in any sport. There was something intimidating about those yellow-and-black Bruins banners and the green-and-white Celtics banners hanging from the rafters. And the people . . . they seemed to be right on top of you. If there was a logical place for an undefeated streak to end, it was this antique of an arena, where the Flyers had won only four times in thirty previous regular-season games. They would have to play an exceptional hockey game to win on this day, and they knew it.

And they did it.

"The streak wasn't important," coach Pat Quinn said after the 5–2 victory. "Boston was important. We knew they were a good hockey club coming off probably the two best games they played this year [one-sided wins over Buffalo and Toronto by a combined score of 15–1]. Instead of thinking about the streak, everybody's saying, 'Oh geez, we're playing Boston.' "

They were playing Boston *in* Boston, and they knew what that meant: hitting . . . digging in the corners . . . never letting up. That was the way this team had played hockey for seventy days, and that was the way it played hockey on this day. "You might never see this happen again in 100 years," Joe Watson said when the streak had officially reached a staggering, an unprecedented twenty-nine.

Even the traditionally partisan Boston Garden fans recognized the significance of what the Flyers had done. There was applause for the visiting skaters as they left the ice. Once inside the locker room the Flyers encountered a mob scene that had to remind them of their Stanley Cup years. The place was jammed, filled by strange faces from faraway cities. There were television cameras, tape recorders, flashbulbs, the works. People were walking up to players, sticking out their hands, and saying, "Congratulations." It could have been the seventh game of the Stanley

Cup. But it wasn't, and the players—particularly the veterans—were very much aware of that. This wasn't the climax of the season, even though it surely must have seemed like it to some; the Stanley Cup playoffs were still months away.

"It [the streak] is in our minds, and it's in our hearts," Jimmy Watson said, "and it's a tremendous feeling for us all. But we think pretty straight here, and we're not going to let it go to our heads. . . . I'm not going to downplay the streak. It means a lot to us. But that doesn't seem to be the most important thing in hockey. The final game of the year, *that's* important. You've got to win that game."

"The streak's in the record book," said Bob Kelly. "Your name's on the Cup. There's no comparison."

His meaning was clear. No line in a record book—not even one that reads "most games without defeat"—could match the thrill of seeing your name inscribed on that old, battered, silver cup. But that line in the record book was all they'd get in 1980.

The streak kept going for a while. There was a 4–2 victory over Hartford at the Spectrum and a 4–4 tie at Hartford. Next came a 5–3 win at Winnipeg and now another record was in sight: the all-time pro mark of thirty-three in a row set by the NBA's Los Angeles Lakers. The Flyers matched it with a 3–2 win at Colorado, broke it with a 5–3 victory over the Rangers in New York, and extended the streak to thirty-five games by rallying to knock off the Sabres, 4–2, in Buffalo.

But the victory that mattered most to them—in the last game of the playoffs—never came. The New York Islanders beat them, 5–4, in overtime in the sixth game of the Stanley Cup championship series before a delirious crowd at the Nassau Coliseum. It was a bitter ending for a Flyers team that had proved its greatness four-and-a-half months before, and it was made all the more bitter by an incorrect linesman's call that enabled the Islanders to score their second goal.

Even in defeat, this Flyers team showed its toughness by rallying from a 4–2 deficit in the third period and very nearly winning it. But moments after Bob Nystrom scored the title-clinching goal for the Islanders, on a marvelous setup by John Tonelli, thoughts flashed back to the "offsides goal" that counted, to the whistle linesman Leon Stickle had failed to blow. Officials are human.

They make mistakes too. But things were said after that hockey game that never should have been said—ugly, angry words that stripped the class from the losers. The erring linesman, Flyers owner Ed Snider told the press, "should be shot."

It was a thoughtless, senseless thing to say, but hockey people have a way of doing things like that. Anyway, long after the frustration and the anger disappeared, there would still be a line in the National Hockey League record book to tell the world of the greatness of that "losing" hockey team.

*   *   *

There was a time when *great* seemed a proper word to use in connection with the 1980–81 76ers. On the night that the "greatest NBA team in history"—the 1967 Philadelphia 76ers—returned to the Spectrum for a reunion, the 1980–81 club won its twenty-seventh game in thirty-one tries. A couple of weeks later the record was 33-and-4, and people were wondering if the Chamberlain-Greer-Walker-Cunningham-Jackson-Jones Sixers of '67 would have been able to beat the Julius Erving-Caldwell Jones-Darryl Dawkins-Maurice Cheeks-Lionel Hollins-Bobby Jones-Steve Mix-Andrew Toney 76ers of '80-'81.

We'll never know for sure which of those two 76ers teams would have come out on top in a head-to-head battle. What we do know is that the team that opened up with a 33-4 run ended the season by losing three in a row to the Boston Celtics in the Eastern Conference finals. What made that even more painful to Philly fans was the way the Sixers lost, letting the Celtics off the hook after opening up a 3-1 lead in the best-of-seven series. Shades of 1968—except this was even worse. The '68 team lost the last three games to the Celtics by eigtheen and eight and finally four points. The '81 team lost the last three games by two and two and finally one.

And even that only told part of the story. In game five the Sixers had a ten-point lead at the half, a six-point lead *with possession of the ball* with 1:40 to go . . . and lost. In game six, at the Spectrum, they opened up a seventeen-point lead in the second period, still had the Celtics down by fifteen in the third period . . . and lost. And finally in game seven, with the previous two games still haunting them and an emotional Boston Garden crowd taunting them, they moved ahead by nine points in the first period, by eleven in the second, by eleven again in the third, by seven with 5:23 to go in the fourth . . . and lost. Some teams have a "killer instinct." Here was a team that had an instinct to self-destruct. It seemed inconceivable that a team with an Erving, a Bobby Jones, a Dawkins, and all the rest could fail to score a field goal in the final five minutes of a game with the Eastern championship—and almost surely the eventual NBA championship—at stake. But that's what happened.

"On Sunday at six o'clock [when the game ended with Bobby Jones' desperate lob pass intended for Erving bounding high to the top of the backboard], I doubt if there had ever been more tears shed in the Delaware Valley over a game than were shed over this one," Sixers' GM Pat Williams would say a few days later. He may have been exaggerating a bit; the unofficial tear count following the third game of the '77 Phillies-Dodgers playoff series and the fourth game of the '78 Phillies-Dodgers playoff series was so high there was danger of a flood. But the fact remains that even people who didn't care that much about pro basketball got caught up in the 76ers–Celtics drama.

"Chuck Daly [76ers assistant coach] put it best," according to Williams. "He said, 'We are in a suffering business.' "

The Philadelphia 76ers, you might argue, have turned suffering into an art form. From the time they lost to the Trail Blazers in the 1977 finals, they seemed intent on torturing themselves and their followers. To compound their misery, the Sixers hired an advertising agency to come up with a juicy slogan following the '77 fadeout. The choice was a pip: "We Owe You One." All that did was constantly remind Philly fans of the Sixers' past failures. The unfortunate slogan has followed the team ever since—through a semifinal series loss to Washington in '78, a quarterfinal loss to San Antonio in '79, a championship series loss to Los Angeles (even though Kareem Abdul-Jabbar sat out the final game) in '80 . . . and finally the startling collapse of '81.

It took Billy Cunningham a while to recover from the latest disappointment. When he did, the coach of the '81 Sixers talked about "the pressure of the way our team is looked upon in this city."

"If you don't win the championship," Cunningham said, "you've failed. And if you do—well, it's about time, isn't it? . . . I think it all goes back to the 'We Owe You One' slogan."

Maybe yes, maybe no. Pat Williams wasn't ready to accept that theory. "To me," he said, "the slogan was always presented in good fun. 'We're coming back [we were saying], we've got a score to settle.' If the public perceived it as an ongoing, ten-year promise—well, we have to live with it."

Harder to live with than that were some of the things that happened in the closing minutes of those last three games against the Celtics. "I think about any one of a dozen plays," the general manager said. "If Bobby Jones hadn't dribbled the ball off his foot out of bounds [in the closing minute] in game five . . ."

If. If. If. If Erving had done this . . . if Dawkins had done that, maybe then Billy Cunningham wouldn't have been standing in front of the door to the visiting locker room in Boston Garden a few minutes after the seventh-game, 91–90 defeat blaming the officials for calling a one-sided game. Maybe he wouldn't look back on that day now as "the toughest day I've ever experienced in basketball." Maybe all those Philadelphia sports fans wouldn't be nodding their heads knowingly and saying, "Those bums; I knew they wouldn't win the big one."

"The bottom line," said Pat Williams, "is that it's awfully hard to win one of those things. Occasionally in this business you get a piece of the cake. When you do, you'd better enjoy it because there may not be another. We had a chance, and we let it slip away."

But look at the bright side. For the first thirty-seven games of the regular season—if you can remember back that far—the 1980–81 Philadelphia 76ers were great, maybe the greatest.

Why did the 76ers of 1981 lose their aggressiveness and their composure with the championship seemingly theirs for the taking? Why did the 76ers of 1968 go suddenly cold when they had the Celtics set up for a five-game kill? Why did the 76ers of 1977 lose four straight to the Portland Trail Blazers after winning the first two games? Why did the 76ers of 1980 get clobbered by the Los Angeles Lakers at the Spectrum on a night when Kareem Abdul-Jabber was 3,000 miles away? Why has failure to produce in the clutch become the trademark of this franchise? Why has it reached the point that one Philadelphia daily, *The Journal*, saw fit to announce in a page-one headline the day after Boston put the '81 Sixers to rest, "Sixers Choke"?

That's awful, isn't it? I mean, accusing a team of choking—and on page one, no less. If you're going to choke, you'd much rather choke on an inside page, where some guy casually walking past a newsstand isn't going to see you.

If the people who have been so hard on the 76ers in the last decade or so would only stop and think. Better yet, if they would only study the contents of that newspaper memo concerning the 76ers; you remember, the two-if-they-win, three-if-they-lose memo. Maybe then they'd have some compassion for this unfortunate franchise. Maybe then they'd come to understand that when the Philadelphia 76ers keep snatching defeat from the jaws of victory they aren't choking. They're just subconsciously thinking about that newspaper memo and trying to get an extra graph in the morning paper.

14

The Big Green Machine

THE PHILADELPHIA EAGLES WEREN'T ALWAYS FOR THE BIRDS. IT just seemed that way to those who followed the club from 1962, when it landed—Kerplunk!—in last place with a 3-10-1 record, through 1977, when Dick Vermeil's second Eagles team went 5-9. In that sixteen-year period, the Eagles had one winning season (9-2 in 1966), and six head coaches. Their overall record was a sickly 73-142-8.

But as miserably as the Big Green Machine sputtered and died in that era, it couldn't erase the memories of brighter days in Philadelphia pro football when the Eagles were champs, not chumps, and when stars named Van Buren and Bednarik and Van Brocklin and McDonald and Retzlaff had the Birds in full flight.

Steve Van Buren was *the* pro-football runner of his day, and he sent the Eagles thundering to their first two National Football League titles in 1948 and 1949. The first came on the frozen turf of old Shibe Park in a snowstorm; Van Buren plowed five yards for the fourth-quarter touch-down that beat the Chicago Cardinals, 7-0. The second came in the rain and mud in Los Angeles, where Van Buren gained 196 yards in 31 carries—"The greatest running on any gridiron ever," Coach Greasy Neale called it—and the Eagles whipped the Los Angeles Rams, 14-0.

Van Buren was a powerhouse runner. Also a shifty runner. As a college player at Louisiana State, he gained 160 yards to lead his team to a 19-14 victory over Texas A & M in the 1944 Orange Bowl. Two seasons later he led the NFL in rushing with 832 yards in a ten-game season and inspired a young United Press sportswriter named Walter Byers, who went on to become the czar of college athletics in this country as executive director of the NCAA, to describe him as "a 200–pounder who runs like a deer." Walter always did have a way with words.

As great as he was, Van Buren was only part of that Eagles story. On the day he was rolling up all that mud-splattered yardage against the Rams in the '49 title game, the Eagles rose to the occasion on defense, holding the home team to twenty net yards in twenty-four rushes. Among the defensive heroes for the Eagles was Mike Jarmoluk, a tackle who played most of the second half with broken ribs.

The weather was so bad in Los Angeles that the owners of the two clubs requested that the game be postponed a week to Christmas Day. Commissioner Bert Bell promptly ruled that the game must go on as scheduled, citing a network radio contract as the primary reason. The broadcast was worth $14,000 to the players' pool. In those days that was big money. So was the winner's share. Each Eagle received $1,090.

How good was Steve Van Buren? Following the '49 title game, Greasy Neale said, "Maybe Red Grange was better than Van Buren today. Maybe Bronko Nagurski was better. But I'll bet nobody ever ran like Van Buren did in this mud." And Rams coach Clark Shaughnessy, the "father of the T-formation," called Van Buren "the equal of any player I've ever seen."

On another occasion, Greasy Neale had this to say about the greatest running back of the era: "First off, let me say that Red Grange can't even compare with Van Buren. Grange was only an elusive runner who had a great blocker in front of him. Steve is as elusive as Red ever was, and he doesn't need a blocker lots of the time, for he provides his own interference. He's a power runner, which Grange never was. Red only ran around an opponent. Steve goes around and through them. With Grange out of the way, the only man left is [Jim] Thorpe. They are alike in the way they ran. Thorpe was shifty, with high knee action, and plenty of power. Steve also runs over his opponents, and knocks over men thirty and forty pounds heavier than he is. When Steve meets a tackler, he lowers his head and bores over top of the man. There's many a big tackle he's knocked unconscious. He has a wonderful knack of bowling over the man, staying on his feet, and keeping his motion forward."

Since Greasy Neale played a year with the legendary Thorpe,

he was in a rare position to compare the two. So was John Kellison, an assistant to Neale in the late '40s who also played with Thorpe on the Canton Bulldogs.

"Remember Thorpe was a bigger man than Van Buren," Kellison was quoted in a newspaper article prior to the 1948 title game. "Yet Steve does the same things as Thorpe. Of course, when Thorpe hit you, he used his knees. Steve uses the shoulder and with terrific power. I'll never forget the way he knocked that blocking back of the Giants out cold last year. He did the same thing to Ray Evans in the Steelers game in Pittsburgh this year."

Clearly, Steve Van Buren was one in a million, the Grange, the Thorpe, the Jimmy Brown, the O. J. Simpson, the Earl Campbell of his day. And he was still playing for the Eagles when another superstar, Chuck Bednarik, arrived on the scene.

Personality-wise, the two had little in common. Van Buren was once described by a Philadelphia sportswriter as "almost pathologically bashful." When he displayed his happiness in the locker room following the Eagles' second straight title victory, long-time Van Buren watchers seemed amazed. "Steve Van Buren," wrote one, "usually as excitable as an Indian, leaped all over the Eagles dressing room yesterday, pounding playmates on the back and yelling, 'We did it, we did it. We're in again.' " Bednarik, on the other hand, always let his emotions flow. Chuck was the Tug McGraw of his day. When he was happy, he let the world know it. When he was sad, the world knew that too. The former Penn All-American put everything he had into playing football, and he had plenty.

Bednarik's exuberance led to an unfortunate scene at Yankee Stadium in 1960. Buck Shaw's Eagles were beating the New York Giants, 17–10, courtesy of a jolting Bednarik tackle that caused Mel Tripplett to fumble the football into the arms of the Eagles' Jimmy Carr, who plucked it out of the air and ran thirty-six yards to score. Now it was late in the fourth quarter, and the Giants were on the move. With two minutes left Frank Gifford caught a pass on the Eagles thirty and Bednarik hit him. Oh boy, did Bednarik hit him. The ball bounced away . . . into the possession of the Eagles' Chuck Weber . . . and Bednarik, his competitive juices flowing, his emotions bubbling, began jumping for joy. The game, he knew, was as good as over. The Eagles' seventh straight victory in that championship season was finally secure. So he jumped. And he hollered. And he celebrated. And all the while Frank Gifford remained motionless on the ground. He was out cold.

Giant fans saw Bednarik doing his victory dance, and they were incensed. They thought Chuck was emoting over Gifford's injury, that he had intentionally injured the Giant star. Emotions ran so high in the crowd that an Eagles fan told me years later that he had refrained from displaying his rooting interest the rest of the game; no telling what those infuriated New York fans might do.

"I made a perfectly clean play," Bednarik said. "I knew I had to meet him head on. I hit him with my shoulder and right arm high on the chest."

It *was* a clean play; the pictures proved that. But it wasn't the play itself that sent emotions soaring; it was Bednarik's dancing around *after* the play. Even as the Giants' trainer and team physician came running out to attend to Gifford, Chuck was jumping around and gesturing, happily oblivious to the fact that the man he hit hadn't moved since. "The game's over, we got the ball," Bednarik was shouting. But some thought he was gloating over the fallen Gifford, and some of those who thought so wrote for New York newspapers.

"I didn't even know Gifford had not gotten up at the time," Chuck said later. "I'm emotional. I knew we had the game won because we had the ball. That's why I was jumping around. Everybody in Philly knows I always do that. You should have seen me when Jimmy Carr grabbed that other fumble and ran for the touchdown. I was jumping all over the place. I ran up and kissed him."

If you knew Bednarik, you knew he spoke the truth. The man just loved playing football and winning football games. And his presence led to a lot of Eagles victories.

His career was winding down when he made perhaps his greatest contribution to the Eagles cause in 1960. An injury to Bob Pellegrini put the Eagles in a hole . . . and along came Chuck to dig them out by playing both ways. That's right. *Both ways.* In a game that was fast becoming a sports of specialists, Chuck Bednarik emerged as the last of the iron men. At thirty-five, an age when most athletes slow down, he played on offense *and* defense for the Eagles because they needed him.

When the Eagles had the ball, Chuck was at center. When the other guys had the ball, he was a linebacker. Writer-broadcaster Dick Schaap once told about hearing a sportswriter he knew going up to Artie Donovan, a veteran Baltimore lineman, and saying, "Hey, Artie, Bednarik's just as old as you are, and he's been around just as long. He's playing both ways. Why don't you?" And Donovan, Schaap related, gave the writer a dirty look and replied, "There's one big difference between Bednarik and me. He's nuts!"

Ah, but what a delightful nut. And what an effective one. Chuck's first double-duty effort that year came in Cleveland against a very tough Browns team that had opened the season by beating the Eagles, 41–24, at Franklin Field. He went fifty-two-and-a-half minutes in the rematch, which the Eagles won, 31–29, on a late field goal by Bobby Walston. By then, Bednarik should have been ready to pass out. Not Chuck. "I was jumping up and down when the ball went through," he recalled.

He was jumping despite a pulled muscle sustained early in the game, an injury that would have sidelined a lesser man. "I don't know what we would have done if I had to go out," he explained.

It was an afternoon Bednarik would remember—and savor—for years. "Early in the game," he said, "I was knocked flat on my back right in front of the Cleveland bench. Brown [Cleveland coach Paul Brown] was laughing at me. 'We're playing football now,' he said, just like he was saying, 'This is no place for you, you old bum.' I told him off. I wouldn't repeat what I said. After the game I apologized because I respect him. He's a great coach. But in the heat of battle, I told him plenty."

Later, at a Philadelphia luncheon honoring Bednarik, Pete Rozelle would call his two-way effort in the Cleveland game the turning point of the Eagles season.

Chuck kept doing the seemingly impossible, kept finding a hidden reserve in that thirty-five-year-old body. After his second two-way effort, against the Giants, Norm Van Brocklin remarked, "If Bednarik had played for the Giants, they would be erecting a statue of him under the flagpole in Yankee Stadium."

The success of the '60 team was remarkable in view of the fact the Eagles had finished last, with a 2–9–1 record, two years before. Buck Shaw and GM Vince McNally wasted no time putting together a contending team. They got Pete Retzlaff from Detroit, Jim McCusker and Chuck Weber from the Cards, Marion Campbell from San Francisco, Bobby Freeman and Timmy Brown from Green Bay, Norm Van Brocklin and Don Burroughs from Los Angeles, Jimmy Carr from Baltimore, and signed Eddie Khayat and Joe Robb as free agents. The new arrivals joined the likes of Bednarik and Walston, Jess Richardson and Tom Brookshier, Clarence Peaks and Tommy McDonald, Ted Dean and Max Baughan and Bill Barnes. Presto-chango: The doormats became champions.

The Eagles carried a 10–2 record into the title game at Franklin Field. Their opponents were Vince Lombardi's second Green Bay Packer team, which finished with a rush to dethrone Baltimore. Although the Packers were only 8–4 that year, they were generally considered to be a better balanced team than the Eagles, and most observers gave them a slight edge.

It was one of those rare championship pro football games that lives up to expectations. Van Brocklin threw a thirty-five-yard TD pass to the acrobatic Tommy McDonald and fired a forty-one-yard strike to Pete Retzlaff that set up a short Bobby Walston field goal. The biggest play of all may have been a fifty-eight-yard kickoff return by Ted Dean to the Green Bay thirty-nine in the fourth quarter, a run that set up what proved to be the winning touchdown after the Packers had taken the lead. "When we went ahead and then he ran that one back—well, you've got to consider that the big play of the game," Lombardi would say later.

The finish was classic. The Eagles, leading 17–13, were forced to punt with 1:20 to go. Green Bay took over on its thirty-five . . . and the race against the clock began. Downfield they moved behind the quarterbacking of Bart Starr until, with time left for just one more play, they were twenty-two yards away from the championship. Starr flipped the ball to Jim Taylor and Eagles converged on him. Taylor ducked and spun and dodged and weaved on a wild journey through the Philadelphia secondary. Finally, he went sprawling nine yards from the goal line, pinned down by the body of —who else?—Chuck Bednarik. That's how Bednarik's most memorable iron-man performance ended: stretched out on top of Jim Taylor while the final seconds ticked off.

"I came up helling," Chuck said. "I knew I had to make a perfect tackle there if I ever made one. He bounced off somebody—I think it was Maxie [Baughan]. We just had to stop him from going all the way."

No way Jim Taylor was going to escape Bednarik. No way in the world. "I was on top of him," said Chuck, "and I stayed there. I made up my mind I was gonna lay on him until it was over."

That was the final game for Buck Shaw, who climaxed a thirty-nine-year coaching career by winning the NFL title, and also the final game for Norm Van Brocklin. "I'm getting out now, when I'm at the top," the brilliant quarterback said. "It's like retiring unbeaten."

"I don't think I've ever coached a team that had more desire," Shaw said at the Philadelphia Sports Writers Banquet a month later, "or a team that had more 'beyondness.'"

It wasn't immediately clear what Shaw meant by *beyondness*. Danny Ozark hadn't arrived in town yet, so there was nobody to turn to for a definition. However, Shaw—noting that the Philly writers looked even more puzzled than usual—put their minds to rest. Beyondness, he explained, was the ability to play beyond one's capabilities.

Many years would pass before an Eagles team would be saluted for displaying "beyondness" again.

* * *

The Leonard Tose Era started in 1969, when the trucking magnate bought the Eagles from Jerry Wolman for $16,155,000. For quite a while, Tose's reign was more error than era. If Danny Ozark beat long odds to remain manager of the Phillies for seven years, Leonard Tose faced even longer ones in his battle to keep control of the Eagles into the '80s.

Tose had become a dedicated football fanatic at the side of Frank Leahy, the old Notre Dame coach. Spending all that time with Leahy prepared Tose for all the sleepless nights he would spend as owner of the Eagles. Leahy was a notorious worrier, the ultimate pessimist, a coach who always expected to lose even though he almost always won.

"He used to make me believe the worst," Notre Dame alumnus Tose said. "I've seen Notre Dame three touchdowns ahead with three minutes to go ad him walking up and down in front of the bench saying, 'We're going to lose the game,' and I'm saying to myself, 'Can we really lose the game?' "

They couldn't, of course. Not very often, anyway. But the hard-driving coach and the gung-ho old grad became very close. "Leahy used to come to my house," Tose said. "He'd spend the summer with me when I lived in Norristown. We'd spend our Christmas vacations together."

That was back in the '40s when Leonard Tose's fall weekends revolved around Notre Dame football. Tose would board the train in Paoli on Thursday night and rumble out to South Bend to hear the latest forecasts of doom from the great man . . . and see the latest victory. On Friday night Leahy and Tose would bunk out in the firehouse, where the famed coach always slept the night before a game. "His brother, Tom, he used to bet all the games," Leonard remembered. "You could never talk betting in front of [Frank] Leahy. He'd kill you. Tom was scared to death of him, so he'd say to me, 'Now how do you think we're going to do?' and I'd say, 'The coach says we're going to lose.' I told him that every game, and he'd look at me like I was lying. But Frank always said he didn't have a chance."

Finally even Tose got his fill of the Leahy pre-game pessimism. "One day," said Leonard, "I got so damn mad at him. He had convinced me we were going to lose, and we won, 57–6. So when I got home the next morning, I called him. I said, 'Frank, what impressed you about the game?' I was trying to needle him. He said. 'That linebacker of ours who was picking his nose when they got their six points.' "

For a time Tose sat on the Notre Dame bench on game day, together with Moose Krause, but that wore thin after a while too. "Leahy was the kind of guy, if you recruited a kid and got him to Notre Dame and if he made a mistake in the game, he'd turn to me and say, 'That's *your* fault,' " Tose said. "He'd say, 'You got that kid,' and he'd really get emotional. Finally Moose and I said, 'We aren't going to sit on the bench.' It just got too much."

If being on the sidelines while his beloved Fighting Irish rolled up the score got to be too much, imagine how Leonard Tose felt watching the Eagles during the seemingly endless period when the other team did the rolling. For years Tose had been conditioned to expect the worst and get the best. All of a sudden here he was, expecting the worst and getting it. It must have come as an awful shock. So he tried a different approach. Ignoring all that Leahy had taught him, Leonard began speaking of the future with great confidence. One time he got so carried away that he actually "guaranteed" an Eagles victory. That didn't work, either. Fortunately for Leonard it wasn't a *money-back* guarantee.

On the field, the Eagles were a disaster. Off the field, they were no great shakes either. Tose went through hell those first nine years. Not only did his club lose, but he almost lost his club. He fought in court with former owner Jerry Wolman. He fought with banks. He hired and fired coaches at a pace that must have made George Steinbrenner green with envy. And through it all he got ripped apart in the press. Leonard Tose was paying the price of being on the firing line, in full view of the public. It was just as Leahy had told him years before. "You can go back to your trucking company," he had said. "You can make all the damn mistakes in the world, and nobody sees it. I make one mistake, and millions of people criticize me." Now it was Leonard Tose, not Frank Leahy, on the firing line . . . and it was rough sailing.

When he named Jim Murray, a Philadelphia Irishman with a public relations background, as general manager of the Eagles, the critics really had a field day. But it was Tose—and Murray—who had the last laugh. Together, they came up with a coach, Dick Vermeil, who turned things around.

"Leonard always uses the term *staying power*," Murray said recently. "I've gone through the whole gamut of telling him he should sell the team because it was destroying his health and his life."

But Tose didn't sell. Maybe he was just being stubborn. Maybe all the attacks—some of them vicious personal attacks—brought out the fighter in him. Whatever, Jim Murray was at his side, fighting too. "I also like to consider myself a fighter when I believe something's right," he said.

Murray, a charming, outgoing man, had the ability to bounce back with a smile on his face, but the long struggle for survival took its toll on Leonard Tose. "We were really at Dunkirk a lot of times, he and I," Murray said. "A lot of Decembers it was just the two of us in the office trying to figure out how we were going to make it to January. Nobody will ever know how low he's been or how much the attacks hurt him."

"When the banks came down on me, they *really* came down on me," Tose said. "They came down on me, they came down on the trucking company. They wounded me."

To this day, Leonard Tose is convinced that all the criticism, all the pressure, all the worrying, all the attacks led directly to the open-heart surgery he underwent in his tenth year as the owner of the Eagles. "I'm not sure this operation I had wasn't a result of it," he said after making a full recovery. "It had to be. *That's* pressure. How many nights, weeks, months didn't I sleep? I might sleep for two hours, get up and think about what these people were trying to do to me. . . . We've gone through some tough times here. They've tried to take me to the wall. The bank ran the place for nine days [early in the Vermeil years]. We kept it a secret from everybody—pretty much of a secret, anyway. One of the things they said was we didn't know how to run a football team. We didn't know how to hire a good coach. The big thing was 'fiscal irresponsibility.' "

But he and Murray survived all that. Remarkably, they managed to keep most of the problems from Vermeil, who was working virtually around the clock in an effort to build a decent football team. It wasn't until the crisis had passed that Vermeil learned how close Tose had come to losing his team.

"My low point," Jim Murray said, "was when the bank took over the team for nine days. It was our job to keep our word to Dick Vermeil that we would give him what he needed. He was insulated from all this. I'll tell you, I probably had the most 'Henry Kissinger-type' job of anybody I know in my position as far as the personalities and the plots and all the byplay off the field. I always say when I write my book it'll really be a best-seller because it's an amazing thing. I really believe that only through God's help did we sustain ourselves. I just have a lot of faith, and it's sustained me through a lot of this. Look, I'm a sinner; I'm not a saint. But it's taken a lot of praying to get through this."

It appeared as if praying wouldn't be enough to help the Eagles on the field when Leonard Tose's fourth head coach, Mike McCormack, failed to turn things around after a promising start.

Under McCormack the Eagles went 5-8-1 in '73—a sharp improvement—and finished fast to go 7-7 in '74. But some hard-to-swallow, late-game defeats—a two-pointer at Chicago, a three-pointer to Dallas at the Vet, and a one-pointer to St. Louis at the Vet—dropped the team to 4-10 in '75. In fairness, it seemed Mc-Cormack deserved more than three years. He was a first-class individual, a man of principle. But some members of that '75 team let him down. "It was evident every time he went in on Mondays to watch the films," linebacker John Bunting would say later. "Every single Monday it was that way. It was very discouraging to watch three-quarters of your defense putting out and a quarter of it taking the day off. Our coach then [McCormack] was a damn good coach, but I think he learned something from the Philadelphia situation. That is, he said, 'We'll tolerate you until we can replace you.' Dick said, 'Bullshit on that; we'll get rid of you right now.' "

With a little more luck, or a little more time, Mike McCor-mack—now head coach of the Baltimore Colts—may well have been the man to put Leonard Tose's Big Green Machine in working order. But it wasn't to be —and so Tose and Murray embarked on a search for yet another coach in the winter of 1975-76. They made a pitch for Frank Kush, who was still at Arizona State at the time. They went after Joe Restic of Harvard, who merely had to say yes and the job was his. (The Eagles have since denied that, but Restic, a most honorable man and a first-class football coach, has left no doubt that he was offered the position.) Ultimately, the Tose-Murray traveling show got to the West Coast, where an energetic, single-minded, young man named Dick Vermeil had made a gigantic splash by upsetting a Woody Hayes-coached Ohio State powerhouse in the Rose Bowl with a second-half rally that destroyed the losers' bid to become no. 1.

"We didn't kid him about what he was coming into," Tose said. "We laid it out for him. We said, 'No draft picks, morale's low.' We gave him all the negatives. The only thing we said was, 'It's your ball game, and we'll support you.' "

Other Eagles coaches—Jerry Williams in particular—may have felt that Tose sold them down the river. Not this Eagles coach. From day one, Vermeil and Tose hit it off beautifully. Dick remains Leonard's biggest booster; Leonard remains Dick's biggest booster. After all those years of going through hell, this was a "marriage" made in heaven. Even through the franchise's rockiest times, Tose protected his coach to the very best of his ability.

"We were so close [to losing the team]," Tose reflected one day. "They [the banks] said we had too many coaches, that the box lunches we were providing were too much. The last game I went to when they had control of it was an exhibition game with the Giants. They made me pay for the ticket in the owner's box. They wanted to approve every contract, take all of Dick's power away. If Dick had ever known it. . . . But we kept all that away from him."

Looking back on it, it all seems impossible. Here was an owner fighting for his financial life, hanging on by a thread, while his new coach, oblivious to much of the turmoil around him, went about the awesome task of turning a losing football team into a contender. But it happened. By Vermeil's second season, Tose was convinced he had struck the coaching jackpot. "It took me as long [to realize that] as it took to observe him getting rid of guys even if they had ability because they weren't the 'character guys' he wanted," the owner said. "I saw him weeding those guys out. Then I saw the team starting to believe in his hard-working schedule."

For a couple of years Vermeil got rid of players he didn't want even though the men behind them weren't quite as talented. "Then," John Bunting said, "Dick started having to release some 'character people.' It hurt him, and it hurt me to see some of my good friends go. But he was replacing them with people with the same type of attitude that had a little more ability."

First, Dick Vermeil raised the attitude level. Next, he raised the talent level. And he produced results. Even those who initially questioned his approach became convinced when the Eagles' winning percentage began a steady climb.

Linebacker Billy Bergey, one of the "character people" who was already there when Vermeil arrived, admitted that he experienced some early doubts. "I liked the guy a lot," Bergey said, "but I thought some of his ideas were a little flaky. He wanted to restore the discipline that had been lacking, I guess, but when he said, 'Keep your chin straps buckled,' and, 'Nobody grab a knee on the field [after being injured],' and, 'Keep your helmet on at all times,' I just said, 'That's got to be the hairiest high-school stuff I ever heard of in my life.' "

But Dick Vermeil was determined to do things his way. And his way worked. There would be adjustments, of course. As Vermeil surrounded himself with his kind of people, the "high school approach" eased off. At no time, however, did the new coach let his players forget he was the boss. They came to realize that when Vermeil said something he meant it. Those who were slow to adjust their thinking to his soon became ex-Eagles.

One thing Leonard Tose found out in a hurry. Dick Vermeil was no Frank Leahy-type pessimist. He expected to succeed and made no effort to hide those expectations. "Leonard Tose has done everything he said he would do and more," the new coach said after his first season. "I'll say this. If in five years I haven't shown as head coach of the Eagles significant reason to be rehired, it won't be Leonard Tose's fault. It'll be mine. You can't work for a better owner. He has never walked in here and said, 'Dick, trade this guy. Don't pay this guy this much money. Do this on first down on the goal line. Throw a pass to Harold Carmichael.' The only thing he's ever done is say, 'What can I do to help?' . . . I feel I'm at the right place at the right time with the right owner."

Those words, mind you, were spoken after a 4-10 season, in which the Eagles lost five of their last six games. But Vermeil wasn't kidding. His Eagles went from 4-10 to 5-9, from 5-9 to 9-7 and a wild-card playoff berth, from 9-7 to 11-5 and a wild-card playoff victory, from 11-5 to 12-4 division champions, who went on to gain a berth in the Super Bowl.

The '79 team, Vermeil's fourth, made believers out of the city's long-hungering football fans by beating the Pittsburgh Steelers at the Vet, 17-14, on the way to a 6-1 start. Then the Eagles faltered, losing on successive weeks to Washington, Cincinnati, and Cleveland. The season was in danger of blowing up for them; their next game was against the Cowboys in Dallas. "I think we'll play like hell against Dallas," Vermeil said. "I don't know if we can beat them. I really don't. But it's about time we do. If I know this squad like I think I know 'em, I think they'll play Dallas right out of that stadium."

With a Monday night TV audience looking on, the Eagles beat the Cowboys, 31-21. When the game ended, the contrast between Vermeil and Dallas coach Tom Landry was startling. Vermeil bubbled over with emotion; Landry, of course, was his usual, stone-faced self. "Tom Landry is Tom Landry," Vermeil would say later when the subject was raised. "He is himself, and I think everybody that's ever been around him describes him as the same kind of person. And I'm myself. That doesn't make me right and him wrong or me wrong and him right. We're two different people, that's all."

Emotion, Vermeil kept saying, didn't win football games by itself. "I've heard John McKay say his wife was very emotional, but she couldn't win a football game," he said.

The key, Vermeil explained, was in directing that emotion toward winning. "I think that's what we did the best job of [against Dallas]," he said. "We took enthusiasm and intensity, and we directed it toward winning."

The Eagles were for real. The doormats had grown into honest-to-goodness contenders. In one season they had beaten both the Steelers and the Cowboys, the two clubs that had met in the previous Super Bowl. What's more, they had beaten the Cowboys in Dallas, and they had come from behind to do it. "It was like a heavyweight championship fight," general manager Murray said. "We got knocked down in the first round for a nine count. Then we went way ahead on points, but in the fifteenth round the champ comes back, puts you on the ropes, but you end up winning. It's hard to define it, it was so special. The enthusiasm in that locker room was just phenomenal. They actually lifted Dick up. They picked him up and carried him after Carl Hairston gave him the game ball. That's sincerity. You don't fake that. That's just spontaneous sincerity, which is missing in the world today, not just in sports."

If so, the Eagles found it that Monday night in Dallas. Later, the Cowboys would win a rematch at the Vet, 24–17, to prevent the Eagles from winning the division championship. And still later, after beating the Chicago Bears, 27–17, with a less-than-scintillating performance at the Vet, the Eagles would come up shockingly flat in a divisional playoff game at Tampa Stadium, losing to the Bucs, 24–17. Still, for the fourth straight year, Vermeil's Eagles had moved up a step; in 1980 they would be shooting for dizzying heights.

One of the things that impressed you most about Dick
Vermeil . . . he was his own man. "I don't try to be any one of
those head coaches I worked for," he said before the start of the '77
season. "There are seven NFL [head] coaches that I either worked
for or with. I've seen a lot of guys, and I'm convinced the only way
to do it is be yourself. If that isn't good enough, then you shouldn't
be in this business. I think players can spot a phony."

It takes all kinds to coach football. One of the men Vermeil
worked for in his formative years—and still looks up to today—is
George Allen. Like Allen, Vermeil approaches the game as if it
were a matter of life and death. Like Allen, he is an emotional
man. But the similarity ends there. Vermeil is far more outspoken,
far more direct in his dealings with the press, and with others.
Directness has never been one of Allen's strong suits. Ken Den-
linger, a columnist for *the Washington Post*, tells the story of a
typical George Allen incident that occurred at Veterans Stadium.
Allen's teenaged son, Bruce, had a sideline pass, and the kid was
getting carried away. Finally, one of the officials grabbed him and
led him back to Papa George. "Is he yours?" the official inquired.
Allen, apparently fearing that such an admission would carry a
fifteen-yard penalty, stared at his son with an I-never-saw-him-
before-look on his face and assured the official that he had no idea
who the kid was.

"Well, who is he then?" asked the official.

"He must be a ball boy the Eagles sent over," George replied.

Somehow, I don't think Dick Vermeil could ever bring
himself to disown, however temporarily, his own son—even if fifteen yards *were* at stake.

*   *   *

There would be many emotional scenes in the Eagles locker
room during the Tose-Vermeil years, but the day that the '78 team
closed its season by beating the Giants, 20–3, at the Vet was
special. With the victory the Eagles assured themselves of a winning record (9–7) in the NFL's first sixteen-game season. What's
more, that was good enough to gain a wild-card berth in the
playoffs.

No small accomplishment, that. In three years Vermeil had

taken a 4–10 team with no high draft choices and transformed it into a playoff team. The owner, the general manager, the coaches, the players were so happy that the locker room was opened immediately after the game so the press could be part of the postgame scene.

The prayer was first. "Heavenly Father," intoned the priest in the suddenly quiet room, "I ask to forgive the coach for all the times that he wanted you players to go out and kick ass. Heavenly Father, we thank you for all that transpired in training camp and in the six months since then."

Among the visitors in the locker room that day was Steve Van Buren, the running star of three decades past. In a particularly touching scene, Wilbert Montgomery, the soft-spoken man whose ball-carrying ability had helped to turn this Eagles team into a winner, and Van Buren met in the midst of that mob and shook hands. "You're a great football player," Van Buren told Montgomery. Wilbert, one of the most self-effacing stars who ever flashed across Philadelphia, nodded his thanks and replied, "You were too."

It was a day when the Eagles' offensive line rose to the occasion. "I was glad to see those holes," Montgomery said. "Today they were really blowing them off the ball."

"They played some very fine football games this year," said quarter-back Ron Jaworski. But never before, he went on to say, had the emotions of the Jerry Sisemores, the Wade Keys, the guys who had been through the long, losing years, reached the level that it did on that Sunday afternoon against the Giants. "Today it was in front of us," Jaworski said. "We just had to take it. They realized that. They couldn't get to the line of scrimmage fast enough. They just wanted to get out there and get after them. They were mad when we called passes because they just wanted to take 'em on."

"For me," said Jim Murray, the general manager of a million well-chosen words, "what this victory meant was the ultimate. To see Wilbert Montgomery and Steve Van Buren standing there, getting their picture taken. . . . It's just two quiet gentlemen from two eras stepping across a bridge. You just look at the two of them. Just look. A picture *does* say a thousand words.

"It's not just the winning. You have to understand what went into this. There was so much adversity. This is sort of our birth-day. We sort of came of age today. Leonard was in a fight for sur-vival, a fight to keep his team. A month ago he was in a fight maybe to keep his life, and here he is today to get the game ball. I just think it's a great moment in Philadelphia sports."

You had to remember all the bad moments to fully appreciate what Jim Murray meant. You had to be at Giants Stadium in East Rutherford, New Jersey, a month before when the Eagles won a game that seemed hopelessly lost on a day when their owner was in a Houston hospital, recovering from open-heart surgery, to understand what receiving that game ball meant to Leonard Tose.

If the 20-3 win over the Giants at the Vet had triggered an emotional response, the Eagles' incredible, 19-17 victory at Giants Stadium wasn't far behind on the tear-jerking scale. It was the twelfth game of the season and the Eagles were about to drop to 6-and-6. The game was as good as over, and the Giants had won. They had beaten the Eagles, 17-12. It was as simple as that.

Oh sure, a little time remained on the clock, but not enough time to save the Eagles. The Giants had the ball—third down and two to go on their twenty-nine. The Eagles had used up their last time out. All Joe Pisarcik, the Giants quarterback, had to do was take the snap from center, fall down, and compose a post-game victory statement for the press.

But a crazy thing happened. Instead of instructing Pisarcik to fall down, word came in from the bench to hand off to Larry Csonka, who had just ripped off a big chunk of yardage on the previous play. "You run that play 500 times [and] you don't fum-ble that son of a gun," Giants coach John McVay would explain. "That's one you just don't fumble."

Aha, little did he know that this was the 501st time. Pisarcik bobbled the snap from center, then let the ball slip out of his hands as he turned to give it to Csonka. Suddenly, inexplicably, the foot-ball wound up in the arms of Eagles cornerback Herman Edwards, who romped into the Giants' end zone. The impossible had hap-pened. The sure-fire, 17-12 loss had been magically transformed into a 19-17 win. The team that was on the verge of dropping to 6-and-6 was 7-and-5 and still in the playoff picture.

Minutes later, Jim Murray stood near the door in the visitors' locker room at Giants Stadium and placed a long-distance call to

Houston, where his boss had undergone open-heart surgery a few days before.

"Get me Mr. Tose, please," Murray was saying in a voice loud enough to be heard over the din. "Tose!" Murray screamed into the phone. "Tose, as in miracle."

There was a long wait. "What's the matter," quipped comic Jack Edelstein, a camp follower, "wouldn't he accept the charges?"

Murray was shouting into the phone again. "Hello . . . hello . . . hello." Finally, he got through to Tose's room and handed the phone to Bill Bergey.

"Mr. Tose, how you feeling?" the linebacker thundered. "While I got you on the phone, the defense is asking for a raise." Bergey laughed to show he was only joking. "Hang in there, Mr. Tose," he said. "You're tough."

Then Dick Vermeil grabbed the phone. "What did that [game] do to your new valve?" he asked. And then he started telling Leonard Tose what had happened.

"Oh," Vermeil finally said, "you heard it, huh?"

The owner had indeed heard it—over a special phone hookup. Medical history had been made. Never before had a man recovering from open-heart surgery received therapy like that.

*   *   *

The wild-card playoff loss in Atlanta—a game that got away from the Eagles when a late field-goal attempt veered wide—couldn't erase the fact that the team had finally reached competitive status in the NFL. The Eagles had gone into Atlanta Stadium without an experienced placekicker, and it cost them. But nobody could deny that, for the first time in years, the future looked bright. Compared to the way it had looked only a year earlier, it was absolutely incandescent.

Leonard Tose frequently reflected on the bad times now that the Eagles were no longer a bad Philadelphia joke. He talked openly about the time Vermeil—hearing bits and pieces about his boss' problems despite efforts to keep such matters away from him—walked into Tose's office at the Vet in an effort to help. "He came to me with his contract," the owner said, "and he told me,

'Here it is. Tear it up if you want.' I said, 'Thanks, Dick. I know you're my friend, but that's not necessary.'

"He's my friend," Tose would say at that point in a voice filling with emotion. "That's the only way I can describe him. What he offered to do that day was no grandstand. Just the two of us were in the room. He didn't tell anybody. He didn't embarrass me. He just did it. That's Dick Vermeil."

And this was Leonard Tose, a man thoroughly wrapped up with his football team. For years he had been an object of ridicule. His team was a laughingstock. He was a laughingstock. And then, just when things seemed utterly hopeless, it all turned around. The Eagles started winning . . . and Leonard Tose became a sympathetic figure instead of a buffoon. When the winning continued, he became almost a heroic figure to some, a man who refused to give up, who fought on in the face of extreme adversity.

"Jimmy Murray talked to me many times," the owner of the Eagles said on the eve of that playoff game in Atlanta, "He'd tell me, 'For your own sanity and health, why don't you sell?' I knew it was probably the right thing to do. I thought about it many times . . . but I don't know what I'd do with my life without the Eagles. I have to admit I enjoy owning a football team. I'd be lost without it. Anybody who owns a football team and tells you it's not, in part, an ego trip is not telling you the truth."

For nine years it had been more of an ego-shattering trip than an ego-building trip. But all that was changed now. No longer did the fans decorate the Vet with anti-Tose signs. No longer did Philadelphia sports-writers refer to the team as Tose's Big Green Mistake. No longer did coaches come and go so fast that the Vet could have used a revolving door. After nearly a decade of acting on impulse, of letting his emotions run wild, of depriving the Eagles of the stability that a successful pro football franchise needs, Leonard Tose had found Dick Vermeil, a man he believed in, a man he thoroughly trusted. This became Dick Vermeil's football team. Tose stepped into the background . . . and a bright, new era had begun.

By '79 the Eagles had come so far that Vermeil would often startle his Frank Leahy-trained owner by assuring him that his team would win the next game. "We beat Green Bay," Tose said late in the '79 season, "and I thought that was a milestone. Then I started worrying about Detroit. Dick said we should really be able to beat Detroit. I said, 'Dick, please don't tell me that.' "

But this was Vermeil, not Leahy. When Dick Vermeil thought his team was good enough to win, he said so. Tose would just have to get accustomed to that.

The 11–5 Eagles beat the Chicago Bears, 27–17, in the wild-card playoff game that year, although they looked so flat in the first half that the Vet Stadium crowd, growing spoiled now, actually directed some boos at Ron Jaworski. A week later, playing the Tampa Bay Bucs, the Eagles were even flatter. They fell behind, 17–0, and never fully recovered. Ricky Bell ran through defenders. Lee Roy Selmon disrupted the Eagles offense. And, at the very end, when the Eagles had rallied to within seven points, there was even a break in Eagles discipline, something that rarely happened under Vermeil. After an attempted onside kick went out of bounds, the coach ordered Tony Franklin to kick deep. But Franklin decided to play hero on the spur of the moment, tried to drop a short kick in an open area—and the Bucs got the ball in excellent field position. Vermeil was livid and, to make sure Franklin didn't forget the message, hit him with a stiff fine.

That was the Vermeil way. Some coaches might make up excuses for an erring player. Not this coach. Some coaches, when asked at the post-game press conference about that second straight outside kick, might have passed it off as sideline strategy that went wrong. Not Vermeil. Without hesitation he explained what really had happened. When the blame was his to take, he took it. When it belonged on somebody else's shoulders, that's where he put it. Players learned quickly to do things Vermeil's way or do them elsewhere.

*   *   *

Nobody had a more difficult time of it in the Tampa Bay game than Bill Bergey. While his team was losing on the field, he was in the CBS broadcasting booth, spotting for Chris Schenkel and Hank Stram. "With about three, four minutes to go, I just couldn't take it any more," Bergey said. "They told me they were going to give me fifty bucks, and I thought it was going to be kind of neat to be up there, but I got so wrapped up in the game, and I got to feeling so sick about what was happening out there, that I had to leave the box."

To many people, for many years, Bill Bergey *was* the Eagles, the All-Pro who kept making those terrific hits, kept playing with the greatest of enthusiasm no matter what it said on the scoreboard or in the standings. Then, in the third game of the '79 season, Bergey tore up his knee in New Orleans. There was cartilage damage. And ligament damage. Bergey was thirty-five years old. No way you could expect a man that age to come back from an injury like that. But Bill Bergey did.

Merrill Reese, the Eagles' radio play-by-play broadcaster, phoned Bergey's wife from New Orleans to let her know that the injury was serious. "She picked me up at the airport," Bill recalled, "and took me to the hospital. As we're going up the Schuylkill Expressway she says—and she knows how much I love the game—she says, 'Well, what if this is it?' I said, 'What do you mean?' She says, 'Well, you know what I mean.' She didn't really want to say it, but I made her say it. I made her say, 'Well, what if you can't play any more football?' I said, 'Micky, I don't care how bad this thing is, I've got to play more football.' "

John Bunting, another veteran Eagles linebacker, had come back from a similar injury the year before. It took a lot of doing, a lot of desire, a lot of dedication. To come back from an injury like that and play football again a man had to put the game ahead of everything else—ahead of his family, his social life, *everything*. Bunting did that. The rehabilitation period was hell, but he did it. Now it was Bergey's turn. He had missed just one game in eleven seasons as a pro; now, at age thirty-five, this had to happen.

Bill Bergey is a remarkable man. When that serious injury occurred, he got up and walked off the field. "The only thing I said was, 'Damn, that hurts,' " he recalled. "I was putting a little ice on it, and Petey Perot came up to me and I said, 'Pete, I want you to hit me just like I was hit out there.' " So Perot hit him, just like he'd been hit out there. The pain must have been excruciating. "I knew then," Bergey said, "something wasn't right."

When he came home from the hospital following the operation, his wife had a note pinned to the wall. "We'll make this thing work out together," it said. And they did. The star linebacker whose career nearly ended in a mangled heap at the Superdome at thirty-five, was back playing for the Eagles at thirty-six.

"Any time anybody would tell me, 'You're thirty-five,' I just kind of snickered to myself," Bergey said. "I don't know how old a thirty-five-year-old person should feel, but I don't feel like a thirty-five-year-old person."

Above all, he didn't want his career to end like that. He wanted to go out his way and besides, he simply wasn't ready to quit playing that kid's game he loved so much—least of all now that he sensed the Eagles were closing in on something big.

"I'm not going to talk about wearing a ring or getting a big, fat check at the end," he said one day during training camp in 1980. "The way I look at winning the world's championship, football has never been a job or an occupation with me. It's been a fun, wonderful way of living. Now if I can go all the way to the top on the field and accomplish that championship, that would really be icing on the cake. I mean that would be probably the most beautiful thing that ever could happen to me because when I'm an older-type person and I have maybe my young grandchildren running around, I don't want to tell them I was All-Pro all these years, this kind of stuff. I would love to tell them I was a hard worker that was part of a Super Bowl championship team. I just think that would be something beautiful."

And, after spending all those years with an also-ran, Bill Bergey became part of a Super Bowl team—if not a Super Bowl championship team—in his comeback season. It began the way all those other Eagles seasons began, with this marvelously enthusiastic little boy in a man's body standing up on the final day of training camp and singing *Sentimental Journey*. The song was never more fitting.

For Bergey, for all of them the big date was September 7, 1980, the day the long journey to the Super Bowl would officially begin. Bergey kept thinking about it, kept talking about it; he wouldn't let anybody forget it . . . as if they could, anyway.

Jerry Robinson, the top draft choice who lived up to his advance billing, and then some, remembered laughingly how the old pro had kept emphasizing that date. "He said, 'Jerry, be looking forward to September 7,' " Robinson said. " '*The Star-Spangled Banner* . . . me and you, side by side, hands over our hearts, and then we'll go out and kick some butts.' "

And they did kick some butts, holding the Denver Broncos to a pair of long field goals. The outcome was no longer in doubt when Bill Bergey made the play the 70,000 fans had come to see. He wrapped his arms around Matt Robinson and dragged him down for a ten-yard loss, and the Vet exploded. "Bergey . . . Bergey . . . Bergey," the people hollered as he came off the field. "It made me drop a tear," Bergey said. "I guess it was their way to say, 'Welcome back.' "

And that ten-yard sack was Bill Bergey's way of saying, "It's good to be back."

He had returned in time to take part in a memorable season. There were difficult times, to be sure. There were moments when the 1980 Eagles appeared to be in serious trouble. For instance, there was the knee injury that felled Wilbert Montgomery, keeping him out of some critical early-season games. What happened? Vermeil's nephew, a little guy named Louie Giammona with Uncle Dick's hard-as-nails approach to the game, filled in and got the job done. Against the Chicago Bears, Little Louie gained seventy-nine yards on the ground, matching Walter Payton yard for yard. That was the day a Chicago defensive end named Mike Hartenstine blindsided Ron Jaworski, nailing the quarterback helmet-first on a play that knocked Jaworski woozy and enraged Vermeil. "It almost seems like the cards are against you with all the aces injured," Keith Krepfle said. "It shows the quality and the character of this team [that it managed to win, anyway]."

Would Jaworski be able to bounce back from that devastating hit by Hartenstine? "Subconsciously," the quarterback knew, "those things can bother a lot of players."

Not that player. The very next week Jaworski was back at his old post, directing a fifteen-play, eighty-four-yard drive that pulled out a come-from-behind victory over the Seattle Seahawks in the Kingdome.

On and on, the Eagles rolled. They beat the Redskins in Washington—a top priority item on Vermeil's list—and they pulled out a tough, home victory over the Oakland Raiders. The team was 11-and-1 when it stumbled, dropping a road game to San Diego, despite a big second-half comeback, and a home game to Atlanta. Suddenly, they were in danger of being relegated to wild-card status again.

It all came down to the final Sunday of the regular season in—where else?—Texas Stadium. The National Football League's tie-breaking procedure, only slightly less complex than Einstein's theory of relativity, created a rather incredible situation. Although a Dallas victory would leave the teams tied for first place with 12–4 records, the Cowboys had to beat the Eagles by at least twenty-five points to wrest the title—and a precious week off—away from them.

All week long the Dallas Cowboys' party line was that they'd be satisfied to win by any score, that the twenty-five-point mountain was too high to climb. Maybe the Eagles believed that propaganda. More likely, they weren't psychologically prepared to play a game in which a three-touchdown defeat would be seen as a victory. Four-and-a-half minutes into the fourth quarter the score was Cowboys 35, Eagles 10, and the place was going bonkers.

We found out a lot about the Eagles then, and they found out a lot about themselves. Their best running back, Wilbert Montgomery, was woozy, his head throbbing from a thunderous hit delivered by linebacker D. C. Lewis late in the first half. And that wasn't all.

The Eagles' record-breaking pass-catcher, Harold Carmichael, was on the sidelines, unable to run his routes because of a vicious shot he absorbed at the hands of free safety Dennis Thurman late in the first half; as a result, Carmichael failed to catch a single pass for the first time in 128 regular-season games. Also, Charles Smith, another of the team's top receivers, was out. So was Billy Bergey and defensive end Carl Hairston. If ever there was a time for the Dallas Cowboys to destroy somebody, this was it. But it didn't happen. The crippled team in green came back. Seventeen more points were scored that Sunday afternoon—and the Eagles got all of them. Guys named Rodney Parker and Scott Fitzkee made the catches that Carmichael and Smith weren't able to make. Montgomery, his mind still foggy, returned to the game and caught a twenty-five-yard pass to set up one score and ran six yards for another. "We had come a long ways to turn over the division championship to Dallas," Montgomery said.

The post-game scene was bizarre. Years before, at Franklin Field, a brutally bad Eagles team had muffed its chance of getting O.J. Simpson by winning the last game of the season. Now a very good Eagles team won a division championship *by losing*. Maybe only a gifted few in the world understood Pete Rozelle's tie-breaking scheme, but on that day at least the people of Philadelphia had to love it. Their heroes had given up five touchdowns and scored only three. They had missed three of the five field goals they tried. They had scored twenty-seven points and yielded thirty-five. And still they "won." Don't ever say anything bad about Rozelle. The man is a miracle worker.

Off the field the Eagles ran, whooping, hollering, celebrating. They had lost many games before at Texas Stadium, but this was the first time there was champagne awaiting them when they got to the locker room.

"This wasn't an ordinary game," general manager Murray said, just in case there was anyone left who thought it was. "How many games do you come in twenty-four points 'ahead' [before the opening kickoff], and lose it, then win going away? It was a bizarre football game. I don't ever remember a game with more plays in it. I don't think Shakespeare had that many plays. There were comedies, and there were tragedies."

And there were the Philadelphia Eagles, newly crowned champions of the National Football Conference East. "A moment like this makes it all worthwhile," said Bill Bergey, standing on his aching, puffed-up left knee, so badly damaged that it would cause him to be placed on the injured reserve list before the start of the 1981 season. "I'm so excited, I'm almost speechless. I know what it was like here at one time. There were times we'd get this excited just winning a ball game, let alone winning a championship."

But never had there been a time when the Eagles got so excited about getting outscored in a football game. On a day when they scored twenty-seven points and gave up thirty-five, they had come up with the biggest "victory" by an Eagles team in two decades. Only in America.

*   *   *

The Eagles had lost three of their final four regular-season games; fears mounted that the team had "peaked" too early. When the Minnesota Vikings scored the first two touchdowns in a playoff game at the Vet those fears grew stronger. But the Eagles had something left. Wilbert Montgomery, his knee twisted, his thigh bruised, his head aching, wouldn't quit. Time after time he went limping, staggering, reeling off the field surrounded by concerned teammates and trainers. And time after time he'd return a few plays later, carrying the football, lunging for that extra yard. Montgomery's two second-half touchdowns put the Vikings to rest, and set up the confrontation all of Philadelphia couldn't wait to see: the Eagles and the Cowboys for the championship of the National Football Conference and a trip to the Super Bowl.

All those sorry Sundays at Franklin Field in the '60s and at the Vet in the '70s were shoved into the background on this day as the Eagles took charge and stayed in charge. On the very second play from scrimmage, Wilbert Montgomery took a handoff from Ron Jaworski and raced forty-two yards through a gaping hole for the game's first score. At halftime it was 7–7, but the Eagles had outplayed the Cowboys by a wide margin. And in the second half, their supremacy showed on the scoreboard as well. Big defensive plays caused crucial fumbles, and the Eagles capitalized. There was a short field goal by the slump-ridden Tony Franklin, a nine-yard touchdown run by Leroy Harris, and another field goal by Franklin. Through it all, Montgomery was absolutely magnificent, rolling up 194 yards, two short of Van Buren's all-time playoff record. Final score: Eagles 20, Cowboys 7.

The Eagles hadn't merely beaten the Cowboys; they had dominated them, and a city celebrated. The fact that the Eagles had been down for so long added to the excitement of the occasion. "The last time the Philadelphia Eagles did anything this outrageously glorious," wrote *The Bulletin's* Sandy Grady, "Ike was in the White House, gas was thirty cents at the pump and cars had tailfins. The Eagles played on real grass in an old brick stadium with board seats."

Now gas was closing in on a buck and a half a gallon, Jimmy Carter was turning the White House over to Ronald Reagan, and the Eagles were playing football games on a hard, green rug known as AstroTurf in a modern, multi-purpose stadium.

"It's just so rewarding and gratifying," said Bill Bergey, who had gone through so much to be a part of it. "There are peaks and valleys in this game, and there are a helluva lot more valleys. Just to be able to say this moment, right here, is worth it all would really be an understatement."

The Eagles had spent most of two decades in the Valley of the Dead and now, for the first time in the Super Bowl era, they were scaling the heights over the prone bodies of the team they most wanted to beat. "If we had to write a script," said offensive tackle Stan Walters, "this was how I'd like it to go." Walters, like Bergey, had been on losing Eagles teams. On this day, with the NFC, title in sight, he played the second half despite a back spasm. "I had to go out and try it," the veteran explained. "I had to give it my best shot in the second half. For nine years I've always been shooting for this. I couldn't see myself lying on the training table."

So they shot his lower back with novocaine. And they packed ice on his bruised right leg. And he played in the second half. So did John Sciarra, who did a tremendous job of running back punts despite a broken left hand that was far from healed. On this day, it seemed nothing was going to stop this team.

* * *

Almost since its inception, the Super Bowl has been synonymous with unfulfilled expectations. The buildup is staggering; the game, more often than not, is stultifying. for the Philadelphia Eagles, Super Bowl XV lived down to many of the Super Bowls they had viewed from afar in years past.

Nobody can say they didn't take it seriously. Maybe that was the trouble; they took it too seriously. Maybe no first-time Super Bowl team can hope to put forth a top effort in that crazy, hyped-up atmosphere. One thing's for sure: the Eagles didn't go to New Orleans for a joy ride. They didn't spend half their waking hours on Bourbon Street. And they didn't live in the lap of luxury.

Some luxury! The good hotels in New Orleans were operated by people smart enough *not* to want to put up a Super Bowl team. Why give special rates to the participants when the city is crawling with suckers willing to pay top dollar? So the Eagles were assigned to the Airport Hilton, some fourteen miles from the French Quarter. The place's main claim to fame was that an airplane had once crashed there.

The surroundings were—for want of a better word—interesting. Directly in front of the motel was Airline Highway, a heavily traveled road over which trucks and buses roared most of the day and night. In all honesty, though, the rumble of the trucks and buses seldom bothered the guests. It wasn't that the place was soundproof because it wasn't; it was just that the roar of the jet planes taking off and landing nearby drowned out all other sounds. Those with a yen for sightseeing had merely to walk out the front door, glance to the right . . . and get a close-up view of the friendly, neighborhood Gulf station. Wonderful how those orange signs brighten up the street. And just behind the Gulf station was—no, not an eighteen-hole, championship golf course; you're not paying attention. Directly behind the Gulf station was Buddy's Auto Repair Shop, a great place to browse for lovers of decaying, old cars.

This was the Eagles' Super Bowl Shangri-la. And they voiced nary a complaint. The NFL, in its infinite wisdom, could have housed the Eagles in the basement of the Y in Baton Rouge, and they wouldn't have said a word. That's how happy they were to be in Super Bowl XV. And how closely they listened to Dick Vermeil when he told them, "Let's make the best of it."

Bill Bergey, for one, thought it was great. Either he did public relations work for Hilton on the side, or he had remembered to bring along ear plugs to keep those jets from ruining his beauty sleep.

"Hey," he said, "the last time I was down here for a Super Bowl I came with a travel group. They put us in like an old folk's home—it was an old hotel downtown, about ten blocks from the Dome—and so help me there was a roach two inches long that was right in the bathroom. I called for room service, and they didn't know what room service was."

Hmmm. Well, one thing was clear. Bill Bergey *wasn't* working for the New Orleans Chamber of Commerce.

The assembled journalists, seeking to make this Super Bowl something out of the ordinary, turned it into a battle between the good buys and the bad guys. The Oakland Raiders, natch, were the bad guys. Tales of John Matuszak filled the nation's sports pages. For days the country learned that "Tooz" had turned over a new leaf. And then came the inevitable day when "Tooz" tripped over the leaf and landed smack dab in the middle of Bourbon Street—after curfew. The Raiders made no big deal out of that slight indiscretion. They slapped Matuszak with a fine and let it go at that. When asked about it at a press conference, Dick Vermeil made it plain that he would never stand for one of his players running around on Bourbon Street—or on any street—in the wee hours on Super Bowl week.

Strict discipline was the name of the game that Vermeil coached. "Jerry Robinson was late for the airplane [on the way down to New Orleans]," Vermeil told the writers. "He broke off the key in his ignition. We were taxiing down the runway, and we realized we were a player short. So we backed up and there he was. He'll be fined for that."

The Eagles coach left little doubt that if one of his players should happen to turn up on Bourbon Street after curfew, the guy—no tatter how key a player—would be invited to take the first plane home. "I think each player has a commitment to himself and his teammates," Vermeil said. "I'm not criticizing how Oakland handles anything. Hey, I just do things my way. I just think that Claude Humphrey has a commitment to Charlie Johnson, that Ron Jaworski has a commitment to Wilbert Montgomery, and that Wilbert Montgomery has a commitment to him, and to me. Something like that is a display of lack of respect for your teammates, a display of a lack of discipline. There's no way it can help a team."

The only way to handle such things, he went on to explain, was to take quick, firm action. "If you don't do it when you're confronted with it," Vermeil explained, "chances are you're going to be confronted with it more often somewhere down the road. And if you don't act when you're confronted with it with the best football player you have, then you better never act with any other football player because it'll never hold up."

When the Raiders, following their Bourbon Street exposure, won the football game, some took it as proof that their approach was superior, a rather ridiculous conclusion to draw and one that annoyed Vermeil.

"I've never said my approach was right or wrong," he reiterated. "It's just our approach. It hasn't hurt our organization. A lot of people [other coaches] have come to Philadelphia, and they haven't won and they haven't been to the Super Bowl. I believe in the way we do things. Our players believe in the way they do things. I believe in them.

"Since the two approaches to doing things are in contrast, it creates the impression—well, the Eagles approach is wrong. If the approach of surrounding yourself with quality people is wrong, then I'm in the wrong business. A National Football League player should be something that all kids and people and fans can identify with. I thought we had a chance to symbolize to the country the meaning of character and hard work and dedication because that's how we got here."

Eagles fans mobbed New Orleans on Super Bowl week. The day before the game, Canal Street was jammed with visitors dressed in green shirts, green sweaters, green jackets. If you didn't know better you'd have thought it was St. Patrick's Day. But even in their moment of triumph, Philadelphia sports fans retained that special quality that made them so, uh, endearing. Former Eagles coach Mike McCormack laughingly told of standing in line outside a well-known French quarter restaurant during Super Bowl week. In front of him, he said, were several Eagles fans, resplendent in their green garb. They didn't recognize Mike but kept chattering away about the upcoming game. "One of them said, 'The trouble with Vermeil, he's too conservative,' " McCormack said. "I had to smile."

There they were in New Orleans, the promised land, and they were still critical of the coach who got them there. The Eagles had changed, Mike McCormack discovered that day, but Philadelphia fans—bless their hearts—hadn't.

The game itself, in keeping with Super Bowl tradition, was nothing to write home about, especially if your home happened to be in Philadelphia. The Eagles won the toss and elected to receive. On their first play from scrimmage, Wilbert Montgomery ran left for eight yards. On the second play Leroy Harris smashed up the middle for three yards and a first down. The cheers from those green-clad Philadelphia fans had scarcely died down when Ron Jaworski faded back to pass on the next play—and threw the football into the hands of Oakland's Rod Martin. The Eagles never seemed to get untracked after that. It was Oakland 14, Eagles 0, at the quarter, and Oakland 27, Eagles 10, at the end. Philadelphia's only real chance to get back in the game vanished in the closing minute of the first half. Trailing 14-3, they moved to a first down on the Oakland 11, then stalled. Three passes failed; so did a twenty-eight-yard field goal attempt by Franklin. In a regular-season, 10-7 victory over the Raiders the Eagles had rushed Jim Plunkett off his feet; on this day the Raiders gave their quarterback all the time he needed. The Eagles had been favored to win in their first Super Bowl appearance . . . and they had been decisively beaten.

"We just passed up a tremendous opportunity, the opportunity to be no. 1," John Bunting said. "I don't know if I'll ever get that opportunity again, or if Bill Bergey will ever get that opportunity again."

"It was still a great season," a man said to Leonard Tose, but the owner of pro football's no. 2 team, looking very tired, very sad, shook his head and replied, "I don't think so."

Outside the locker room door Tommy Lasorda's friend, Don Rickles, who also happens to be a friend of Leonard Tose, stood patiently, quietly, waiting for the owner to come out. Even Rickles couldn't think of anything funny to say at a time like this.

It would take a while for the Eagles to wipe away the result of that last game and recall, with justifiable pride, the twelve regular-season victories and the two playoff victories that preceded it. But the day would come when they, and their fans, could look back on the 1980 season as a very special one in Eagles history. In five years Dick Vermeil had driven this team from the brink of oblivion to the Super Bowl. One loss—even a Super Bowl loss—couldn't destroy that achievement.

"We had a good season," Vermeil said the next day as the Eagles prepared to make that treacherous trip across Airline Highway and jet back to Philadelpia. "As an organization we brought some smiles to the faces of a lot of loyal fans. They were excited. We ignited the community and brought 'em together in a common cause. We had a telegram—I don't know how many thousands of names were on it—but we let 'em down. Still, I would not call the season a failure."

It was anything but a failure. It was a season filled with joyous moments—like the one that occurred when a large group of Super-Bowl-bound Eagles fans boarded a jet out of Atlanta a few days before the game. As is customary, the stewardess welcomed the new passengers aboard. Then she made a serious mistake. She announced that "the Dallas-based crew" would be pleased to serve them.

To this day the poor girl probably can't understand why all those seemingly nice folks who had boarded the plane in Atlanta saluted the Dallas-based crew with a rousing, raucous, heartfelt BOO-O-O-O.

15

They Had 'em All the Way

NOT THAT MANY PEOPLE EXPECTED THE 1980 PHILLIES TO GO ANY-where—except home after the last game of the season in Montreal. Many of the "experts" were picking them to finish behind the Pirates, behind the Expos, even behind the Cardinals. The season was seen as a "last chance" for the players who had come up to-gether, won divisions together, lost playoffs together and, in '79, collapsed together. "If someone had told me we'd get Manny Trillo and Nino Espinosa and Pete Rose, and we'd be .500 going into September, I'd have laughed," Larry Bowa said at the end of the '79 season. "It's a joke."

The joke was on the Phillies. The team that Rose was sup-posed to lead to the World Series fell to fourth place in the Na-tional League East instead. It seemed at times as if some of the players went out of their way *not* to let Rose influence them; cer-tainly his rah-rah, gung-ho approach didn't spread very far or very fast in 1979. The '79 Phillies (and it carried into '80) had the reputation of being "fat cats"—lazy, overpaid, undermotivated stars. The fans booed. The press ripped. It was a miserable situa-tion that Dallas Green inherited when he took over from Danny Ozark late in the '79 season, and it didn't improve overnight. If anything, it got worse at times. The war between the players and the press heated up, and while that was going on a new war broke out—between some of the players and the manager.

Before the '80 season ran its rocky course to a storybook end-ing, there was a "drug scandal" that made headlines coast to coast and turned a difficult relationship between the Phillies players and the press into a near-impossible one. Larry Bowa may have found it hard to believe that the '79 Phillies could fail; many observers found it even harder to believe that the '80 Phillies could succeed.

261

The switch from Ozark to Green was a jolt, to put it mildly. Danny was low key; he rarely blasted players, rarely got involved in shouting matches. Dallas, on the other hand, always seemed to be shouting. Even when he thought he was whispering it came out sounding like a shout.

"You know what I want to do?" the new manager asked before the '80 team headed for spring training. "I want to get our guys talking about 'we.' That's oversimplifying it, but we've got too many guys talking about 'I.' It's always, 'I don't want to do this. I don't like that.' Let's think about 'we,' about the team."

When Dallas Green spoke, people listened. Hell, they had no choice. His voice registered 1.6 on the Richter Scale. There were suburban radio stations that didn't have the carrying power of Dallas Green's voice.

The new manager was in a unique position. He hadn't sought the job; it was thrust upon him. As heir-apparent to Paul Owens as the Phillies' general manager of the future, he obviously had a lot of clout in the organization. If the players didn't like him, that was their problem. Danny Ozark had managed his way . . . and come up short. Now Dallas Green was about to do things his way. He had become convinced, he said, that all those "I's" in the Phillies clubhouse really wanted to become a cohesive, winning, "we."

"You can see the different personalities that we have down there," he said. "They're so diverse that I don't think anything really got them together totally. They say [the desire] is there, and I believe it. I believe it. Otherwise I would've told Paul at the end of the thirty days [the final month of the '79 season], 'Hell, these guys don't give a damn about Philadelphia.' But they do. Deep down, they do. It's not all lip service. But we've got to tie it all together. There are a lot of loose ends down there right now in the clubhouse."

There was no certainty when Dallas Green replaced Ozark late in '79 that he would remain as Phillies manager the following season. After all, he had only had two previous years of managerial experience in the pros —both deep in the Phillies farm system. But that month on the job in September of '79 inspired him to keep at it for a while. Managing one month in the big leagues is like eating one potato chip; it's damned difficult to stop.

Among those available to take the job in the event Green had returned to the front office was Whitey Herzog, who had won three straight division titles—and lost three straight American League playoffs to the Yankees. Fired by Kansas City at the end of the '79 season, Whitey was free . . . and interested. "Bing Devine [former Cardinal general manager] really wanted me to get that ball club," Herzog—now manager *and* general manager of the Cardinals—said. "Actually Bing talked to the Phillies more than I did . . . Paul said, 'Look, I've promised the job; it's Dallas' if he wants it, and he's going to let me know by the end of the World Series. If he wants it, it's his.' "

Dallas wanted it . . . and the "We, Not I" signs sprouted in the Phillies clubhouse. The easy-going Ozark era was history. Now Dallas Green, a tall, imposing figure with a booming voice and no hesitation about using it, was sitting in that office near the clubhouse door. If Danny had treated the players with kid gloves, his successor favored the iron-fist approach. If Danny prided himself on never publicly knocking one of his players—unless, of course, the guy's name happened to be Jay Johnstone—Dallas made it a point to say what was on his mind. For the Phillies, it was more than a whole new ball game; it was a whole new world.

The bad year, he felt, would provide some added motivation. "I'm counting on that," Dallas said. "They got their tails beat. They got kicked around pretty good by the press, and by the fans—as well they should. And I kicked them pretty good for thirty days because I kept reminding them that they were the ones that got Danny fired. Not me. I didn't fire Danny. They did. And they didn't like to hear that because it was true."

Dallas Green would say many things in the course of the 1980 season that his players liked hearing even less than that. It got to be a stormy scene in that clubhouse. He ripped the players; the players ripped him. But the bottom line is, he won. And they won. And Philadelphia won. Maybe it happened despite his tactics, as some players would have you believe. Maybe it happened because of his tactics. The fact remains that it did happen. A parade of managers had led bad Phillie teams, mediocre Phillie teams, and good Phillie teams in the three decades since Philadelphia last hosted a World Series. Steve O'Neill had tried. And Mayo Smith. And Eddie Sawyer (in a return appearance). And Gene Mauch.

And Bob Skinner. And Frank Lucchesi. And Danny Ozark. Even Paul Owens had taken a brief turn at it. But it took a one-time, sore-armed pitcher with minimal managing experience in the low minors and his sights set on being a general manager to put the Phillies over the top. He drove them, he taunted them, he angered them . . . and he won with them.

A number of players contributed mightily to the Phillies' first world championship. Mike Schmidt was a terror, leading the major leagues in home runs with 48, scoring 104 runs, driving in 121, and hitting higher (.286) than he'd ever hit before. Second baseman Manny Trillo had an outstanding year, batting over .300 most of the season on the way to a .292 finish, his best ever. Rookies Lonnie Smith and Keith Moreland contributed significantly on offense: Smith hit .339 in 100 games and stole 33 bases; Moreland, one of those good hitters who gets even better in clutch situations, batted .314 and knocked in 29 runs with his 50 hits. Bake McBride hit .309 with a career-high 87 RBIs.

Even those who struggled at times—Larry Bowa, Bob Boone, Garry Maddox, Greg Luzinski—rose to the occasion at some key times. And then there was the pitching staff filled with questionmarks that became exclamation points instead. Nobody doubted Steve Carlton's ability to lead the staff one more time, but his Cy Young Award-winning, 24–9 season was above and beyond the call of duty; his earned run average dropped from 3.62 in '79 to 2.34. There were doubts about Dick Ruthven's ability to come back from elbow surgery—the second time he'd gone under the knife in his career. However, the righthander bounced back brilliantly, winning seventeen games in the regular season and then, under the greatest pressure imaginable, winning the biggest game of them all: the fifth game of the championship series against Houston. A couple of kid pitchers helped too. Bob Walk, who had spent the previous season in Double A Reading, got yanked up in an emergency and won eleven games, then started—and won—the first game of the World Series. Marty Bystrom was even more amazing. Called up in September almost as an afterthought and not expected to pitch in the stretch drive, he got pressed into service when Larry Christenson was injured and did nothing but win, going 5–0 in the regular season and holding Houston to one earned run in five and one-third innings as the fifth-game starter in the playoffs.

And then there was Tug McGraw, for half a season as great a relief pitcher as ever stifled an enemy rally. Out for a while with tendonitis in his shoulder, the lefthander with the hard-to-hit screwball and the easy-to-love personality returned in mid-July and was virtually untouchable the rest of the way.

But if all that makes it sound easy—believe me, it wasn't. In fact, if not for the presence of the man the Phillies had grabbed in the free-agent market prior to the '79 season, another Philadelphia baseball season most certainly would have gone down the drain. Maybe Pete Rose was unable to snap this club out of its lethargy in his first season at the Vet, but he worked wonders that second season. It didn't matter that he hit "only" .282 and that he collected "only" 185 hits and scored "only" 95 runs. The man was there when the Phillies needed him most—in the playoffs. When a run had to be scored, he was the guy who found a way to score it. When the championship series seemed irretrievably lost, he was the guy who stood in front of the visiting dugout in Houston, clapping his hands together, talking up a storm, constantly reminding his teammates that there was still time, still hope. In that nerve-shattering playoff series against the Astros, Pete Rose did all the things the Phillies expected him to when they got him—and then some. Watching him in Houston brought back words spoken by Rawly Eastwick, a teammate of Pete's in Cincinnati who was a member of the '79 Phillies. "I think just the one asset Pete has that would benefit this team," Eastwick said, "is that once this team got into a playoff he'd be one of the main ingredients. I think just having him around and having that attitude and having that leadership, that's what the Phillies were after [when they signed Rose] and that's what they're going to get."

First, though, the Phillies had to get into the playoffs. For a long time in 1980 their chances didn't seem awfully bright.

At the All-Star break, they were second, only a game off the lead, but that was more a result of Pittsburgh and Montreal failing to take charge than the Phillies' great play. With all of Green's prodding and pushing, they were only six games over .500. What's more, they simply didn't have the look of winners. The friction between the manager and some of his players had been on the rise, and then, to complicate matters further, the drug story broke in *The Trenton Times.* Several Phillies, it was revealed, had been obtaining amphetamines, pep pills, greenies, call them what you will, from a doctor in Reading, Pennsylvania. There was an investigation, and some of the Phillies would be asked to testify.

The story broke during the All-Star break . . . and the war between the Phillies and the press became hotter than ever. Some of the players—Larry Bowa, in particular—attacked the press for writing half-truths and worse. To a certain extent their anger was understandable. A front-page headline in *The Philadelphia Journal* read, "Narcs: 'We're After the Phils.' " Basically responsible journalism in Trenton had led to sensationalized headlines elsewhere. Still, if the media overreacted at the time, the ball club overreacted even more. Simply by being totally honest the Phillies probably could have taken a giant stride toward diffusing the story.

Their players were charged with no crime. Several of them—Luzinski, Carlton, Bowa, Rose, Lerch, Christenson—had obtained amphetamines through prescriptions made out by Dr. Patrick Mazza, a Reading physician who had once been team doctor of the Reading Phillies (Philadelphia's Eastern League farm club). Pitcher Randy Lerch would testify under oath in February of '81 that he had obtained an amphetamine known as Preludin in that manner. OK then, why the run-around? Why did Paul Owens tell the press that he knew nothing of an investigation until *The Trenton Times* broke the story on July 8, when, in fact, two drug investigators employed by the Commonwealth of Pennsylvania, Phoebe Teichert and William Johnson, met with the general manager on June 26? Chances are, the Phillies were afraid of further damaging an image that was none too good in the first place, and fearful of what baseball commissioner Bowie Kuhn might do if the facts were made public.

So the Phillies screamed "irresponsible journalism" and tried to make it appear that the *Trenton Times'* story was a figment of somebody's imagination. When the young man who wrote the story showed up in the press room at the Vet, Phillies executive vice-president Bill Giles unleashed a withering verbal attack. In the end, the Phillies were left with greenies on their shelves and egg on their faces.

The Great Pep Pill Caper was still smoldering when the war between Dallas Green and his players became headline news. It was late July, and the Phillies were stumbling through a six-game losing streak that dropped them to third place, a mere three games over .500, when that story added a new touch of controversy to an already stormy season.

Triggering the latest commotion was the usually quiet, even-tempered Greg Luzinski. He had worked tremendously hard in the off season, reporting to spring training in such good shape that a casual observer might have mistaken the slimmed-down left fielder for his kid brother at first glance.

And the hard work paid off. On his very first at-bat the man they called "the Bull" unloaded a three-run homer against Montreal's Steve Rogers at the Vet.

In May, Luzinski hit eight homers; he seemed headed for a big year. But it wasn't to be. He slumped in June, hurt his right knee on a slide in St. Louis in early July, and underwent surgery in late July. It was just a week before he entered the hospital to have his knee taken care of that the disappointment and the frustration and the anger he felt bubbled over. Several hours before the Phillies were to take on the Cincinnati Reds at the Vet—and go crashing down to their fifth defeat in a row—Luzinski nodded in the direction of the manager's office and said, "I think he's hurting us. He's trying to be a fucking Gestapo. I stay at home and read his quotes, and it really disappoints me. It's terrible. He put in [the papers] yesterday, 'I hear us saying we want to win; we're going to win. I hear us saying we're grinding it out, but I don't see it.' He pisses me off, putting quotes in the paper like that. He's like a Gestapo. I thought from spring training to opening day, when they opened the gates and it was for real, he changed."

That was the first round in a feud that became very vocal and very personal, a feud that would lead to the sale of Luzinski to the Chicago White Sox in the spring of '81. "I like playing for the guy," Greg said that day in July of '80, "don't get me wrong; it's just some of the things he says." With that, he pointed to the big sign hanging above the door. "It says We, Not I," he said, "but I dunno. You get the feeling sometimes that he doesn't think we're trying. He says 'We' when we win, but he says 'they' when we lose."

Dallas Green and his largely unhappy band of athletes staggered along, battling with the press and each other as they went. In early August the team went to Pittsburgh for a four-game, three-day series against the defending world champion Pirates. If ever the Phillies were going to make a run for the division title, this seemed like the time. But the run disintegrated into an all-out retreat. The Pirates beat them 6-5 on Friday night, and 4-1 on Saturday afternoon, then kicked them out of Three Rivers Stadium with a 7-1, 4-1 double thumping on Sunday, after which Dallas Green roared at them in such a loud voice, accusing them of "quitting," that Bill Conlin, of *The Philadelphia Daily News,* wrote that the manager's not-so-dulcet tones could be "heard through bolted steel doors." Who would have guessed the Phillies team that went reeling out of Pittsburgh on the night of August 10 would be the toast of Philadelphia two months later?

Veteran relief pitcher Ron Reed recalled that four-game series with the Pirates the following spring, and talked about how the club was able to take an apparent disaster and build it into eventual triumph.

"We lost those four straight to the Pirates," he said, "and we left there and everybody wrote us off. Then we got together in Chicago—just the players—and we said, 'Hey, let's don't go [back] to fourth place. We're better than a fourth-place club. Forget all the other stuff and play for ourselves. Get together as a team, but play for us.'

"We had a meeting," Reed said. "The heck with Dallas," we said. "The heck with the coaching staff. Let's win it for us. And it seemed like we came close together after that. It was a very brief sort of thing, but we turned it around.

"That was the closest I've ever seen guys come together as a team," Reed went on. "I mean it was all there as a team. No rah-rah stuff, no cheerleading, but the guys actually pulled for each other in their own way. Individual performances were out the window. We finally realized we wanted to be in a damn World Series, and that's what it takes."

The drug story faded into the background. The feuding, fussing, and fighting faded into the background. Oh sure, there were still some sparks, but the game became the most important thing. Needing a quick about-face following the Pittsburgh debacle, the Phillies achieved it. They won two out of three in Chicago, then blasted the Mets five straight times in New York. They were back in the race—right back where they'd been *before* the Pittsburgh series. Now it would be the Pirates, riddled with injuries, who couldn't keep up the pace. By the beginning of September the

Phillies team that had been counted out on August 10 was in first place.

The Phillies clubhouse still wasn't the friendliest spot on earth, but the atmosphere did seem to improve a bit. Actually, it couldn't have gotten much worse. Things were so bad in '79 that Tug McGraw went on record about it in an interview with Stan Hockman of *The Philadelphia Daily News*. "I said the one area where there should be peace and tranquility was the clubhouse," Tug said. "I told him the players seem to hate the fans, they seem to hate the press, and then, when they come in the clubhouse, they act like they hate each other."

Now, all of a sudden, they all seemed to be pushing for one goal: a chance to play in a World Series. "I think Dallas helped ease some of that [clubhouse tension]," McGraw would suggest later. "He made things so controversial, he had the guys so mad at him with some of his quotes that the dark cloud from over the clubhouse settled right over his door. It was probably one of the best things he did, although he might have lost a few friends on the team by doing so. I think that was inadvertently one of the good things that happened. I know toward the end it was sure a lot more pleasant walking in there. Before, there was so much tension in that clubhouse every day when you walked through the door that you wondered if this was going to be the day that a riot was going to break out, that somebody was going to jump on somebody."

Maybe Tug had a point. Maybe Dallas Green got some of the players so angry with him that they stopped being angry with each other and put all their energy into striving for a common goal. If a feeling of "The hell with Dallas, let's win" was what his team needed, so be it. Ozark's pat-on-the-back approach hadn't produced any National League pennants; the time had come to test Green's kick-'em-in-the-butt approach.

Everybody was contributing now. Larry Bowa, so upset by the drug story that he refused to speak to the local press for several weeks—a "penalty" that must have been harder on the talkative Bowa than on the writers—was playing brilliantly again. "Up until two or three weeks ago, I couldn't do anything," he said in mid-September. "I wasn't mentally in the game. Thoughts would go through my mind when the guy's in the windup. You can't play baseball like that."

But there was another one of those clubhouse meetings that

helped snap him out of it. "I didn't realize that I was doing some of the things that I was doing," Bowa said. "Then the general manager came down and aired out a couple of us. My name was mentioned as one of the guys that really wasn't playing up to his capability. . . . I said, 'Hey, the most important thing right now is to try to help us get in the playoffs.' "

Bowa is a born worrier. If there isn't anything to worry about, never fear, Larry Bowa will think of something. But with it all, the skinny, little guy—"Gnat," they nicknamed him in the minors—was a helluva ball player, the most consistent shortstop in the history of the big leagues. Don't say, "Yeah, but he had the advantage of playing on artificial turf." Bowa broke in at Connie Mack Stadium, on the grass. He made all the plays there too. The man virtually never messed up a routine play and that, in the final analysis, is the greatest attribute a big-league shortstop can have. Even when Bowa blew his top—a not uncommon occurrence—he had the ability to set his anger aside when the next ground ball came his way. Larry's temper tantrums became legend; once, after making a big out in Houston, he walked the length of the runway that led to the clubhouse, using his bat to smash all the light bulbs along the way. But when the Phillies made their stretch run in 1980, Bowa channeled his competitive instincts in the way you'd expect an All-Star-caliber athlete to channel them. Forget the early months of the '80 season; Larry Bowa was an All-Star again when it mattered most.

The year had been a difficult one for Bob Boone too. The starting catcher for the National League in the 1979 All-Star game in Seattle, he sustained a serious knee injury late in the season and had to undergo surgery. The injury, comparable to that which felled the Eagles' Bill Bergey in '79, cut into Boone's effectiveness in '80. A .280–plus hitter for three straight seasons, he slipped to .229. It got so, the mere mention of his name by the PA announcer at the Vet triggered a torrent of boos. But Boone kept plugging away, kept crouching behind the plate, even when the pain was severe, kept doing a bangup job of handling the pitchers.

"It [the booing] probably was tougher on my wife and family than it was on me," the Stanford grad said. "It's allowed me to recognize what fans are—and *fans* is short for *fanatics*, and I think that's what we have in Philadelphia. It allows you to keep everything in perspective as far as baseball goes. You recognize that, 'Yeah, I can be on top with one swing of the bat or I can be at the bottom with one swing of the bat,' and you recognize that that's the way it is, and so you don't get too eaten up with your successes or your failures. I think it's a matter of being mature enough to accept it."

It would be hard to find an athlete more mature than Bob Boone, or more intelligent. He got through those difficult times in 1980 . . . and at the end delivered some vital clutch hits.

"It's something my dad taught me," said Boone, whose father, Ray, was a major-league infielder for thirteen years. "I guess it was '75, the year Danny Ozark sat me down as a punishment and played Johnny Oates, and Johnny did a great job for us, and it was very upsetting to me every day not to be in the lineup. I felt that I should be, and at the end of the season my initial feeling was, 'Get me out of here.' Maybe the most important thing my dad ever said to me was, 'Well, I'll be damned if I'd let anybody else run me out of a job.' I think he was right, and I think it applies the same way to fans. I don't care what they do; they're not going to run me out of town. It's the only way to survive. It goes along with the ups and downs of baseball. You have 162 games. You're going to have good days, you're going to have bad days, and you've got to stay on an even keel, or you're on an emotional roller coaster and you'll go crazy."

So Boone didn't let the boos get to him in '80, although there was one time when he admits he got more than a little upset. "You know where I had the most trouble?" he said. "It was sitting and watching some Eagles games. I remember, the Eagles were playing the St. Louis Cardinals; they beat 'em, but they weren't playing particularly well. I was sitting in the stands, and to hear the fans booing Jaworski. . . . There was a lot of wind. It was cold. I know what it's like to throw a baseball on a day like that, let alone throw a football. It was tough on me being in the stands with that going on. I wanted to argue with every fan there."

But that, Bob Boone had come to realize, was part of the game, part of the price a man must pay for being a professional athlete in a city like Philadelphia, where the people care so terribly much about their teams.

The National League East race rolled into the next-to-last

weekend of the season. The Phillies, half a game ahead of Montreal, prepared to host the Expos in a three-game series. When Bake McBride won the first game with a ninth-inning home run, it appeared the Phillies were ready to open up some daylight. They had their ace, Steve Carlton, ready to pitch the second day; the Expos seemed to be in trouble.

A funny game, baseball. Appearances are often deceiving. Montreal beat Carlton to close within half a game again, then won the Sunday afternoon rubber match going away when center fielder Garry Maddox, temporarily blinded by the sun, was unable to catch a sixth-inning drive by Chris Speier that went for a game-breaking, two-run triple.

The Phillies had blown their chance to take charge in the race. Once again, they looked like a team that couldn't get over the hump. By the following night when the sad-sack Cubs came to town to open a four-game series, the tension that Tug McGraw had talked about was evident in the clubhouse. Dallas Green had shaken up the lineup, benching three veterans —Garry Maddox, Greg Luzinski, and Bob Boone. Before the game began, Maddox confronted a writer, The Inquirer's Jayson Stark, and told him he felt he was responsible for his benching, blaming it on a story that made a big thing out of the line drive Garry lost in the sun.

A veteran of Vietnam, a man who spends countless hours doing charitable work for kids, Maddox is an introspective, highly sensitive person. When he is hurt, it shows. And it showed very glaringly that last Monday evening of the 1980 season. At a time when he wanted to play, when he wanted to be a part of the pennant push, he was riding the bench.

Larry Bowa had a few things to say too, when he saw the lineup that Green had posted before the game. And the shortstop had a forum for those words; he did a nightly sports show on a local FM station, WWDB. "Dallas has said he's going to let the veterans go to the hilt," Bowa said on the air. "To me, this is not letting the veterans go to the hilt. If he's going to let Lonnie [Smith] and Keith [Moreland] play [against the Cubs], then I'm sure he's going to let them play [against] the Expos in Montreal [the final weekend of the season]. He can't sit down Boonie and Luzinski for four days and then when we go against Montreal say, 'OK, go get 'em again.' In order for them to find their batting stroke or find

their batting eye, they have to play every day. If they're not going
to play every day, don't just throw them in against the Montreal
Expos. Dallas," Bowa told his listeners, "is trying to shake things
up, which is very understandable, but on the other hand he's talking out of both sides of his mouth by saying he wants to stay with
the veterans."

Yessir, things had returned to normal, or abnormal, or
whatever you'd call the usual state of the Phillies clubhouse, circa
1980.

They had just lost two big games to the Expos; they had just
fallen out of first place, and now they were snarling, bickering,
feuding again. The all-or-nothing, do-or-die final week of the pennant race had the look of an impending disaster as the Phillies took
the field that night. And things got worse before they got better. It
was one of those games that looked like it would never end. The
Cubs rallied for two runs in the seventh off Larry Christenson to
take a 3–2 lead; the Phillies came back to tie it in the home
seventh . . . and then the goose eggs started going up. The Phillies
wasted a one-out double by Del Unser, Maddox' center-field
replacement, in the eleventh, a two-out single and stolen base by
Lonnie Smith in the twelfth, a leadoff walk to Bake McBride in the
thirteenth, a one-out single by Manny Trillo in the fourteenth.
Into the top of the fifteenth they went, and when the Cubs followed a walk and a throwing error by Dickie Noles with a sacrifice
fly and a double against Kevin Saucier, the Phillies trailed by two.

A loss there might have polished off the 1980 Phillies. Left-
handed reliever Doug Capilla gave them an opening, walking Lonnie Smith and Pete Rose to start the bottom of the fifteenth and
wild pitching them into scoring position. Bake McBride's grounder
got in one run and moved the tying run to third. In came
righthander Dennis Lamp to pitch to Mike Schmidt. The Phillies'
big hitter took a ball, then popped weakly to second. The tying
run was still on third, but now there were two out.

The next batter was Garry Maddox, who had come in to play
center field after Del Unser was lifted for a pinch runner in the
twelfth. It was one of those truth-is-stranger-than-fiction situations. Here was Maddox, upset because the manager had taken
him out of the starting lineup, coming to the plate with the
game—maybe even the pennant—on the line. He ripped a clean

single to center, tying the score, and came around to score the winning run on singles by Keith Moreland and Manny Trillo. The night that had started so badly ended, nearly four and a half hours later, with a happy band of Phillies whooping and hollering around home plate. Maddox' hit may have been the single most important hit of the Phillies' stretch drive.

"I'll tell you what," said Mike Schmidt, one of Maddox' closest friends and admirers, "that was a special moment for me too. Just going back to the bench [after popping up] and watching Maddox walk up to home plate. . . . I wasn't verbally yelling at him or screaming at him or anything like that. I wasn't showing a great deal of emotion. But I guarantee you inside I was—you know, concentrating as hard as I could concentrate. I could sort of see the look in Garry's eyes. I could tell that he knew this was an important at-bat, a big hit, and when he got it you just sort of feel like, that's what it takes to win divisions. The time when people least think you're going to pull out a ball game, you do it. People in the stands are saying, 'It's over.' "

They were, in fact, booing the Phillies after the Cubs scored those two runs in the top of the fifteenth—a fact that prompted the emotional Bowa to shout, within earshot of the press immediately after the game, that they were "the worst fans in the world."

That quote received wide circulation the next day, and the boos rained down on Bowa's head the rest of the home stand. His response was typical Bowa. He got two hits in each of the next three games and played brilliantly in the field as the Phillies swept the Cubs and headed for Montreal in a flat-footed tie for first place.

The Expos had chased the Pirates down to the wire the year before and come up just short. This time they expected to win, and why not? They were hot, and they were playing at home.

But Dick Ruthven, Sparky Lyle, and Tug McGraw cooled them off.

Mike Schmidt gave them all the runs they needed, knocking in one with a first-inning sacrifice fly, another with a sixth-inning homer. Ruthven blanked the Expos on two hits until the sixth, then gave up his third hit—a double by Jerry White—and his first (and last) run. Lyle got Warren Cromartie on a checked-swing grounder to strand two Expos in the sixth and forced White and

Rodney Scott to hit the ball in the air with runners on first and second in the seventh. Then in came Tug. The Expos might as well have turned off the lights to save some money; it wouldn't have made any difference. He struck out pinch-hitter Bob Pate, Andre Dawson, and Gary Carter in the eighth and, after Cromartie lined to left, threw called third strikes past Larry Parrish and Jerry Manuel to close out the ninth. The Phillies were one victory away from the Eastern Division title.

Normally, Tug McGraw would have come leaping off the mound, brandishing a fist, celebrating the big victory. Not this time. "Last Friday [when McBride homered to beat the Expos in the ninth], we got all keyed up," he explained, "and then we went out and lost Saturday and Sunday. So I thought maybe we should change our program a little bit—not get too emotional about winning tonight, and it'll be easier getting it together tomorrow."

"Tug made a good point when he came in here [immediately after the game-ending strikeout]," Dick Ruthven said. " 'Key down, key down,' he said. 'There's one more to win, *then* we'll go nuts.' "

That one more came in the kind of baseball game that drives people nuts. Nobody could have written this script. The Phillies made five errors, one of them an inglorious muff of a pop fly by the usually sure-handed Manny Trillo. They ran the bases like a Little League team gone mad; in one particularly zany sequence a two-run single by Greg Luzinski wound up being an inning-ending double play. Seventeen hits they pounded off four Montreal pitchers . . . and yet they were one out away from losing it. The Expos led, 4–3, in the ninth and Woodie Fryman, after walking Pete Rose, got Bake McBride and Mike Schmidt to pound the ball into the turf. With two out and the tying run at second, Fryman faced Bob Boone, the slump-ridden catcher who had been benched in favor of rookie Moreland on that rainy Saturday afternoon.

Boone had just two hits in his last twenty-five at-bats as he stood up there, facing Fryman. A minute later he was 3–for–26 with a solid, line single to center, and the game was tied. What Maddox had done in the fifteenth inning at the Vet, Boone did in the ninth inning at Olympic Stadium.

In came Tug McGraw to prove that the previous night's heroics had been no accident. He struck out the first two Expos he faced, retired the next on a foul pop to rookie catcher Don McCormack, and the game went into extra innings.

McGraw and Stan Bahnsen pitched a scoreless tenth; then Rose grounded a single to right to open the eleventh. Bake McBride, first-ball swinging, fouled out . . . and now it was Schmidt's turn to hit with McCormack on deck and the bench bare. Moreland had been lifted for a pinch-runner in the eighth. Boone had been yanked for a pinch-runner in the ninth. There are people who will tell you there's no way the Expos could let Mike Schmidt knock them out of the pennant race at a time like that, no way Stan Bahnsen could have given him a pitch to hit out of sight. But the count went to two balls, no strikes . . . and then Bahnsen got one over. Schmidt swung and there was no doubt about it. Home run no. 48 went soaring deep into the left-field seats.

Later, Larry Bowa, that noted journalism critic, would talk about the difference between the press in Philadelphia and Montreal, using that eleventh-inning situation as an example.

"Mike Schmidt wins the game with McCormack coming up on deck," the shortstop said. "We're out of players. I'll be damned if I'm going to let Mike Schmidt beat me when there's a kid coming up next. But not one thing was written in the paper up there. I'll guarantee you, if that happened in Philadelphia, if we pitched to an established hitter in that spot, we'd have been picked apart. We couldn't believe nothing was written about it [in Montreal]. I was sitting on the bench saying, 'There's no way they can pitch to Schmitty. There's no way.' Pow! Home run. I said, 'Williams [Expos manager Dick Williams] is going to get ripped tomorrow.' Next day I'm looking all over in the paper. Nothing except, 'Wait 'til next season.' "

McGraw made sure that the Expos would have to wait by retiring Carter, Cromartie, and Parrish in order in the home eleventh. This time, when Parrish went down swinging for the final out, Tug did one of his patented high jumps off the mound. "Today's ball game," he said later, "was probably one of the most outstanding head-to-head ball games that I can ever remember. It was just an incredible show of two teams that wanted it real bad."

"Maybe we have more heart now than we used to have," Mike Schmidt told a group of writers in the clubhouse as the champagne flowed again. "If we'd lost that game today and lost tomorrow you could have had a field day—and justifiably so."

Phillies' Division Clincher
(October 4, 1980, at Montreal)

Philadelphia	ab	r	h	rbi		Montreal	ab	r	h	rbi
Rose, 1b	5	2	3	1		White, lf	3	1	2	3
McBride, rf	5	2	3	0		Scott, 2b	4	0	3	1
Schmidt, 3b	5	1	3	2		Office, rf	5	0	1	0
Luzinski, lf	4	0	2	2		Dawson, cf	5	0	1	0
Reed, p	0	0	0	0		Carter, c	4	0	0	0
Lyle, p	0	0	0	0		Cromartie, 1b	5	0	0	0
Boone, ph	1	0	1	1		Parrish, 3b	5	0	1	0
Dernier, pr	0	0	0	0		Speier, ss	3	0	0	0
McCorm'k, c	1	0	1	0		LeFlore, pr	0	1	0	0
Unser, cf-lf	4	0	1	0		Manuel, ss	1	0	0	0
Smith, lf	1	0	0	0		Rogers, p	1	1	0	0
Moreland, c	4	0	0	0		Montanez, ph	0	0	0	0
Loviglio, pr	0	0	0	0		Tamargo, ph	0	0	0	0
Brusstar, p	0	0	0	0		Raines, pr	0	1	0	0
Aviles, ph	1	0	0	0		Sosa, p	0	0	0	0
McGraw, p	1	0	0	0		Fryman, p	0	0	0	0
Trillo, 2b	5	0	1	0		Wallace, ph	1	0	0	0
Bowa, ss	4	1	1	0		Bahnsen, p	0	0	0	0
Christenson, p	2	0	1	0						
Gross, ph-lf	1	0	0	0						
Maddox, ph-cf	2	0	0	0						
Totals	**46**	**6**	**17**	**6**		**Totals**	**37**	**4**	**8**	**4**

Philadelphia	000	010	201	02 — 6
Montreal	002	000	200	00 — 4

Philadelphia	IP	H	R	ER	BB	SO
Christenson	6	6	2	2	3	3
Reed	1/3	0	1	0	0	1
Lyle	2/3	1	1	1	1	1
Brusstar	1	0	0	0	0	1
McGraw (W, 5-4)	3	1	0	0	0	4

Montreal	IP	H	R	ER	BB	SO
Rogers	7	11	3	3	3	4
Sosa	2/3	2	0	0	0	0
Fryman	1 1/3	1	1	1	2	2
Bahnsen (L, 7-6)	2	3	2	2	0	0

Game-winning RBI—Schmidt.
E—Trillo 2, Christenson 2, Parrish, White, Moreland. DP—Philadelphia 3, Montreal 3. LOB—Philadelphia 12, Montreal 6. 2B—Schmidt, Scott, HR—(White (6), Schmidt (48). SB—Dawson, LeFlore, Raines. SH—Scott. SF—White. WP—Rogers. T— 3:51.

But they hadn't lost. And now, after all the controversy, all the squabbles, all the bitterness, there they were, laughing, shouting, dumping champagne over each other's heads. Truth is indeed stranger than fiction.

The team that was supposed to fold under pressure had won two straight games away from home—hell, out of the country—on the last weekend of the season with the division title on the line. Trailing by half a game with a week to go, they had put together a six-game winning streak. It was a week when it all came together for the Phillies, as if by magic; a week that began when a center fielder (Maddox) who wasn't supposed to be able to swing a bat—because of a bad finger—drilled a game-tying, two-out hit in the bottom of the fifteenth against the Cubs, a week that ended with the help of a bases-loaded single by a left fielder (Luzinski) who was battling a 4–for–34 slump, and a two-out, game-tying, ninth-inning single by a catcher (Boone) who was mired in a 2–for–25 slump. "If you want to write a story," Greg Luzinski told a member of the press, "it's all there."

Indeed it was. The team that couldn't win had transformed itself into the team that wouldn't lose. It was a week when Mike Schmidt, who had never been considered a great pressure player despite all those homers, all those runs batted in, put on an October power display worthy of a Willie Stargell or a Reggie Jackson. When the Phillies needed a long ball, Schmidt provided it for them. Four games in a row he sent baseballs rocketing into the stands, and in the two title-clinching victories in Montreal—playing in front of crowds that Ruly Carpenter described as "intimidating"—he hit the homers that made the difference. Clearly, Mike Schmidt had come of age. At thirty-one, he had learned how to concentrate on the most difficult of sports challenges: hitting a baseball under pressure-cooker conditions.

"It's probably the most emotional time of my career," Schmidt had said as the team entered that all-or-nothing final week of the regular season. "I don't think this is our 'Last Hurrah' or anything like that. Speaking for myself, I feel simply that it's a time in my career where I can have a great year and be part of a winning cause. Who knows what's going to happen over the winter, the rest of your life—you may never get an opportunity like this again and you've got to make the most of it while you've got it. There are people all over wondering if we *are* trying to make the most of it."

That was the reputation Schmidt and his teammates had to live down. With a few notable exceptions—McGraw, Bowa, Rose, and some of the kids—they were generally perceived as an ultra-cool bunch, and that cool approach was interpreted as an "I-don't-give-a-damn" approach. In that final week of the regular season, and in the couple of weeks that followed, they proved that they *did* give a damn.

It took a lot of doing. "At times," said Mike Schmidt, "we're out there trying to beat the other team, trying to beat the mood of the crowd, trying to beat all kinds of external forces that we shouldn't have to be trying to beat in our own minds. It's tough enough when you've got your mind tuned in to what you want to have it tuned in to—but man, if there are other things clouding that thinking you'll see more pop-ups than you'll ever want to see."

All those negative thoughts had to be put to rest in a game that is overwhelmingly mental. "I'm not sure you can say the press affects or ever has affected anyone's play during a ball game," said Schmidt. "I don't think it ever has. I'm talking about something you can feel while you're up there hitting. You can't feel the power of the pen while you're hitting a baseball in the middle of a game, but you sure as hell can feel—your ears can *hear*—boos. And the press can affect the mood of a crowd."

In their minds, right down to the end, they were battling the press and the mood of the crowd, as well as the team in the other dugout.

"The only way to put a damper on this stuff," Schmidt had said, "is to scrape out a divisional title and a playoff title and a World Series title, and all you've got to do is do it once. The Flyers are the greatest thing in this town, and they only did it once or twice or whatever. I don't know what they did; all I know is they got a Stanley Cup somewhere and that's all it took. They became a 'team of winners.' The term 'always find a way to lose a big one' or 'never play well under pressure' will never be applied to them. Never."

Schmidt might have been exaggerating somewhat, but his point was well taken. The Flyers, by winning those two Stanley Cups in the mid-'70s when the rest of the city's teams were a joke, had become synonymous with success. The Phillies, by going nearly a century without winning a World Series, by going the last three decades without even getting into one, by losing three consecutive National League playoffs in the late '70s had become synonymous with failure. Overcoming that stigma may have been the toughest thing the 1980 Phillies had to do.

"At times," Mike Schmidt said, "I think this team gets too high. I think we get too cocky as a result of winning [a game]. Sometimes I don't think we're good winners. I believe in drawing positive vibrations from victories. I really do. I believe in drawing positive vibrations from any kind of hit you get. I believe in learning and adjusting even if you get a broken-bat hit. I believe in learning and adjusting after a victory where you didn't score for ten innings, then somebody hits a home run and you go crazy. You feel like pouring champagne because you beat 'em when really one swing of the bat won the game for you. You didn't hit well. You may not have played well. But you won so [the feeling is], 'Keep it the same. Use the same lineup. Do the same thing. Wear the same underwear.' I don't believe that. Like hitting a golf shot that hits a tree and goes on the green. You putt it in for a birdie, right? I believe in saying, 'What did I do wrong on that shot?' so I can improve it the next time. Not, 'Hey, I'm on the green!' "

Well, they had butchered plays in the field on that last Saturday of the season in Montreal, and they had squandered a pile of hits . . . and, lo and behold, they were on the green. They were back in the National League playoffs. And they had Pete Rose, soon to become the all-time base-hit champion of the National League, on their side. And Steve Carlton, the best starting pitcher in all of baseball. And Tug McGraw, one of the best relief pitchers. And Mike Schmidt, far and away the outstanding power hitter.

What did winning the division . . . and the pennant . . . and the World Series mean to Michael Jack Schmidt? Only this: "You know," he said just before that division-clinching, six-game winning streak started, "if I don't get a hit the rest of the year, I'll still have good numbers. But man, I'll tell you what . . . it could be the greatest season I ever had or it could be a mediocre season as far as I'm concerned. The numbers will be there. It's the asterisk by the numbers that means, 'They were in the playoffs and the World Series,' and it's the possible ring on my finger that's going to make it all worthwhile."

And now the Phillies embarked on the next step toward making it all worthwhile: the championship series against the pitcher-rich Houston Astros.

The name *Astros* didn't have the ring to it that *Reds* had had in '76 or *Dodgers* had had in '77 and '78. But if pitching was the name of the game, then the '80 Houston Astros were a team to be reckoned with. Beating out the Expos had been tough, but the Phillies hadn't seen anything yet.

First thing they had to do was win a post-season game at home. Sounds easy, right? Not for the Phillies, it wasn't. On October 8, 1915, at old Baker Bowl in North Philadelphia, the Phillies won a World Series game from the Boston Red Sox. The score was 3–1. The winning pitcher was Grover Cleveland Alexander. (You were expecting maybe John Boozer?)

Well, that was it, the *only* time Phillies fans saw their heroes win a post-season baseball game at home—until the 1980 team beat the Astros, 3–1, on the night of October 7 at the Vet. In the sixty-four years between victories Phillies teams had found ways to lose a total of ten post-season games in three Philadelphia ball parks. The 1915 club lost twice at Baker Bowl to the Red Sox on the way to losing the World Series in five games. The 1950 Phillies lost twice at Shibe Park to the Yankees on the way to losing the World Series in four games. The 1976 Phillies lost twice to the Reds at the Vet on the way to losing the National League championship series in three games. The 1977 and 1978 Phillies each lost twice to the Dodgers at the Vet on the way to losing the playoffs in four games. In those ten post-season games spanning six-and-one-half decades of frustration, the Phillies lost in almost every way imaginable . . . and in some ways that were almost unimaginable. There were two ninth-inning losses to the Red Sox in '15. There was a 1–0 loss and a 2–1, tenth-inning loss to the Yankees in '50. There was that numbing, two-out, three-run rally by the Dodgers in the third game of the '77 playoffs. And the grim let-it-rain, let-it-rain, let-it-rain game that followed.

But all bad things have to end. In 1915 it had been a Hall of Famer-to-be named Alexander who gave the home fans a victory to cherish. In 1980 it was a Hall of Famer-to-be named Carlton, with a late-inning assist from McGraw, who turned the trick. But it wasn't easy. With the 1980 Phillies, nothing was ever easy. For five-and-a-half innings, Ken Forsch had Carlton down, 1–0. Then with two out in the home sixth and Pete Rose on first, Greg Luzinski, who had struggled so mightily since returning from knee surgery, sent a 3–2 pitch crashing into the seats in left center. It was the twelfth straight playoff game in which Luzinski had hit safely; the streak would reach thirteen games before Joe Niekro would stop the Bull in game three.

The Phillies went on to win the first game, 3–1, but let the second game get away when consecutive ninth-inning singles by Bake McBride, Mike Schmidt, and Lonnie Smith merely loaded the bases, and Houston reliever Frank LaCorte squirmed out of trouble by getting Manny Trillo on strikes and Garry Maddox on a foul pop. Third base coach Lee Elia took the heat this time—for holding up McBride at third on Smith's looping hit to right. In the very next inning the Astros exploded for four runs . . . and held on for a 7–4 win. So it was on to the Astrodome, called the "eighth wonder of the world" by some Texans, called some things I'd rather not repeat by National League power hitters. This indoor playpen was a pitcher's park. Runs came hard there and, it seemed, especially hard for the Phillies.

They squandered ten innings of shutout pitching in game three—the first six by Larry Christenson—and finally lost, 1–0, in the eleventh when Joe Morgan led off with a triple against Tug McGraw, working in his fourth inning, and Denny Walling followed two intentional walks by hitting a sacrifice fly to left. The Phillies, who managed five hits off Joe Niekro in the first four innings, picked up only one more hit off the knuckleballer—an infield single by Trillo—in the next six. Dave Smith pitched the eleventh, gave up a two-out double to Garry Maddox, but fanned Del Unser for the third out. The Phillies were in their favorite position again: backs to the wall, facing a firing squad.

There had been something poignant about the game-ending scene. Walling's fly ball had floated out toward left field. Not very deep, but with Rafael Landestoy pinch-running and Greg Luzinski throwing, deep enough. From the instant the throw left Luzinski's hand it was obvious that Landestoy would score, but Schmidt cut if off anyway and made a hopeless, off-balance relay as the 44,000-plus Houston fans hollered themselves hoarse. In the stands the people were waving Texas flags and Astros pennants. Near home plate the Astros were celebrating the victory that moved them to within one game of the World Series. And near third base, while all the commotion went on around him, while his teammates trooped slowly, silently down the runway to the clubhouse, Mike Schmidt stood, bent over from the waist, hands on his knees, as if frozen there.

Most likely he was thinking about all the wasted opportunities, all the hard-hit balls with runners in scoring position that *didn't* fall safely —like the sharp bouncer he had hit to third with runners on second and third and one out in the third. No, he said later. He was merely waiting to make sure that Landestoy hadn't left third base too soon. "He might've left too soon; who knows?" Mike said. "But the umpires were off the field. Everybody ran out of there. I guess he didn't." The very next day, though, a Houston runner would be called out for leaving third base too soon on a fly ball to the outfield.

There were many low points for the 1980 Phillies, but that 1-0, extra-inning loss in Houston had to be the lowest. They had come so close to winning game two at the Vet, so close to winning this game at the Astrodome, so close to beating the Astros in three straight . . . and yet there they were, one defeat away from losing yet another championship series.

"I'd like to be in their shoes over there right now," Mike Schmidt said in the clubhouse. "But right now I still feel we're the best team. No question in my mind. I don't think there's any question in anybody's mind."

Maybe not. But the '77 Phillies were sure they were the better team . . . and the Dodgers beat them. And the '78 Phillies felt they were the better team . . . and the Dodgers beat them.

"Sometimes," sighed Larry Bowa, "you wonder if you're even supposed to get into a World Series. You wonder if maybe it just isn't in the cards."

After what happened in the top of the fourth inning the following day, Bowa must have been wondering even more. The Phillies had runners on first and second, nobody out in a scoreless duel between Carlton and Vern Ruhle. Garry Maddox swung and hit a ball off the handle of the bat toward the mound. Ruhle reached for it, appeared to trap it. The throw went to first. The Phillies had two runners in scoring position with one out. But wait. After a lengthy debate, the umpires decided that Ruhle had caught the ball on the fly. The Astros thought they had a triple play. But wait. It was decided that time had been called before Bake McBride had been "tripled" off second. So the Astros wound up getting a double play, and both teams played the game under protest.

The craziness continued. Carlton, by now trailing 2-0, walked the bases loaded in the sixth and had to be yanked. Luis Pujols hit a fly ball to right against reliever Dickie Noles. Gary Woods tagged and scored ahead of the throw. The Astros led, 3-0. But wait. The Phillies appealed, claiming that Woods had left third too soon. Third base umpire Bob Engel agreed. Cancel that third Houston run.

It didn't seem all that important as the Phillies went down meekly in the seventh, making it eighteen innings in the Astrodome with twelve hits and no runs. In the bottom of the seventh, the Astros filled the bases again on walks . . . and again they failed to score. Somehow three Phillies pitchers—Carlton, Noles and Kevin Saucier—had managed to walk a total of six Houston batters in two successive innings without giving up a run. Maybe the time had come for the Astros to start wondering if it was in the cards.

Anyhow, the Phillies were down to their last six outs. There was so much noise in the Astrodome that the place actually seemed to be shaking. The people were ready to celebrate Houston's first National League pennant.

"I honestly couldn't see it ending that way," Mike Schmidt said. "I couldn't see us leaving here without scoring some runs."

And finally they *did* score some runs. Finally, ground balls started finding holes and the noise abated; the Astrodome stopped shaking. Greg Gross singled to center. Lonnie Smith grounded a single to left. Pete Rose failed to bunt, then bounced a single to center. When the throw went to third, Pete scampered to second. Now it was Schmidt's turn. He bounced one up the middle. Joe Morgan backhanded the ball, glanced at Rose, and then threw to first. Too late. Schmidt had an infield hit. The score was tied.

The go-ahead run scored on a play that was in keeping with the day's madness. Manny Trillo lined one to right. Jeff Leonard charged it and fielded it on a short hop. Bruce Froemming, the right-field umpire, was in perfect position to make the call. So he made it—incorrectly. The Astros, grateful for small favors, came up with an inning-ending double play. But at least Rose scored the third run before the play was completed.

Had this emotional roller coaster ride ended? Don't be silly.
The Astros tied it on Terry Puhl's RBI single in the last of the ninth

Fourth Game in National League Championship Series
(October 11, 1980 at Houston)

Philadelphia	ab	r	h	rbi	Houston	ab	r	h	rbi
L. Smith, lf	4	1	2	0	Puhl, rf-cf	3	0	1	1
Unser, lf-rf	1	0	0	0	Cabell, 3b	4	1	1	0
Rose, 1b	4	2	2	1	Morgan, 2b	3	0	0	0
Schmidt, 3b	5	0	2	1	Woods, rf	2	0	0	0
McBride, rf	4	0	2	0	Walling, ph	1	0	0	0
Luzinski, ph	1	1	1	1	Leonard, rf	1	0	0	0
G. Vukovich, lf	0	0	0	0	Howe, 1b	3	0	1	1
Trillo, 2b	4	0	2	2	Cruz, lf	3	0	0	0
Maddox, cf	4	0	0	0	Pujols, c	3	1	1	0
Bowa, ss	5	0	1	0	Bochy, c	1	0	0	0
Boone, c	4	0	0	0	Landestoy, ss	3	1	1	1
Carlton, p	2	0	0	0	Ruhle, p	3	0	0	0
Noles, p	0	0	0	0	D. Smith, p	0	0	0	0
Saucier, p	0	0	0	0	Sambito, p	0	0	0	0
Reed, p	0	0	0	0					
Gross, ph	1	1	1	0					
Brusstar, p	1	0	0	0					
McGraw, p	0	0	0	0					
Totals	40	5	13	5	Totals	30	3	5	3

Philadelphia	000	000	030	2	— 5
Houston	000	110	001	0	— 3

Philadelphia	IP	H	R	ER	BB	SO
Carlton	5 1/3	4	2	2	5	3
Noles	1 1/3	0	0	0	2	0
Saucier	0*	0	0	0	1	0
Reed	1/3	0	0	0	0	0
Brusstar (winner)	2	1	1	1	1	0
McGraw (save)	1	0	0	0	0	1

Houston	IP	H	R	ER	BB	SO
Ruhle	7†	8	3	3	1	3
D. Smith	0‡	1	0	0	0	0
Sambito (loser)	3	4	2	2	1	5

*Pitched to one batter in seventh.
†Pitched to three batters in eighth.
‡Pitched to one batter in eighth.
Game-winning RBI—Luzinski.

E—Landestoy. DP—Philadelphia 3, Houston 2. LOB—Philadelphia 8, Houston 8. 2B—Howe, Cabell, Luzinski, Trillo. 3B—Pujols. SB—McBride, L. Smith, Landestoy, Woods, Puhl, Bowa. SH—Sambito. SF—Howe, Trillo. U—Harvey, Vargo, Crawford, Engel, Tata and Froemming. T—3:55. A—44,952.

and, once again, the teams careened into extra innings. Pete Rose was on first with two out when Greg Luzinski, benched on this day, was sent up to pinch hit against Joe Sambito. He roped the ball into the left-field corner, where Jose Cruz played the carom off the fence. The ball was hit so hard, it got to Cruz so fast that there didn't seem to be any way the runner on first could score. But that runner was Pete Rose . . . and in a mad, give-'em-hell dash around the bases he showed why the Phillies had been wise to bid so high for his services. If there was any way to score on that hit, Rose was going to find it. No third base coach could possibly have stopped him. And you could only pity the poor catcher who tried.

"I know Pete Rose," said Joe Morgan, his old Cincinnati teammate. "Pete Rose was never going to stop."

And Lee Elia, the third base coach who went through the meat grinder after the second game for holding up Bake McBride, wasn't going to try to stop this runaway locomotive of a ball player as he tore around the bases.

"Only Pete Rose can score on that play," Elia said. "He *wants* to go from first to home."

Left-fielder Cruz threw the ball to shortstop Landestoy on one bounce. Landestoy wheeled and fired home. The ball got there ahead of Rose, but Bruce Bochy had to handle a difficult short hop—and with Pete Rose thundering toward him that difficult short hop became an impossible short hop. The ball was rolling on the ground even before Rose arrived, touching the plate with his right foot, ramming Bochy with his left forearm. The Phillies led, 4–3, and when Manny Trillo drilled a double to left-center, it was 5–3. Somewhere Tug McGraw found the strength to pitch the bottom of the tenth and retire the Astros in order. There would be a fifth game on Sunday night, after all.

As Art Howe's game-ending fly ball settled into Garry Maddox' glove, Paul Owens stood up in his front-row box alongside the Phillies dugout, grabbed his wife, and kissed her. Ruly Carpenter, in shirt sleeves, leaped over the low railing and disappeared into the dugout. They had finally gotten over this toughest of hurdles. They had forced a championship series *past* a fourth game. They weren't claiming a pennant yet, but the confidence was surging back. The Astros had let the sleeping giants off the floor.

"I never saw a game like that," Owens said.

"This was the weirdest game I've ever played in my life,"

Larry Bowa was saying in front of his locker. "Hey, now it's down to one game. There's no advantage. There's no disadvantage. There's nothing now. You just go out and battle."

Bowa's emotions had spilled over in the midst of the fourth-inning furor over Maddox' soft liner to the pitcher. He had thrown his bat in anger. He had screamed and stormed until coach Bobby Wine and others had restrained him, fearing that he would be thrown out of the game. "They're saying, 'Take it easy. Take it easy,' " Bowa said, grimacing. "Take it easy! If you're playing just a regular league game, OK, then I'll take it easy. But this is for everything. This is to try to get in a World Series."

You'd have thought the Phillies and Astros would be hard pressed to equal the stirring drama that was game four. But, if anything, they surpassed it in game five, the single most important baseball game played by a Philadelphia team since that Sunday afternoon at old Ebbets Field in Brooklyn, thirty years before, when Richie Ashburn threw out the potential winning run at the plate in the ninth and Dick Sisler hit the ball into the seats in the tenth. Any kind of a victory for the Phillies in that final game at the Astrodome would have gained a special place in Philadelphia sports lore. But the way they won—in a game that should be the new standard by which all league championship series games are measured—was fantastic. Yes, there had been memorable fifth games before: in the '72 National League playoffs when Johnny Bench's homer pulled the Reds even with the Pirates in the last of the ninth and a two-out wild pitch by Bob Moose brought Cincinnati the pennant, and in the '76 American League playoffs when George Brett's three-run homer tied it for the Royals in the eighth and Chris Chambliss' homer won it for the Yankees in the ninth. But never had there been a fifth game to top this.

It took twenty Phillies players—six of them pitchers—to win the game and to put to rest forever the theory, widely held in Philadelphia before this night, that the 1980 Phillies lacked what it takes to win a championship.

It took them ten innings to bring Philadelphia its first-ever National League pennant. It took them three hours and thirty-eight minutes. It took so much heart, so much character, so much of all the things that Pete Rose was hired to instill in this team as to be almost beyond belief.

And, yes, it took some luck too.

The tension was brutal. One minute the Phillies were leading, 2-1, and just twelve, then eleven outs away from the World Series. Then suddenly the countdown stopped. The game was tied and, before that shock had a chance to wear off, the Astros were three runs ahead and the Astrodome was shaking again. Louder and louder, the people yelled, waving their orange hats, their orange banners, their Texas flags, chanting, "We're no. 1," doing all the things sports fans do when their team has wrapped up the big one. Now the Astros were counting down to the big celebration, to the moment the champagne would start flowing. Six more outs and the pennant would be theirs. No way the Phillies—no way *anybody*—could be expected to come back from a 5-2 deficit in this ball park against Nolan Ryan.

But the Phillies found a way.

Sure, they needed a break to do it. A big break. After Bowa's lead-off single to center, Bob Boone hit one back to the box. Had Ryan handled it cleanly, it would have been a double play; the rally would have been killed almost before it began.

Ryan tried to snatch the ball backhanded, and failed. It bounced off his glove for an infield hit; instead of two out there were two on. Now it was up to the Phillies to take advantage of the break.

Greg Gross put down a perfect bunt toward third. No play. The bases were loaded. Ryan was permitted to face one more batter, Pete Rose. He walked him on a 3-2 pitch, and the Astros' lead was cut to 5-3.

The rally very nearly died there. Joe Sambito relieved and got pinch-hitter Keith Moreland to bounce into a force at second. Now it was 5-4 and the tying run was at third with one out. In come righthander Ken Forsch, the first-game starter, to face Mike Schmidt. The count went to two balls, two strikes. Forsch threw . . . Schmidt took. Strike three called.

Surely, that was the crusher, the final blow that would bury this Phillies team with all those other Phillies teams.

No. Not this time. Dallas Green sent up Del Unser to pinch-hit and the veteran outfielder stroked a clean single to right center. The game was tied. Then Manny Trillo slashed a triple down the left-field line, and the game was untied.

Back came McGraw for yet another game-saving appearance, but even Tug is human. A couple of hits around a couple of strikeouts, and the Astros had two on with two out in the home eighth. Rafael Landestoy's hit trimmed the Phillies' lead to 7–6; Jose Cruz' single to center tied the score. Who was writing this script, Alfred Hitchcock?

The Phillies threatened in the ninth but failed to score. A sudden-death situation faced Dick Ruthven as he came in to face the Astros in the last of the ninth.

Ruthven had expected to be the fifth-game starter for the Phillies and he was more than a little upset when he wasn't handed the ball. Instead they sent him to the bullpen . . . and bypassed him again, calling on Larry Christenson in the seventh inning with the score 2–2. By then Dick Ruthven was an extremely angry young man.

"I got mad when they brought Larry in with one day's rest," he said. "I'm saying, 'What the hell is this—a sacrificial lamb? I've got more rest. Why don't you use me?' "

Dick sat there and smoldered as the Astros jumped on Christenson for the seventh-inning runs that put them temporarily in command. "I was emotionally spent," Ruthven said. "I had never seen a game or participated in a game which had so many comebacks, so many disappointments, so much elation, then another disappointment on top of that."

Yet when the time finally came, when they brought him in to pitch in a situation where one slip, one bad pitch could end the Phillies season, Dick Ruthven was in total control, mentally and physically. "By the time I got out there," he said, "I was a robot, which is exactly what I wanted to be."

The robot righthander set down the Astros in order in the ninth. Into extra innings the teams went—for the fourth consecutive game. Mike Schmidt, the magic of the stretch drive misplaced for a while, went down swinging. Del Unser doubled over first and moved to third on Manny Trillo's long fly. It was up to Garry Maddox . . . and he delivered.

A notorious first-ball hitter, Maddox wasted no time. He lined the ball to center. Terry Puhl came charging in, but he couldn't quite get there. The ball landed in front of him and bounced away. Maddox had a double. The Phillies had an 8–7 lead.

Ruthven held it with another three-up, three-down inning. It was nearly midnight, Philadelphia time, when Enos Cabell, who

Fifth Game in National League Championship Series
(October 12, 1980 at Houston)

Philadelphia	ab	r	h	rbi	Houston	ab	r	h	rbi
Rose, 1b	3	0	1	1	Puhl, cf	6	3	4	0
McBride, rf	3	0	0	0	Cabell, 3b	5	1	1	0
Moreland, ph	1	0	0	1	Morgan, 2b	4	0	0	0
Aviles, pr	0	1	0	0	Landestoy, 2b	1	0	1	1
McGraw, p	0	0	0	0	Cruz, lf	3	0	2	2
G. Vukovich, ph	1	0	0	0	Walling, rf	5	2	1	1
Ruthven, p	0	0	0	0	LaCorte, p	0	0	0	0
Schmidt, 3b	5	0	0	0	Howe, 1b	4	0	2	1
Luzinski, lf	3	0	1	0	B'man, pr-1b	1	0	0	0
Smith, pr	0	0	0	0	Pujols, c	1	0	0	0
Christenson, p	0	0	0	0	Ashby, ph-c	3	0	1	1
Reed, p	0	0	0	0	Reynolds, ss	5	1	2	0
Unser, ph-rf	2	2	2	1	Ryan, p	3	0	0	0
Trillo, 2b	5	1	3	2	Sambito, p	0	0	0	0
Maddox, cf	4	1	1	1	Forsch, p	0	0	0	0
Bowa, ss	5	1	2	0	Woods, ph-rf	1	0	0	0
Boone, c	3	1	2	2	Heep, ph	1	0	0	0
Bystrom, p	2	0	0	0					
Brusstar, p	0	0	0	0					
Gross, lf	2	1	1	0					
Totals	39	8	13	8	**Totals**	43	7	14	6

Philadelphia	020	000	050	1 — 8
Houston	100	001	320	0 — 7

Philadelphia	IP	H	R	ER	BB	SO
Bystrom	5 1/3	7	2	1	2	1
Brusstar	2/3	0	0	0	0	0
Christenson	2/3	2	3	3	1	0
Reed	1/3	1	0	0	0	0
McGraw	1	4	2	2	0	2
Ruthven (winner)	2	0	0	0	0	0

Houston	IP	H	R	ER	BB	SO
Ryan	7*	8	6	6	2	8
Sambito	1/3	0	0	0	0	0
Forsch	2/3	2	1	1	0	1
LaCorte (loser)	2	3	1	1	1	1

*Pitched to four batters in eighth.
Game-Winning RBI—Maddox.

E—Trillo, Luzinski. DP—Houston 2. LOB—Philadelphia 5, Houston 10. 2B—Cruz, Reynolds, Unser, Maddox. 3B—Howe, Trillo. SB—Puhl. SH—Cabell, Boone. WP—Christenson. U—Vargo, Crawford. Engel, Tata, Froemming and Harvey. T—3:38. A—44,802.

had been unable to check his swing on a 3–1 pitch that would have been ball four, sent Ruthven's 3–2 pitch soaring to center field. Where else could the final out have gone on this night of redemption but to the man who dropped that line drive in Los Angeles in the final playoff game two years before?

Maddox had been sorely tested down the stretch. When Green sat him down in the final week of the regular season, he was tremendously upset. "For four or five days," he said, "I was as mad as I could be."

Yet he had come off the bench to get a vital hit to save the Phillies from losing a game to the Cubs, and now—in the biggest game of all—he had delivered a two-out, tenth-inning double to beat the Astros and win the pennant.

Garry Maddox clutched that game-ending, pennant-clinching fly ball off Enos Cabell's bat and, even three hours away by jet, you could hear the gigantic, collective sigh of relief that swept through the city of Philadelphia; you could feel the happiness that Philadelphia baseball fans hadn't felt since that Sunday afternoon in 1950.

It was a moment to savor, a moment to throw your arms around somebody—as Paul Owens did; a moment for Pete Rose to leave the mob scene at the mound and run toward the outfield to greet Garry Maddox with outstretched arms. For a long time people on this Phillies ball club had resisted following Rose's example; not any more. Seeing him make a beeline for Maddox they charged after him, and there was another jubilant mob scene in short right-center field.

Finally, when the back-slapping and the hugging was completed, there was Maddox, the man some thought didn't have his heart in playing for this team—and this manager—being carried toward the infield by, among others, Dallas Green.

"I think," said Greg Luzinski, whose two game-winning playoff hits had helped make all this possible, "we proved to the world that we don't have a quitter on this team."

Not even the 1980 Phillies, with their flair for the dramatic, could hope to top the Great Battle of Houston. The first World Series in Phillies history was almost—not quite, but almost—an anticlimax. Both managers left themselves wide open to the second-guess. "The Series," said Cardinal manager Whitey Herzog the following spring, "was lost in the first game" (when the Kansas City Royals couldn't hold a 4–0 lead as Bake McBride's three-run homer capped a five-run Phillies rally in the bottom of the third). "And then," Herzog added, "Dallas tried to give it back to them.

He let [Bob] Walk go out there and face [George] Brett and [Willie] Aikens in the eighth with a three-run lead."

Brett doubled, Aikens hit his second home run of the game, and the 7-4 game had become a 7-6 game. In came Tug McGraw, and it remained a 7-6 game.

"McGraw had to come in and do a helluva job," Herzog said. "What the hell? He had McGraw up anyway. Why didn't he just bring him in and let him face Brett and Aikens?"

Because, as explained earlier, the 1980 Phillies did things the hard way. Even things they had never tried before—like the World Series. Game two nearly got away from them in the seventh when Steve Carlton hit a wild spell and Amos Otis ripped a two-run double that erased a 2-1 Phillies lead. KC's ace reliever, Dan Quisenberry, breezed through the home seventh, then let the 4-2 lead get away in the eighth. A walk, a pinch double by Unser, and a chopping single to right by McBride tied it; Schmidt's double to the gap in right center untied it, and Moreland's line single to center provided insurance.

The Series turned abruptly in Kansas City. Willie Aikens' smash to deep left center with one out and bases loaded beat McGraw, 4-3, in the tenth inning of game three and the Royals pounded Christenson for four consecutive extra-base hits in the first inning of game four on their way to a 5-3 win. Then it was KC manager Jim Frey's turn to provide fuel for the second guessers. The Royals led, 3-2, going into the top of the ninth in the pivotal fifth game. Although the situation seemed to cry for a defensive move—Willie Aikens had performed more like a lead glover than a gold glover at first base—Frey left him in.

Schmidt opened the ninth against Quisenberry with a single off Brett's glove at third. Then Unser—that man again—bounced off the Phillies bench and hit the ball sharply down the first base line. A good first baseman might have made the play. Aikens didn't. The ball went into the right-field corner for a game-tying double. A two-out single by Manny Trillo, who smashed the ball off the pitcher toward third, put the Phillies ahead.

They stayed ahead, but Tug McGraw added a touch of high drama in the bottom of the ninth. He walked Frank White, then he threw a called third strike past George Brett. He walked Willie Aikens, then he got Hal McRae to bounce into a force play at second. Two on, two out, and the hot-hitting Amos Otis was at the plate. Tug walked him on four pitches, and the bases were loaded.

The game, perhaps the World Series, came down to a confrontation between two veterans, McGraw and ex-Phillie Jose Cardenal. Tug won it, hands down. As Cardenal missed the third strike McGraw, that one-man House of Thrills, thrust both arms in the air, then braced himself to meet the charge of the Bobby Wines, the John Vukoviches, all the Phillies who had grown accustomed to charging off the bench at times like that.

Tug McGraw had done it again. Not according to the book, mind you. But he had done it. "*Nobody* walks White to strike out Brett, you nut," Dick Ruthven called out to Tug as the lefthanded reliever returned from the post-game interview room. Well, hardly anybody.

The Phillies were going back home with a 3–2 lead in the World Series, and Steve Carlton primed to pitch the sixth game. They were worried. Not so much that the Royals would beat them, but that those victory-starved Philadelphia fans would destroy the ball park and everything —and everybody—in it. "Hell," said Ruly Carpenter, "when they tore old Connie Mack Stadium up, I saw guys with three-piece suits carrying toilets out of the men's room."

"Sounds like a riot to me," Dick Ruthven said about the possibility —no, the probability—that the Phillies would clinch their first world championship at home. "Sounds like insanity. I'm wondering how we'd get out of the ball park to go home."

"It's something you think about," Larry Bowa acknowledged as the team went through a workout on the open date prior to the sixth game. "It's also something you're sort of scared of. I've seen it happen when Chris Chambliss hit that home run [to win the 1976 American League playoffs for the Yankees in New York]. . . . Yeah, I'm concerned about it. I'm really concerned about it. Especially if it ends with a pop fly. They're liable not to let the thing come down."

The fears were groundless. Tug McGraw was on the mound when the 1980 World Series ended. No game-ending pop flies for Tug. The final out was a swinging third strike. Naturally, the bases were loaded at the time.

A one-out walk and two singles set up the final drama.

McGraw got Frank White to lift a pop foul near the first-base dugout. Bob Boone and Pete Rose converged on the ball. Boone reached for it . . . got his hands on the ball . . . and dropped it. No matter. Before the ball hit the ground Rose grabbed it, lunging off to his left. It was, well, a classic Pete Rose play, one of the many plays people will talk about long after Pete retires —if, indeed, Pete ever retires.

The last KC batter was Willie Wilson, the hitting flop of the World Series. The key to beating the Royals was to keep this speedster off the bases, and Phillie pitchers did a bangup job of it. Wilson got only four hits in the six games; what's more he struck out twice in the first game, three times in the second game, twice in the third game, once in the fourth game, once in the fifth game, and three times in the sixth game. Tug got him on a 1–2 pitch to end it . . . and the stadium, the city went wild.

At long last Philadelphians found out how it felt to be a Pirate fan in 1960 when Bill Mazeroski hit the ninth-inning homer against the Yankees, or a Mets fan in '69 when the Orioles fell in five, or a Reds fan in '75 when Joe Morgan's ninth-inning hit beat the Red Sox in the seventh game, or a Pirate fan in '79 when Willie Stargell destroyed the Orioles.

They stood there, 65,000 of them, drinking in the scene as the game ended and the celebration began. They watched "cool" Mike Schmidt leap high atop the mob of Phillie players that surged around the mound. They watched Larry Bowa, capless, dancing off the field, a look of little-boy happiness on his thirty-four-year-old face. And those who were home watching on TV saw Paul Owens, the architect of this team, and Dallas Green, the engineer who finally put the pieces together and made them work, clutch each other in a long, passionate embrace. Tears of joy streamed down Paul Owens' face; he had waited a long time for this triumph and until the very last out the opposition had a chance to snatch it away.

The riot? There was none. The city was ready for this moment. Lord, the city *should* have been ready; it had close to 100 years to make plans. Mounted police circled the field. Policemen, accompanied by German shepherds, appeared out of both bull pens as the magic moment grew near. Some thought it was awful, that show of force. Presumably such critics would have preferred a full-scale riot. Actually, it was handled beautifully—guaranteeing a happy ending to an unforgettable night that would be followed by an equally unforgettable day.

(Sixth (and final) Game of World Series
(October 21, 1980)

Kansas City	ab	r	h	rbi	Philadelphia	ab	r	h	rbi
Wilson, lf	4	0	0	0	L. Smith, lf	4	2	1	0
Washington, ss	3	0	1	1	Gross, lf	0	0	0	0
Brett, 3b	4	0	2	0	Rose, 1b	4	0	3	0
McRae, dh	2	0	0	0	Schmidt, 3b	3	0	1	2
Otis, cf	3	0	0	0	McBride, rf	4	0	0	1
Aikens, 1b	2	0	0	0	Luzinski, dh	4	0	0	0
Concepcion, pr	0	0	0	0	Maddox, cf	4	0	2	0
Wathan, c	3	1	2	0	Trillo, 2b	4	0	0	0
Cardenal, rf	4	0	2	0	Bowa, ss	4	1	1	0
White, 2b	4	0	0	0	Boone, c	2	1	1	1
Totals	31	1	7	1	Totals	33	4	9	4

Kansas City	000	000	010 — 1
Philadelphia	002	011	00x — 4

Kansas City	IP	H	R	ER	BB	SO
Gale (L, 0-1)	2	4	2	1	1	1
Martin	2 1/3	1	1	1	1	0
Splittorff	1 2/3	4	1	1	0	0
Pattin	1	0	0	0	0	2
Quis'berry	1	0	0	0	0	0

Philadelphia	IP	H	R	ER	BB	SO
Carlton, (W, 2-0)	7	4	1	1	3	7
McGraw, (S, 2)	2	3	0	0	2	2

Gale pitched to four batters in third. Splittorff pitched to one batter in seventh. Carlton pitched to two batters in eighth.

E—White, Aikens, DP—Kansas City 1, Philadelphia 2. LOB—Kansas City 9, Philadelphia 7. 2B—Maddox, L. Smith, Bowa. SF—Washington. T— 3:00. A—65,839.

It dawned bright and beautiful, but it didn't really matter. It could have been raining, sleeting, snowing in Philadelphia on the morning of October 22, 1980, and the people who lived there still would have considered it a beautiful day. Their baseball team had won a World Series. It was a time to temporarily set aside all problems and salute the new champions.

It was a day when the honking of horns was the signal of a city feeling good about itself, not of a traffic jam on the Schuylkill Expressway, a day when the boobirds turned to lovebirds. The word *love* kept popping up along the parade route as the Phillies, riding atop flatbed trucks, wound around City Hall, then south on Broad Street, past the Vet to the old, 100,000–seat horseshoe stadium where the Army-Navy game used to be played. The people waved, shouted, held up signs, climbed onto ledges, hung out of windows, threw confetti. They "loved" the Phillies, the signs said. And they "loved" Tug. And they "loved" Schmitty. And, above all, they loved the idea of being no. 1.

Amazing what something like this can do for a city, especially a city that had been the butt of so many jokes for so many years. Most of those jokes had passed away long before the Phillies came to life—gags about Philadelphia had pretty much given way to gags about Cleveland—but this warm, friendly, happy victory parade seemed to underline Philadelphia's resurgence. The City of Losers had become the City of Winners, and that, even more than the new buildings, the refurbished downtown shopping area, all the physical improvements that had been made in recent years, brought out a new spirit, a new feeling of self-esteem. Sports can do that.

Nobody gave a damn about amphetamines now. Nobody cared that Steve Carlton wouldn't talk to the press or that Larry Bowa had called Philadelphia fans "the worst in the world" or that Greg Luzinski was still so upset over the treatment he had received from Dallas Green that he agreed to be part of the victory parade only because Ruly Carpenter made it a point to ask him to be there. All you heard along Broad Street were cheers. All you saw were smiling, laughing faces and signs that said such things as, "How Do You Spell Relief?—T-U-G." The players were having the time of their lives; you could see it on their faces. "It's probably something I'll never forget," Luzinski would admit when it was over. Paul Owens, the general manager who had broken down and cried unashamedly the night before while the nation watched on TV, and Dallas Green, the manager who screamed and hollered and drove this team to the top, stood at the front of one of the trucks, loving every minute of it. Again and again Owens would reach out with his left hand, grasp Green's right hand and hold it up in the manner of a fight manager after his boxer has won the big bout. And then Owens would wave his free hand and blow kisses to the adoring mob.

Finally they reached John F. Kennedy Stadium, the horseshoe-shaped, white-elephant of a structure in South Philly where people had been waiting since early morning. Twice the caravan circled the field while the huge crowd stood and waved thousands of white pennants and cheered.

Jim Murray, the general manager of the Eagles, was in the front row with his kids, drinking it all in. "The power to make people happy is awesome," he said.

Happiness. It was all around you. You could see it and feel it and be a part of it. "There are a few people here today who didn't think this ball club could win," owner Ruly Carpenter told the crowd, "but here they are."

Yes, there they were. . . .

"This is probably the greatest moment of my entire life," Larry Bowa said, his voice echoing through the mammoth stadium, "and I'm glad I can share it with the *greatest* fans in baseball."

Mike Schmidt, the World Series' MVP who would soon be named the National League's Most Valuable Player as well, was next. "I never saw so many sincere faces in my life as I did in that parade today," he said. "Take that world championship and savor it because you all deserve it."

And finally the man these people had taken to their hearts stood at the microphone. Ex-New York Met Frank Edwin (Tug) McGraw waited for the cheers to subside, then said: "All through baseball history Philadelphia has had to take a back seat to New York City. But New York City can take *this* world championship and stick it."

*   *   *

McGraw's shot at New York was prompted by articles that had been written during the World Series by New York sportswriters, among others. They knocked the Phillies, belittled the Series, wrote about how uncooperative, how surly the Philadelphia players were.

All Tug succeeded in doing with his "New York City can stick it" remark was to trigger another round of anti-Phillies stories. In the October 27, 1980, issue of *Newsweek*, columnist Pete Axthelm wrote: "For the Phillies, the Series has been a rite of redemption. In recent years they had earned a solid reputation as pampered and overpaid losers, talented masters of the near miss who had somehow contrived to stay out of Series games since 1950. It took some towering rages by square-jawed manager Dallas Green to prod them into this confrontation. And with the notable exceptions of Rose and McGraw—both refugees from more easy-going clubhouses—the Phillies pursue their glories in a remarkably churlish and thin-skinned mood. Even the imposing Green tends to answer innocuous questions about strategy with a belligerent sneer, as in, 'I plan to do it this way . . . IF it's all right with you.' "

That was just for openers. The following week the talented Axthelm let them have it with both barrels in a column headed, "Those Malevolent Phillies." Using Tug's New York City crack as a starting point, he wrote:

"Perfect. One of the last holdouts was in the fold. The Philadelphia story was complete. The Phillies celebrated as they had played against Kansas City, in bullying and abrasive style. Shortstop Larry Bowa sneered that the boos of the fans had inspired him. Outfielder Lonnie Smith led a few teammates in obscene chants directed at the press. Ace pitcher Steve Carlton withdrew in sullen splendor to the off-limits trainer's room, while sycophants hurled beer at the reporters who maintained their demeaning vigil outside the door of the sanctuary. When McGraw belatedly joined in the mood, there seemed to be only one flaw in the script. The police attack dogs who snarled at the fans during the final inning were aimed in the wrong direction."

Even as winners, the Phillies got rapped. The Los Angeles Dodgers won a couple of National League pennants, and the first image that came to mind was Tommy Lasorda rushing out to hug one of his heroes. The Pittsburgh Pirates won a World Series, and the country read about "Fam-a-lee" and that marvelous gentleman, Pops Stargell. The Phillies won for the first time in their history, and they were knocked from pillar to post. Their reputation, of course, had preceded them into the playoffs and World Series and, despite attempts to live down that reputation, they were stuck with it. Much of the criticism the Phillies had brought on themselves in the course of the season, but you couldn't blame Tug McGraw, one of the most cooperative, most accessible of all professional athletes, for being upset over some of the things that were written.

"It bothered me," he admitted. "I didn't think New York was that way. The writers, and other people outside of Philadelphia, they didn't want us to enjoy some of the things they had enjoyed for so many years. . . . Philadelphia has become a fabulous city and in New York's eyes it's still the same, old Philadelphia that W. C. Fields used to joke about, and these guys were just saying the World Series wasn't an event because it was in Philadelphia. Even with the success the team had, the success the security had, the success the Philadelphia Police Department had, they couldn't see clearly enough to realize that was probably one of the most important precedents established in American sports. I mean the security at the ball park, the way the parade was handled, the way the whole thing was handled. I think they were bogged down by the issue of a handful of our players not having the best relations with the press, and these guys came in from the outside and they couldn't cope with that. They didn't understand it. They more or less let the tail wag the dog. That became more important to them than the event itself."

In fairness to the national press, much of what its members wrote about the Phillies during and after the World Series had been written by the local press many times before that. It would be hard to imagine a professional team—a *winning* professional team, at that—having a worse relationship with the press. But Tug McGraw, the uninhibited one who became to many the symbol of this championship Phillies team, remained the same, fun-loving free spirit who won the hearts of New Yorkers in 1973.

Tug is one of a kind, a man who has never forgotten that baseball should be fun. One St. Patrick's Day he came out on the field with a uniform that was dyed green. ("That wasn't a joke," he said. "That was just an ethnic acknowledgment.") One time at Shea Stadium, when Tug and the great Willie Mays were teammates, McGraw painted himself black on "camera day," put on Willie's uniform and went out to pose for pictures "because Willie didn't want to go out there." Oh yeah, Tug got Mays' permission before he did it.

Nothing, it seemed, fazed Tug McGraw. In the spring of '81, when the drug business was simply something nobody wanted to talk about, Tug cracked jokes about it. When a Florida writer asked him if he'd seen "greenies" in the clubhouse, McGraw replied, "I haven't seen anything stronger than heroin." Asked to identify the biggest problem facing the ball club, Tug shot back,

"Keeping the Food and Drug Administration out of the clubhouse."

The year Tug led some of his teammates on a bicycle trip he was supposed to present a muscular dystrophy award to the Florida Jaycees in Jacksonville. Let him tell it.

"We had just ridden 1,000 miles from Philadelphia to Florida. The Jaycees were having their big convention in Jacksonville—2,500 of them —and I was supposed to go on the program first and give them this big plaque, and it was kind of a serious thing. As it turned out, it was about a two-hour program, and they put me on last.

"I had to sit there the whole time, and we'd been riding those bikes all day. By the time I came on, they were all totally hammered. They introduced me, and nobody even knew anybody was on the podium by that time. They were all wandering around drinking, and I said, 'Thank you, it's a pleasure to be here representing baseball and muscular dystrophy,' and it was like nobody was paying any attention. I said, 'If I just may have your attention briefly here for a second . . .' No response. Just blah-blah-blah. There was so much noise I couldn't hear myself speaking. I said, 'Please bear with me. May I have your attention . . .' Then the guy starts pounding the gavel for me. Still nothing.

"I said, 'OK, if I can't have your attention, if you can't just show me a little respect for a brief moment for this important award you're about to receive . . .' Still nothing. Nothing. So I stepped back from the podium, walked around to the front, turned around . . . and gave 'em a big old moon shot. *That* got everybody's attention. I said, 'Now, ladies and gentlemen, that I have your attention may I please have some silence while I make this presentation.' You could've heard a pin drop.

"I thought maybe they would get ticked off, but I got a standing ovation, and they carried me out of the place, put me in a limousine, and made me an honorary member."

That's the man who pitched so brilliantly the second half of the 1980 season, the man who kept coming through in those tense situations in October. We shouldn't be surprised that Tug McGraw reacted to the awesome pressure the way he did. Any man who can find a way, however daring, to shut up 2,500 drunken Jaycees obviously is well equipped to handle the Expos, the Astros, and the Royals.

*   *   *

In the final analysis, of course, despite all the feuding, fussing, and fighting, despite all the negative stories written about them, the 1980 Phillies will be best remembered as the team that got hot when it had to get hot and brought Philadelphia its first championship baseball team since the days of Connie Mack's A's. "Winning," Tug McGraw said, "is like an eraser."

"I firmly believe we put a lot of ghosts to sleep last year," Dallas Green said in the spring of '81. "We proved ourselves *to ourselves;* we proved as a baseball team we can play with anybody and win big games."

When he took over as manager, Dallas Green said, the Phillies "didn't know how to be a championship baseball team." Maybe he taught them, or maybe the Phillies were just a baseball team whose time had come. The fact is, they won. In pro sports, and in our win-oriented society, that's all that really matters.

"I've done a lot more communicating than a lot of people think," Green said. "I did it in my own way. One thing about Dallas Green, it has to be done my way. I know that Ruly and Paul would probably prefer those one-on-one meetings and big call-ins and let everybody see that you're doing it. I don't believe in that. . . . Everybody's got to live with their own thing. I can live with what I did. I didn't always do everything right, but I know I did it with the one thought in mind—the thought of working hard and doing it for the organization and for the team.

"I know what I did," he went on, "but at the same time I get a little embarrassed at times at all the accolades that I have received because—I'm very sincere in this—I was just a guy working my ass off to do a job, just as I've been all the twenty-five years I've been in baseball. I worked hard at being a player. I worked hard at being a minor-league manager. I worked hard at being director of minor leagues and scouting. I just believe that's the way you become and stay successful in baseball. Hell, I didn't have any talent after I hurt my arm, but I hung in there and played five years at the big-league level. . . . So I had to do something right."

And the 1980 Phillies went all the way . . . so he had to do something right there too. At a time when past Phillies teams would have given up the ghost following that four-game, August debacle in Pittsburgh, this Phillies team had started a pennant drive.

"I think," their manager said, "they decided to put away their personal problems—and there were a lot of personal problems on this ball club. They put those away. They put their dislike for me away. They put their dislike for the fans and the press away, and they started playing the ball they were capable of playing. They played like hell."

*   *   *

There's such a fine line between winning and losing sometimes, such a fine line between reading headlines that say you choked and headlines that say, "We Win!" Another point here, another basket there, and the 76ers would have been hailed as champs, not attacked as chokers in 1981.

Think about it. A bounce here, a call there, and Danny Ozark might have been riding down Broad Street on a flatbed truck in 1977. Or, by the same token, a play here, a play there—had Nolan Ryan handled that comebacker hit by Bob Boone in the final game of the playoffs, for example—and there would have been no victory parade in October of 1980. Amazing what a difference that fine line between winning and losing can make.

It didn't change the thinking of the Carpenter family, however. Ironically, even in the year that the Phillies finally scaled the heights, plans were being made to sell the ball club. Although the public announcement was delayed until spring training of '81, Ruly Carpenter made it clear that this was no sudden decision. Baseball, he felt, was simply going haywire—what with strikes and re-entry drafts and courtroom battles and player salaries that had zoomed out of sight. On the field, it had turned out to be a great year. But all the things that were happening off the field seemed to be sucking the fun out of baseball.

"I sincerely enjoy the-bats-and-the-balls part of the game," Ruly Carpenter said in mid-August of '81. "To me, that's the only enjoyment that's left in this game. Even when you lose, it's still fun to watch a ball game. But I spend 90 percent of my time today battling with agents over salaries and contracts, and with your Marvin Miller problems, your courtrooms, your judges. You just don't have the time to get into the field end of it any more. It's taken all the enjoyment out of the game for me and for my family—except for the two, two and a half hours a day when the game's going on. . . . Our family's just had it. Period."

The possible sale of the Phillies, Ruly Carpenter said, had "been discussed in our family since 1976 privately." Oddly, that was the year the Ruly Carpenter–led Phillies won their first National League East title. How sad that at a time when Ruly, who had grown up in the game, should have been enjoying it the most, he was actually enjoying it the least.

The final straw, said Ruly, came when Ted Turner, owner of the Atlanta Braves, lured free agent Claudell Washington to his team with box-car figures. Dave Winfield, at least, was a star by today's standards. Nobody in his right mind could ever call Claudell Washington a star by any standards—except the salary that Turner gave him.

"Everything was fine," Carpenter said. "We won the World Series. [We were] big heroes and all that. Then I pick up the paper on the Saturday morning after the re-entry draft. It was about six o'clock in the morning. I started reading the sports page, and it says 'Braves sign Claudell Washington for $3½ million.' I couldn't believe it. I thought it was a misprint. Honestly, I thought it was a misprint. So I waited 'til 8 o'clock, and I called Chub [Fenney, president of the National League]. I got his ass out of bed, and I said, 'Chub, what the hell is going on?' There was a big pause on the other end of the phone, and I knew damn well it *was* true then. Right then and there I made up my mind on that Saturday morning. I called my father, and I said, 'We have no alternative.' It's a shame that a family such as ours has to get out of baseball."

And so, even in the happiest of times, there was a large dose of unhappiness. Nineteen eighty-one should have been a gala year for the Phillies. They were defending champions. A hundred and sixty-two times they would take the field as the no. 1 team in all of baseball. They had waited a long time for that—and it was snatched away.

The year the Phillies defended their first world championship turned out to be The Year of the Strike, the year of the split season, the year the owner who treated them like kings—long before they actually became kings—announced he wanted to sell the team.

Nothing ever came easy to the Phillies. For close to a century they had struggled to win a World Series. And now that the championship was theirs, now that they had earned the right to be called the best in baseball, the struggle, if anything, seemed to grow even grimmer.

But always there would be those few marvelous memories from October of 1980, the month—and the year—the Phillies put the fun back into the game for an entire city.

Postscript

IT WAS A STREAK UNPARALLELED IN PRO SPORTS. FIRST THE 76ERS reached the 1980 National Basketball Association finals. Then the Flyers reached the 1980 Stanley Cup finals. Then the Phillies hosted the 1980 World Series. Then the Eagles made it to the 1981 Super Bowl. Four seasons . . . four Philly teams playing for championships. From May of 1980 through January of 1981 the one-time City of Losers was the sports capital of America.

OK, there were a lot of victories, a lot of fun jammed into those nine months. Watching teams that are good enough to play for championships is always fun. But that doesn't mean watching losers all those years was a totally joyless experience. Sports, after all, should provide some fun, a smile or two, even an occasional belly laugh—no matter what the score. That's the great thing about covering sports in Philadelphia. Maybe the talent hasn't always been there, but the laughs have.

Looking back on these past twenty-five years, it's the amusing times as well as the winning times that stand out. It's meeting the owner of a "major league" hockey team who thought the game was played in quarters, not thirds. It's baseball managers and their mad, marvelous malaprops, and the late Joe Kuharich and the lines he used to come up with during football season. You remember; something connected with that ill-fated Eagles team would be described as "rare but not unusual" or perhaps "a horse of a different fire department."

It's the time that awful stick fight occurred at the Arena between Reggie Meserve of the Ramblers and John Brophy, the white-haired terror of the Eastern Hockey League. God, it was a terrifying fight. Blood was flowing. Even those fans who thrive on violence were aghast. Ah, but we were in luck. The president of the league, a gentleman named Tom Lockhart, happened to be in the building at the time. For a change there would be no need for second-hand reports. The prexy was on the spot; he could take immediate action to make sure that such a thing never happened again. The stick fight ended. The blood was wiped away. And the press rushed off to see what President Lockhart was going to do. It took a few minutes but he finally was located between periods in the office of Arena publicist Betty Hardesty. "Well," a writer asked, his ballpoint pen poised for action, "what do you plan to do about that?"

There was a slight pause. Then the president spoke. "About what?" he asked.

"The fight! That terrible stick fight between John Brophy and Reggie Meserve."

The president looked blank. He had seen no stick fight. While Brophy and Meserve were swinging away on the ice, he had been sitting in Betty's office, tinkling the ice in his glass. Don't blame Lockhart. The drinks were free. And besides, there was something about Philadelphia in those days that knocked even presidents and commissioners and the like down to size.

Take Bowie Kuhn (if Henny Youngman will forgive me, may I add *please?*). It was in September of 1970 when the baseball commissioner, with his trusty assistant, Joe Reichler, at his side, came to Philadelphia to take a look at the new stadium that was scheduled to open the following spring.

Off to the unfinished Vet they went, ready for the deluxe tour. It was a beaut. Bowie did it all. He tramped through the dusty, debris-strewn corridors. He sampled the view from the upper deck. He went down to field level and inspected the clubhouses. In his eagerness to see all that there was to see, he even pushed through the door that led to what some day would be a player's lounge, or a large storage closet, or something equally unexciting. The tour group marched on, peering here and there—until suddenly Joe Reichler turned around and a look of distress crossed his face. The commissioner was missing.

"Where is he?" Joe inquired, doing a fair job of keeping the panic out of his voice.

Nobody knew. There was a moment or so of nervous silence; then the tapping sound could be heard. It seemed to be coming from behind a closed door. Soft at first, it got louder and louder. Reichler rushed over to the door, turned the knob and pushed. The door opened . . . and the commissioner of baseball stepped out of the empty room in which he had been locked.

I've often thought how the history of baseball could have changed if we hadn't found Bowie Kuhn that day. The man could have been locked up in that little room for months—maybe until the following April.

Imagine the surprise if, on opening day at the Vet, somebody had opened that door and what was left of the commissioner had fallen out. Bowie Kuhn could have gone down in history as the skeleton in the Phillies' closet.

Big crowds are the norm now in Philadelphia—except when the 76ers are home—but in those fun-filled bygone days it was possible to spot a vacant seat or two, even when the Eagles were playing. Back in the early '50s *The Inquirer* sponsored an annual, pre-season charity football game pitting the Eagles against the best in the West. Pro football wasn't that big a deal then; television had yet to turn it into the really major sport it is today. So it took some doing to sell tickets.

The game that ended that series of "Inquirer Classics" was played in 1955 at what is now John F. Kennedy Stadium. It was the Bears, coached by Paddy Driscoll, v. the Eagles, coached by Jim Trimble. Despite the usual publicity blitz, good seats were still available. Tens of thousands of them.

The moment of truth came when Leo Riordan, the late, great executive sports editor of *The Inquirer*, had to come up with an official crowd figure for the assembled press. Leo put it off as long as he could; then, unable to delay any longer, he leaned out of the press box, looked around at those gaping sections of empty seats, cleared his throat, and said, "Do you think we can say 25,000?"

Bob Paul—now of the U.S. Olympic Committee, then sports information director at Penn—quickly put his mind at ease. "I don't see why we can't," he replied. "There's nobody here to call us liars."

Ah, those were the fun days. The Phillies didn't feud with the press then. Hell, they were glad somebody cared enough to cover them. Some of those Phillies teams were so bad that the *writers* could have used greenies to stay awake. Let it be said, though, that the city still has a sense of humor about sports. I mean, the city *must* have a sense of humor about sports. How else would you explain the success of the Phillie Phanatic, the furry, green creature—played by Dave Raymond, son of the University of Delaware football coach—that cavorts at all Phillies home games? Or the fact that the man who bills himself as "The Clown Prince of Baseball" lives in the Philadelphia area?

I know, it surprises you to find out that Max Patkin—he of the big nose and the baggy uniform with the question mark on the back—is a Philadelphian. Until the last few years you always assumed that all the baseball clowns in town played for the Phillies. Well, you're wrong. For years Max has done his traveling to minor-league parks around the country —and to other countries, as well—out of Philadelphia International Airport. And he's still doing it.

I think we should all be grateful for that. I, for one, find it comforting to know that despite all the successes of the '80s, despite the win-win-win pressure of the World Series, the Super Bowl, the pro basketball playoffs, and the pro hockey playoffs, we still have some clowns left on the Philadelphia sports scene.

Index